Calatonia

Calatonia

A Therapeutic Approach that Promotes Somatic and Psychological Regulation

Editors
Anita Ribeiro Blanchard
Ana Maria Galrão Rios
Leda Maria Perillo Seixas

Copyright © 2019 by Anita Ribeiro Blanchard

All rights reserved. No part of this book may be reproduced, stored in, or introduced into a retrieval system, or transmitted, in any form, or by any means (electronic, mechanical, photocopying, recording, or otherwise), without the prior permission of the publisher, except in the case of brief quotations embodied in critical reviews and certain other noncommercial uses permitted by copyright law.

ISBN: 9781097914357 (Paperback Edition)

Article in Boletim de Psicologia, 1969, by Pethö Sándor, reprinted (translation) by permission from Brazilian public domain rights.

Technical Translation by William Comfort
Copyediting by John Hofton
Designer Felippe Romanelli

First Edition
Revised Printing October 2019

Published by ALMA STREET ENTERPRISE
347 NE 110th Street, Miami, FL 33161

Contents

Preface	vii
Presentation and Acknowledgments	xi
1. Calatonia Pethö Sándor	1
2. The Legacy of Sándor Paulo Toledo Machado Filho	14
3. The Academic Teaching of Calatonia Rosa Maria Farah	26
4. Jung and the Body: Using Calatonia in Individual and Group Psychotherapy Sandra Maria Greger Tavares	46
5. Calatonia and Subtle Touch in the Healing of Trauma Claudia Herbert	70
6. Subtle Touch in Child Psychotherapy: An Alchemical Perspective Maria Irene Crespo Gonçalves	87
7. Subtle Touch in Deep Pedagogy Céline Lorthiois	111
8. Calatonia and Art: Expressing Trauma Through Images Irene Gaeta	132

9. Pethö Sándor's Method
   in the Treatment of Schizophrenia   150
   Leda Maria Perillo Seixas

10. The Psyche in Pethö Sándor's Method   173
    Anita Ribeiro Blanchard

11. The Calatonia of Sight: Learning to See the World
    with Relaxed Eyes and Greater Awareness   202
    Vivian Farah Nassif
    Maria Georgina Ribeiro Gonçalves

12. Calatonia in Child Psychotherapy
    of Early Childhood Trauma   218
    Ana Maria Galrão Rios

13. Petho Sandor's Integrative Method and Drawing:
    A Case Study   231
    Lúcia Helena Hebling Almeida

14. Psychotherapy, Synchronicity and Subtle Touch   253
    Beatriz Vianna Henry
    Luiz Hildebrando Lemos

15. Calatonia and Resilience   263
    Marilena Dreyfuss Armando

16. Calatonia: Novel Insights from Neuroscience   285
    Anita Ribeiro Blanchard

17. Authors   317

18. Annex: Brief Description of the Calatonia Technique   323

Preface

As an academic and a cognitive scientist, I see more than ever the importance of building a bridge over the divide between neuroscientists and experimental psychologists on the one hand, and practising psychotherapists on the other side. Frequently, it seems as if we inhabit the same world but speak entirely different languages, with often vastly divergent meanings for terms such as consciousness, psychophysics and personality. Traditional psychotherapy is often firmly rooted in one or other school of thought, while cognitive neuroscience has had (in)famous difficulty in communicating some of its core concepts (while preserving their scientific validity) to both lay readers and experts in other fields. Modern forms of psychotherapy rightly draw on many theoretical strands, whether from neuroscience or counselling, anthropology or paleontology, medicine or spirituality. Seeking a dialogue and mutual understanding is thus of the utmost importance in interacting with experts across these fields.

It is in this context that I applaud the publication of this book introducing techniques of Subtle Touch and Calatonia to an international audience. Physical forms of contact remain one of the most contentious social issues in many societies, let alone within the framework of therapy. The authors have adeptly covered the cultural, historical and personal issues that frequently lie behind this taboo, and how they may be addressed. Such efforts are important for integrating this key tool into the therapist's armamentarium. Over the course of reviewing and translating this book from Brazilian Portuguese, I have taken care to preserve cultural references and idioms particular to Brazil used by the authors, and, when possible, to direct the reader to their cultural equivalents in English.

While there are significantly fewer barriers to social touch in Brazil than in many other Western countries, the form of affective touch elicited through Calatonia and Subtle Touch can be considered a wholly separate category to social touch, not only in terms of context, but the class of nerve endings which carry signals to the somatosensory cortex through primarily glabrous (non-hairy) skin, only recently the focus of research in neuroscience. Thus, while it is important to consider the distinct cultural mores of the patient when employing Calatonia and other somatic techniques, the therapist should also consider the therapeutic benefit of affective touch in the mental health of the individual, as a tool for recalibrating neural systems related to somatosensory perception, the autonomic nervous system and endocrine regulation. Indeed, the paucity of affective touch in many Western societies itself provides a compelling argument for the inclusion of somatic techniques in psychotherapy, as the under-stimulation of the affective touch system in conjunction with other risk factors, including excessive stress or anxiety, may lead to an increase in many forms of mental illness. Despite cultural mores, which may limit or restrict touch in everyday life, evidence from neuroscience has increasingly revealed the affective touch system to be a universal human need with adaptive evolutionary value.

I have been fortunate to have close contact with several colleagues in analytical psychology at the Pontifical Catholic University (PUC) of São Paulo and the Sedes Sapientiae Institute, a higher-education centre for the study of mental health, education and philosophy in São Paulo. There, Petho Sandór mentored a course of analytical psychology known today as Jung & The Body (*Jung & Corpo*), a key source for analytical psychology in Brazil and one with which most, if not all, the authors in this book have been involved. At PUC, I collaborated with the coordinators of the postgraduate course in Clinical Psychology with a seminar on the "Neuroscience of Consciousness", for Master's and PhD students from a range of therapeutic disciplines including psychoanalysis, analytical psychology, and CBT, as part of their external seminar series. I continue to give a series of courses on "Neuroscience in Clinical Practice" to clinical psychologists and health professionals, alongside my teaching as a Guest Lecturer on the postgraduate course in Neuroscience and Applied Psychology at Mackenzie Presbyterian University. I highly value the outreach and exchange of ideas through these courses and see this communication across disciplines as equally important to my scientific research. To paraphrase Richard Feynman (1918-1988), "if we cannot explain it simply, we don't really understand it".

My encounters with these colleagues have borne fruitful and collaborative discussions on themes related to emotional processing, consciousness and neuroscience, none more so than with my partner. She is a practising Jungian psychologist who routinely employs Subtle Touch techniques with her own patients and is a faculty member on the 2-year Jung & The Body course at Sedes Sapientiae Institute, teaching practical modules on the course to clinical psychologists seeking Jungian specialization.

In that spirit, I feel confident that both the novice reader and those already familiar with Calatonia will find much of interest here, with the application of Calatonia and Subtle Touch in diverse contexts described by inspiring practising therapists who continue to explore and develop new avenues of treatment based on empirical evidence and rigorous professional codes of conduct.

William Comfort, PhD[1]

---

1. William Comfort, Post-Doctoral Fellow, is a cognitive scientist studying different aspects of face perception, including deficits in the recognition of facial expressions in schizophrenia linked to abnormal eye movement, and the electromyographical response to facial attractiveness in healthy subjects when affected by external factors such as cosmetic enhancement, increased sexual dimorphism and greater visual contrast. He received his PhD in Cognitive Neuroscience and is currently a post-doctoral fellow at the Social and Cognitive Neuroscience Lab at Mackenzie Presbyterian University in São Paulo.

Presentation and Acknowledgments

It gives the authors of this book great joy to be presenting the work of Pethö Sándor, placing particular focus on his Calatonia technique. This is a much-needed publication, especially, as over the past fifty years the technique has travelled beyond the borders of Brazil albeit without the background theory which underpins it – until now – the main reason for this having been the language barrier. This has often led to the method being misrepresented or indeed, misused, due to it being employed out of the integral context in which it belongs and deprived of the necessary conditions for which it was ideally created. Our colleague Lucy Penna[1] (1947-2011) describes a situation in which this is very clear:

> I was in London on the occasion of a course given for Health and Education professionals in 1980, at the Gerda Boyesen Institute. Whilst I was there, a technique was presented that came from Brazil via Australia in which

---

[1]. Penna, L. (2008). Dos Fios da Navalha aos Finos Anéis da Sensibilidade. Hermes, 13, 107-113.

the Calatonia touches (the basic sequence on the feet) were shown being done in the wrong order - the patient being told to keep their eyes open and also under orders to "relax, relax". Unfortunately, no mention was made of Dr Sándor, and the technique was presented as the "marvellous BTT (Brazilian Toe Touches)" ... The biodynamic psychology Notebook v. 3 (1983, p. 6) shows a photo of Gerda applying "BTT". It was a surprise for Gerda Boyesen and the group that, at that time of the presentation of the new technique at the institute, there was a person trained by the method's own creator, who had recently completed a master's degree on the subject. I was asked to speak about the origin of Calatonia and also to show the actual sequence of touches on the feet and the head. I did what I could, I quoted from the source material and demonstrated the technique that was then practised in pairs by all participants. (Penna, 2008, p. 109)

In Brazil, there are many books, theses and dissertations written about the method, and presently, an ever-growing enthusiasm for it has been endorsed by recent studies in neuropsychology, cognitive neuroscience and neuroscience of touch, which have offered abundant evidence for future validation of the method. Among the few publications in English, about Calatonia, are the books of Suzana Delmanto (2008) and Rosa Farah (2017), respectively, *Subtle Touches: Calatonia,* and *Calatonia: Subtle Touch in Psychotherapy.*

With the exception of our guest collaborator, Claudia Herbert, all the authors in this book learned the method directly from Sándor and had extensive involvement in his study groups for a number of years. This group of authors also runs workshops and various forms of training in Brazil and abroad (https://calatoniainternationaltraining.com/), using the teaching standards defined by the larger group of professionals who learned with Sándor, available at http://www.calatonia.org/en/requirements-for-becoming-a-calatonia-facilitator-and-trainer/.

Most of the chapters in this book were previously published in the indexed journal "Hermes" (https://www.revista-hermes.org/) between 1996 (when the journal was founded) and 2018. By delving into the articles written during this period, we hope to provide an ample idea of the scope of the method.

The book opens with Sándor's chapter, "Calatonia", published in 1969 in the *Boletim de Psicologia*, in São Paulo, and later in a book edited by him in 1974 (with ensuing editions). Next, Paulo Toledo Machado Filho takes us to meet the teacher and his teachings and gives us a context for Sándor's method. Following on from that, Rosa Farah (1949-2016) briefly describes the teaching of the method within the professional course of psychology at the Pontifícia Universidade Católica de São Paulo, where she taught for over a decade until her untimely death.

In subsequent chapters, Sandra Maria Greger Tavares presents her work with Subtle Touch and Calatonia within the Brazilian public healthcare system, both in individual and group therapy. Claudia Herbert addresses the healing of trauma and offers an exploration of the scientific rationale and specific considerations for the application of Calatonia and Subtle Touch in trauma treatment.

Maria Irene Crespo Gonçalves finds a parallel between alchemical symbolism and psychodynamic processes in somatic psychotherapy with children; and Céline Lorthiois explains Deep Pedagogy, a pedagogic method that takes an integrative approach to child development, in which body, mind, creativity and dreams are essential components.

Irene Gaeta presents to us an adult patient who, having suffered early trauma, was enabled to access, reorganise and integrate her preverbal memories through the use of Calatonia followed by art-therapy. Leda Maria Perillo Seixas expands on the use of Sándor's body-based techniques in the treatment of patients with schizophrenia and discusses central tenets of Jung's psychology in Sándor's method. Likewise, Anita Ribeiro Blanchard writes about the Jungian concept of psyche in psychotherapy and in the ethos of Sándor's work.

Vivian Farah Nassif and Maria Georgina Ribeiro Gonçalves describe a sequence of touches made to the face, the Calatonia of Sight, initially formulated for the treatment of individuals suffering from visual impairment, and later incorporated as a tool in psychotherapy. Ana Maria Galrão Rios describes the case of a child with attachment issues stemming from trauma, abandonment and loss, who was successfully treated with Calatonia. Lúcia Helena Hebling Almeida presents the case of an uncommunicative teenager with body image and self-esteem issues who was able to express herself through a series of drawings, created after receiving the somatic work in session.

Marilena Dreyfuss Armando examines some essential attributes of resilience, and also the ways in which Calatonia contributes to the development of resilience and numinous experiences. Beatriz Vianna Henry and Luiz Hildebrando Lemos discuss how the use of Calatonia produces a distinctive field of transference in psychotherapy and enhances the probability of synchronous phenomena, which may provide directions for the course of the therapeutic process.

In the last chapter of the book, Anita Ribeiro Blanchard presents a summary of the hypotheses about the neuroscientific underpinnings of Pethö Sándor's method.

The authors are indebted to Dr William Comfort for his consultancy on the topic of neuroscience and for his generosity with his knowledge and language skills. Our gratefulness to Beatrice Bartlett for her unconditional reassurance and soulful critique; to John Hofton for his sensitive suggestions and final editing; and to Felippe Romanelli, who patiently and steadfastly produced the actual book. They were beacons of light at different steps of the way and helped to bring about the realisation of this project.

We also express our appreciation to our patients, who shared their healing journeys with us.

And finally, our deepest gratitude to Sándor, a wise and generous teacher who inspired both our professional and spiritual lives.

The aim of this book is to convey the value and reach of his work, and we hope it will be received with openness and interest.

Anita Ribeiro Blanchard, Editor

1

Calatonia

Pethö Sándor

The expression Calatonia means a relaxed and loose muscle tone, but it is not defined solely by its physiological aspects. In the original Greek, *khalaó* indicates 'relaxation' and 'feeding' - 'retreating from a state of anger, fury, or violence', 'opening a door', 'untying the bindings of a waterskin', 'letting go', 'forgiving one's parents', 'lifting all veils from the eyes.'

The therapist performs Calatonia using extremely light touches to the toes, soles of the feet, ankles, and middle of the calves (at the convergence of the *triceps surae* muscle).

The method of Calatonia was created during the Second World War, after the full withdrawal of German troops from Russia. At a Red Cross hospital, a great number of different post-operative cases ranging from patients with phantom limbs and suffering from a nervous breakdown, to depression and compulsive reactions were treated.

In addition to the usual medications and palliative care, it became evident that through interpersonal rapport and gentle manipulation of the neck and extremities of the body complemented by slight changes in the position of the affected body parts, it was possible to induce muscular relaxation, vasomotor reactions, and mood changes of unexpected magnitude in the patients.

There were repeated attempts to implement Schultz autogenic training, but the majority of patients either could not relax or simply did not wish to cooperate. They responded immediately, however, to Calatonia. At that time, there was no intention of transforming Calatonia into a wholly separate technique although there are relatively few differences between the sequence as applied then and now.

Similar experiments were conducted in German hospitals, during a three-year stay in Germany after the end of the war. There, the same technique was applied to displaced individuals preparing for emigration, and to various members of the appalled and ashamed German population. In this setting, the technique was not performed on patients in the surgery ward but on patients suffering from trauma and those with psychological or neuropsychiatric disorders.

At that time, there was a first attempt at formulating an integrative basis to this method which was subsequently consolidated over the years, mainly in Brazil. There, it was possible to study the latest research on the reticular formation, vegetative representations in the cortex, and peripheral proprioceptors. Several colleagues in Brazil who adopted the method, many of whom were psychologists, began to collect and publish a significant number of research papers on Calatonia.

A future analysis will specify the theoretical basis of Calatonia. In this article, there is only a detailed description of the technique.

1) Preliminary instructions:
a) Explain the procedure to the patient, indicating that you will touch his/her toes, soles, ankles and calves very gently symmetrically with both hands for several minutes. The patient should not think about 'relaxing', and the technique

should start with no significant expectations, interference or curiosity from the patient's part.

b) Ask the patient to remove all jewellery, watches, belts, glasses, etc., or any such object that could cause pressure, discomfort or unnecessary stimulation.

c) The patient removes their shoes and socks, or tights and stockings in the therapist's absence. Contact lenses should also be removed.

d) The patient lies on their back with the ankles well-supported on the massage table or mat, arms loose beside the body and palms up. This is always the initial position. Palms may be faced downwards later if needed. When necessary, offer a light towel to cover the legs or a light blanket to protect against the cold. The hands may be placed under the blanket.

2) On the therapist's return to the relaxation room, repeat the instructions: "Try not to expect anything... Also, don't think about relaxing or trying to use yoga or other techniques... Breathe normally, without holding your breath... Let your thoughts come and go without becoming involved with them..." And finally: "it is easier with your eyes closed but you can keep them open if you feel better that way."

3) The sequence of stimuli is as follows:

a) With the thumb and middle finger of each hand, softly hold the middle toe's distal phalanx on each foot – keep your thumbs underneath the toes and the middle fingers over them, without touching the toenails. Do not pinch, move or massage the toes; exert a gentle touch 'as if holding soap bubbles'. Maintain this position for three minutes, keeping one's own body relaxed and being especially careful not to raise the shoulders. Some therapists like to half-close their eyes, but it is important to observe the patient for physical signs (e.g., fasciculation or face tremors, breathing pattern, involuntary movements of hands or fingers, facial expressions, fluttering eyelids, etc.), without verbalising your findings.

b) Move on to the second toe. Repeat the previous procedure by moving thumb and index finger to the second toe of each foot (corresponding to the index finger on the hands). When sensing this change, the patient may want to see or raise his/her head. Gently ask the patient to refrain from doing so. If the patient wants to comment or ask any questions about their impressions or temporary sensations, instruct the patient 'to briefly state in a low voice what he wants, keeping the eyes closed and without raising his/her head)'. Explain that usually, the therapist does not talk while the patient is relaxing. There can be exceptions, naturally. During Calatonia, some people provide valuable material (such as memories, flashbacks, opinions, intuitions) that should not be repressed, ignored or imposed as a topic to be brought up in the following sessions.

c) After three minutes, move on again to the fourth toe. Repeat the same procedure moving the thumb and ring finger to the fourth toe of each foot (corresponding to the ring finger on the hands) for three minutes; keep your own posture relaxed and observe the patient for possible responses. Even if the arms become tired, avoid placing any weight on the patient's toes. In the beginning, while still learning the technique, it may be difficult to find and maintain the right posture.

d) Move on again to the fifth toe (in the initial sequence of Calatonia, each step lasts three minutes). Repeat the same procedure moving the thumb and little finger to the fifth toe of each foot (corresponding to the little finger on the hands). The fifth toes may often be atrophied, crooked, displaced, or pressed out of shape. Even so, execute the sequence with care and patience (for three minutes).

e) Next, hold the big toe (hallux) of both feet using all five fingers – with thumbs providing lower support, the index and little fingers touching the sides, and the middle and ring fingers covering the toes (for three minutes).

Then, move on to touch the soles of the feet. Most often, the soles of the feet receive and transmit the most diverse and extreme forms of stimulation to the nervous system. In Calatonia, contact with this area consists solely of light touches, keeping the touch still at any given point.

f) With your index, middle and ring fingers together, softly touch the sole of each foot approximately at the metatarsal edge of the longitudinal arch for three minutes. There is often individual variation when localising this area. The deep plantar artery of the foot arch runs through this point.

g) The second point on the soles of the feet is the most concave portion of the longitudinal arch. It is easy to find, even in the case of flat feet. Use the same set of fingers, as before, to touch this point softly, for three minutes. Do not exert excessive pressure that could be perceived as 'pushing away' and interpreted by the patient as 'rejection'.

h) Gently lift the heels with your hands, with the palms supporting the heels and the Achilles tendons, without exerting pressure, and with the fingers extending a little below the extremities of the *malleolus medialis* projections (inner anklebones). The *malleolus lateralis* (outer anklebones) should rest in the angle formed by the proximal phalanx of the thumb and the metacarpal edge of the hand.

i) The last position is to shift your hands to the underside of the *triceps surae* muscle (in the middle of the calves). At the same time, the heels should be supported by the therapist's forearms, which will hold them slightly elevated above the surface.

4) After three minutes the therapist gently removes both hands and simply gives the following instructions which will enable the client to come back to the here and now:

> Gently move your toes…and fingers;
> open your eyes…close your eyes…open your eyes again;
> turn your head slowly to the right…turn your head slowly to the left; bring your shoulders towards your ears…relax your shoulders… bring your shoulders towards your ears again…relax your shoulders again;
> take a deep breath…
> turn your body over to one side; bring yourself gradually

up to a sitting position, without any rushed movement; when you are ready, stand up.

5) The therapist leaves the room to wash his hands, instructing the patient beforehand to get dressed (socks, shoes, etc.) and to sit down - giving them sufficient time to make the transition back to a state of normal awareness.

6) When returning to the room, the therapist asks about any (physical or psychological) observations the patient may have, making sure not to ask any leading questions. The therapist may comment that "sensations or experiences don't always arise during a session, and often not at the beginning stages of therapy".

Usually, patients do not know how to convey or report their experiences, and may say "it was just my imagination" or "it's not important". In these cases, just ask the patient to give a brief description in a neutral manner without justifying their experience or making any deprecatory comments on it in any manner. Patients can occasionally make exaggerated or false descriptions of their experiences, but these can be identified. There is no need to immediately prove a lack of authenticity to anything they report.

7) It is useful for patients to keep a journal of what they observe during relaxation. At least twice a day, the patient should do some form of relaxation at home. During the first stages of Calatonia conditioning, a 3 to 5-minute relaxation session will be enough, as follows:

a) Whilst lying or sitting down (somewhere comfortable), with no shoes on if possible, the patient focusses on the sole of one foot (or on any of the touchpoints in Calatonia, without evoking the presence of the therapist), and sustains their attention there for three natural breathing cycles. The patient then focusses on the sole of the other foot, repeating this procedure 3 or 4 times, counting off three breathing cycles for each foot.

b) At a later stage of therapy, this relaxation sequence may incorporate the palms of the hands, the front of the neck (especially for patients who present with symptoms of stammering) and the forehead, enabling the patient over time to elicit a relaxation response under any circumstances, and without any assistance.

c) Once the patient masters this technique, they will be able to start the exercise by focussing on the soles of the feet, allowing the whole body to 'surrender'. Some patients feel it is easier to elicit relaxation responses by focussing on the hands, which is also acceptable. Careful tailoring to individual preferences or practices will facilitate the development of customised aspects in the process, which can be implemented after regular use of the basic sequences.

8) There are cases when, for whatever reason, it is not possible to touch the patient's feet in Calatonia (amputation, mycosis, foot odour, etc.) or it may be necessary to start in the upper regions of the body (with restless or hyperactive children, for instance). In these situations, use the hands in a similar manner, after making some adjustments:

a) The patient raises both arms, which sometimes need to be supported on both sides by cushions or pillows, forming an acute angle just under 90 degrees - to avoid cutting off blood circulation. Keep the palms of both hands in a supine (upwards) position.

b) The stimulus sequence is the same, but this time the therapist's thumb will touch the cuticle of the patient's fingernails, and the corresponding therapist's fingers (will touch the pads (palmar face) of the patient's fingertips (e.g., the therapist's middle finger will touch the patient's middle finger and so on). The patient's fingers should not be stretched out, but rather should be in a comfortable and spontaneous flexion, that is, resting with palms facing upward.

It is easy to find the two points of the palms of the hands, and the therapist touches these points with his index, middle and ring fingers. Next, the therapist supports the underside of the hands and wrists, without clamping down on them, but instead, raising them slightly, being careful to prevent the arms from becoming rigid and/or constricted. The last point of contact will be 'wrists over wrists', with the therapist's fingertips covering the distal half of the patient's forearms. Any necessary adjustment will naturally depend on the relative size of both the therapist's hands and patient's forearms. The therapist should rest their hands lightly on the forearms, without exerting pressure or immobilising them, as this may give an overall negative impression (the patient could feel dominated or imposed upon by the therapist otherwise).

c) It is useful to enable the patient to relax their head, especially with children. The therapist holds the patient's head with both hands (joining both hypothenar eminences); the middle fingers touch the back of the neck in the region where the arteries, veins, and occipital nerves emerge. This technique should be applied gently. When removing the hands after 3 or 4 minutes, be careful not to shake the patient's head, because, in a state of deep relaxation, any sudden stimulus may produce undue emotional reactions, anxiety or embarrassment.

d) At home, the patient may also initiate a relaxation response by focussing on the palms of their hands. In the initial stage of treatment, it is better to avoid including the head in the conditioning sequence. Even later (this depends entirely on the individual), it is recommended that the patient wait for spontaneous relaxation responses, avoiding the imposition or practice of experimental techniques.

The therapist should be extremely cautious and considerate when suggesting or trying to apply new sequences. It is always advisable to be sure about the use of a technique by consulting with a supervisor or clinical team about the technical aspects or context of the application. The feet should always be the starting point for any Calatonia conditioning even when the patient has particular preference for the hands or head.

9) Stokvis and Wiesenhutter (1963) recommend relaxation particularly for spastic states, insomnia, and severe psychological conditions. Self-suggestive exercises are recommended for obsessive-compulsive neurosis, hypochondria (false self-sug-

gestive ideation of illness), self-control disturbances, hysteria (conversion), neurasthenia, addictions, functional somatisation, and for symptoms manifested in organic illnesses. Other uses may be: as a means of differential diagnosis (patients with psychosis have particularly adverse reactions to Calatonia when they are in an active episode); and as an educational tool - this last area looks very promising when applied on a larger scale.

They further emphasise that relaxation exercises utilising self-suggestion are not recommended for patients who:

are uncooperative;
lack self-confidence;
have intense anxiety;
have morbid fixations;
have poor concentration;
have oligophrenia and/or psychosis.

Other ways in which patients may fail to respond to relaxation exercises may be:

the patient wants to impose his/her 'will', is overly controlling or stressed;

the patient cannot relax adequately due to excessive curiosity;

the patient does not give in to the process, finds the technique too strange;

the patient frequently wants to assess, measure, understand, or does not want to engage;

the patient believes he/she must take the opportunity to release emotional tension;

the patient is opposed to the technique, does not take it seriously or only pretends to enter into a state of relaxation during treatment;

the patient intends to profit from a mental or physical illness (e.g., malingering for secondary gains);

the patient is in a hypobulic state (has a lowered ability to make decisions or understand outside stimuli);

the therapist applies the technique before having had

sufficient training, before becoming qualified or due to a lack of rigour;

other therapists disparage the treatment without providing valid criticism.

The distinctive conditioning that occurs during the Calatonia process allows the technique to be applied to and used with the majority of patients (with the exception of the cases and mediating factors listed above) and enables patients to learn and practise self-conditioning relaxation exercises at home.

10) There is a basic difference between Calatonia and other auto-suggestive or hypnotic methods and exercises. Calatonia uses cutaneous sensitivity, allowing for the simultaneous transfer and perception of different sensations (pressure, temperature, and nociception at lower intensities); thus, creating a multisensory experience. Furthermore, tactile stimulation enables the synthesis of aspects of conscious and unconscious perception, which are synchronised in unique configurations and to which each individual becomes attuned.

We now know that cutaneous sensitivity interweaves protopathic (vital-affective content, affective touch) and epicritic (conceptual-logical representations, discriminative touch) neural pathways, which are charged with an intensity that surpasses any occurrences and perceptions of the other sensory systems.

Our languages are rich in expressions borrowed from cutaneous sensation. They are used to describe affective-emotional experiences such as hard, tender, rough, mushy, burning, cold, soft, dry, warm, painful, cutting, hurtful, pleasant, etc. There are also some very complex cutaneous sensations which can be barely expressed in words. The field of sensory plasticity has yet to be sufficiently explored. The ectodermic origin that the skin shares with the nervous system in human embryogenesis explains the wide phenomenology that occurs during Calatonia stimulation. Unfortunately, there is no space in this brief description of the technique for a more detailed account of the biopsychological and neurophysiological aspects involved in the Calatonia process.

11) A trusting relationship can be built up between the client and therapist through a tailored and structured body-based technique. The diversity of material derived through Calatonia provides the basis for a therapeutic dialogue and for exploring the patient's personal history, identifying underlying issues in the present, and subsequent planning of the next steps in therapy.

The patient's observations about their feelings, emotions, ideas or intuitions resulting from experience with Calatonia can be integrated and analysed in the light of a wide array of other sources of information in order to enhance the psychotherapy process. Sources of information such as: a) verbal reports about issues or life difficulties in therapy; b) data about the patient's biological, physiological or religious background, age, sex, education, race and social status; and c) the therapist's observations of the organismic, psychological and noetic clues noticed during Calatonia (which may be directly linked to the patient's history). Thus, we can clearly see the multidimensional aspects of even (apparently) very simple reports made after a Calatonia session.

Observations or comments made after Calatonia can be verbal or non-verbal (e.g., drawings, paintings, artwork, etc.) and the therapist's interpretation will pursue different lines of approach, such as: a) an objective interpretation that considers only concrete evidence; or b) an intuitive or speculative interpretation based on the inherent or supposed symbolism of the material presented by the patient, which can be condensed or amplified depending on the system or school of thought that the therapist follows.

12) Calatonia also greatly enhances proximity to extra-rational areas of the psyche (such as aspects of the psyche that were once conscious and other aspects that have remained unconscious) and transpersonal areas (such as the collective unconscious), and to the holistic core of the psyche which is more than the sum of its components. This publication lists two case studies with descriptions of some aspects of these 'frequen-

cies' or altered states of mind. There are other descriptions of such states listed in the chapter on mental images.

We would also like to mention that this is the first account of the Calatonia technique ever given in a written publication.

References

Stokvis, B. & Wiesenhutter, E. (1963). *Der Mensch in der Entspannung*. Stuttgart, DE: Hipokrates.
This chapter was translated from:
Sándor, P. (1969). Calatonia. *Boletim de Psicologia, XXI*(57/58), 92-100.

2

The Legacy of Sándor

Paulo Toledo Machado Filho

When reference is made to Pethö Sándor and his work, it is almost always in the context of Calatonia and the Subtle Touch techniques. Yet his legacy is much broader than these techniques and is one that I address below, and also one which the reader is able to elucidate from each of the chapters in this publication. Initially, I note that Sándor, a Hungarian physician born in the city of Gyertyámos on April 28, 1916, and who arrived in São Paulo, in 1949, was one of the first Jungian therapists to practise in Brazil and was also the first psychologist to introduce Jung to Brazilian academia.

This happened in the early seventies, when Sándor began teaching Deep Psychology on the Psychology course at São Bento College, which was later transferred to the Pontifical Catholic University (PUC) of São Paulo. It was on this course that he began to teach body-based techniques, founding the study of Psychophysical Integration.

At that time in Brazil, psychology was still being structured as an area of professional training and practice. However, in the effervescent context of the 1960s and the collective changes that ensued, São Paulo boasted two eminent personalities who were particularly sensitive to these societal changes with regards to the body: Gaiarsa[1] and Sándor. Gaiarsa was more extroverted and followed in Reich's revolutionary footsteps, though he referred to Jung as his spiritual mentor, while Sándor was more introverted and contextualised his Subtle Touch approach within deep psychology and the relationship between mind and body. Sándor's viewpoint was to have a major influence on the academic environment at PUC, as previously mentioned, where the body was incorporated into clinical practice. This body-based approach, epitomised by Calatonia, emerged as a new model, having a significant impact on the hitherto stable patterns of psychological theories and behavioural psychology. It was a time of revolution.

Sándor's classes were revolutionary for that time and in that context. I remember that the students radiated a positive restlessness within a very special and distinctive atmosphere, most certainly engendered by the experience of his classes and in tune with the historical events of that time. The method (in fact, Sándor did not like to talk of methodology or any other forms of rigid systematisations) that he used valued both the acquisition of knowledge and of experience. For example, while students gained direct experience in applying body-based techniques, in other classes they also studied human anatomy and physiology, as well as the neurophysiological basis for the Subtle Touch sequences. We studied Jung, Jungian authors and other materials related to psychosomatic phenomena which Sándor translated himself. At the same time as we touched the body, we studied the psychophysical effect of touch, the neural substrates of emotional processing and the symbolism of emergent images. The students were fully involved in class and entered into an intense process of personal transformation. We try to maintain this dynamic on our course today, but in a pe-

---

1. José Ângelo Gaiarsa (b. 1920 in Santo André – d. 2010 in São Paulo): a psychiatrist and body therapist who wrote 35 books over the course of his career.

riod characterised by other configurations.

In the eighties, in the midst of the political crisis that our country was going through and which interfered with his teaching on the courses at PUC, Sándor received an invitation from Mother Cristina Sodré Dória (1916 – 1997) to transfer to the Sedes Sapientiae Institute. At the Institute, he took over the course on Psychomotor Therapy, which, some time later, was renamed "Analytical Psychology Integrated to Body-based Techniques." The course still exists today, but is now called "Jung and the Body", and taught as a specialisation course in analytical psychology and body-based therapy techniques. He went on to take over the course on Psychological Kinesiology, an advanced course in body-based therapy for those students who had already completed the course on "Jung and the Body".

In the context of Analytical Psychology, Sándor's influence is that of an independent pioneer operating outside of institutional constraints and the sphere of international "Societies", comparable to the work of Nise da Silveira, Roberto Gambini and others. The following reference to Sándor is found in Kirsch's encyclopaedia on Analytical Psychology throughout the world:

> Pethö Sandor (1916-1992) was a Hungarian gynaecologist who came to Brazil in 1949. A highly intuitive and introverted man, he taught at the Catholic University in São Paulo, where he made private translations of Jung's "Vision Seminars", and led discussions on the *Collected Works* of Jung. At the time they were not yet translated into Portuguese. He developed his own theory of "Subtle Touch Therapy", a kind of psychosomatic treatment. Though not accepted by the "theoretical" Jungians, he continued to work independently in his own individual way. (Kirsch, 2000, p. 197)

By developing his form of integrative psychology outside of the institutional context of Analytical Psychology, interesting intersections can be found mainly with psychosomatic studies and with organismic psychology, leading the academic study of Sándor's method in a uniquely interdisciplinary direction. Because it is a synthesis of different areas of study, it is loosely sympathetic to the Morinian concept of complexity (Petraglia, 2001), which touches on various holistic perspectives and our interactions with the quantum universe. Understanding psychical energetics is enriched through one's understanding of mind-body interactions. As with any new approach, Sandor's method still awaits a deeper understanding of its relationship with academic models but it is already widely practised and is being constantly improved and adapted through clinical experience.

Sándor died on January 28, 1992, on his farm in Pocinhos do Rio Verde, a town in the state of Minas Gerais, taking his students, patients and relatives by surprise, due to the good health he had enjoyed. The perplexity and emptiness felt in the wake of his loss allowed us to assess the importance of his work and the intense relationship that was established between his work and his complex personality.

Some aspects of his strong and sometimes larger than life personality were common knowledge. Known for his great intuition, Sándor was also seen as a "Great Father", expanding the existential horizon of each of his students, nurturing them intellectually and affectively, showing them paths for exploration, helping them to make decisions and being present at difficult moments, extrapolating yet further the aspect of "friend" in the therapist, a friend who was never limited merely to the common place.

Added to the qualities described above, wherein the strong, generous, sensitive and intuitive sides of the personality of the "Great Father" emerged, Sándor was also "Workman", "Creator" and "Master". As a humble workman and artisan, he left us a huge body of his translations of Jung's texts and of other, mostly Jungian, authors in Deep Psychology in addition to texts from Psychosomatic Medicine and Organismic Psychology, most of which had never before been read in Brazil. He summarised this material and sometimes adapted it for use in his courses and study groups, where they were extensively debated and amplified. I wish, in particular, to highlight his translations of Jung's Vision Seminars; texts of Gustav Heyer (Kirsch, 2000, p. 124), a psychiatrist and a member of the Society for Analytical Psychology, which remain the only existing translations from the German originals; and of the German seminar on Vegetative Lability (VELA; Cortese, 2009) - translated and annotated with his own comments. From a psychosomatic standpoint, the latter two references form an important theoretical basis for the vision of an integrative psychology that Sándor constantly strove towards.

Sándor represented the "Creator", an archetypal reference that overlaps with, but does not exclude, that of the "Sower", terms which I forcibly use, perhaps even improperly so, to replace the term "Artist". Nevertheless, Sándor intuited and developed an immense repertoire of Subtle Touch sequences and other body-based techniques, in which Calatonia and Fractional Decompression stand out in particular.

These techniques are now widely used either as the main components in therapy itself or in conjunction with other psychotherapeutic approaches, creating a modality within Jungian psychology characterised by an integrative, psychophysiological or physio-psychic focus, wherein somatic and psychic processes are not perceived separately but as a coherent whole. A complementary Jungian-oriented theoretical basis for these techniques, which he also proposed, allows for a substantive symbolic understanding of emergent content in the therapeutic process. However, in his writings on Calatonia, Sándor included the possibility of using other theoretical frameworks to interpret the content emerging from his body-based techniques. In the role of "Artist", Sándor's "touch" was familiar to all who knew him, through the creative way in which Subtle Touch sequences were suitably developed, and often came from a seemingly inexhaustible supply of suggestions and experiences made in supervisions of patient cases, in group discussions and readings, so characteristic of his classes. In the same vein, it is interesting to consider that he never assumed the title of "creator", modestly preferring the expressions "propose", "suggest" or "indicate" when referring to the techniques that "were configured" (another of his favourite expressions) on his life's journey, perhaps tellingly aware that knowledge itself is universal.

Finally, it was possibly as "Master" that his image is most deeply fixed in the memory of those who knew him. In his classes or discussion groups, the elucidations, summations and precise comments that he made were always memorable, but the most important aspect was the experience of participating in these groups experiencing and sharing one's knowledge of the body-based techniques under discussion. This learning experience could not and cannot be taught directly by the teacher and must come through the students' own experience, as a modality of "initiatory knowledge" which is acquired only "from the inside out". This condition presupposes that the full knowledge and application of the techniques are only gained through their practice. The latter aspect also points to a fundamental feature of his teachings: *gnosis*, the inner knowing of knowledge.

Inherent to this maxim is the cultivation of a suitable internal attitude towards receiving instruction, which also, when applying one of the techniques, corresponds to the concept of the "Third Point". In Sándor's view, the "Third Point" should be adapted by the therapist according to their individual conduct and is the subject of analysis in my master's thesis (Machado Filho, 1994). To his closest students he also confided his belief that one's spiritual relation to knowledge should elicit and guide the formation of this "point". His way of reasoning was conducted on a consistent theoretical and empirical basis, as well as by his powerful intuition: precisely the point where he differed from the objective, pragmatic and reductive pattern of transmitting knowledge in an academic environment. Yet he remained profoundly systematic and almost ceremonially reverent in his aforesaid reasoning, which led him to suggest methods of study, to inspire postgraduate theses and to recommend research without ever having pursued an academic career, strictly speaking. Despite this, Sándor was often invited to participate on examination panels because of his intellectual range and depth.

All the same, his greatest contribution, together with the legacy of his teaching, was Calatonia and the Subtle Touch technique. He described these techniques as having emerged from his experiences in the Second World War, during which he lost both his parents and his first wife in tragic circumstances. With few resources available for relieving the pain and suffering of patients who had been seriously injured and traumatised as a result of the war, these techniques became more and more invaluable. He also stated that it was a product of a pact he had made when his parents died, to give his own life over to the service of humanity. Thus, once he had booked his passage for Brazil after his experiences in the refugee camps of WWII, our country was blessed by his presence, by Calatonia that is now wide-spread here, and by his inexhaustible creativity.

Sándor's contribution to knowledge arose much more from directly teaching his students and treating his patients; the immense influence that his work held for his disciples also came about through his translations, lectures and practical exercises in body-based techniques. He left relatively few written works, even about Calatonia. As has already been pointed out, this fruitful area of study formed the subject of numerous academic articles, postgraduate theses and book publications, while Sándor himself wrote only two chapters in a short book on Relaxation Techniques, which he also edited. In a concise and objective style, Sándor defines Calatonia as meaning a "loose and relaxed body tone", adding a small mystery for us to decipher: "but not only from a static and muscular perspective".

The key to the above mystery can be found perhaps in his etymological description of the word Calatonia, which in the original Greek derives from the verb *khalaó*, indicating "relaxation", "nourishment", "freeing oneself from anger, fury and violence", "opening a door", "untying the bindings of a water-skin", "letting go", "forgiving one's parents", "lifting the veils from one's eyes", etc. Leaving aside the etcetera for another time, I will focus my attention here on Sándor's original descriptions of the Greek verb khalaó.

Sándor initially describes this etymological precursor as a process of "relaxation", related to the "loose and relaxed body tone" of Calatonia and one which leads to a state of well-being, as commonly associated with this technique. He then continues with "and nourishment as well". As it is a relaxation technique, this idea of nourishment is somewhat curious as one may associate it with the physical act of eating. It leads to the question: what is feeding? The most immediate image that emerges is that of spiritual or psychical nourishment. Another association that can be made with nourishment is that of femininity and maternal care; through breastfeeding, an altruistic act of unconditional love, the mother gives of her very own being to the child. Likewise Calatonia expresses an altruistic, feminine and nourishing quality directed to the spirit instead of the body. This quality is also evidence of the positive relationship Sándor had with the many students and therapists who learned from him.

He moves on to a description of "freeing oneself from anger, fury and violence". An immediate association that springs to mind is that of the very genesis of Calatonia, which occurred during World War II, when Sándor's personal experience of dealing with tragic losses led him to explore and transmute the ghosts of his past. This meaning hints at a change in attitude, as Calatonia allows the individual to establish a degree of inner peace that departs from a crazed condition of violence or fury. The sequence of touches in Calatonia also allows the body to regain homeostasis (a state of neurogenerative balance), after suffering from stress.

He continues on to "opening a door", or even "crossing a threshold", which signifies coming into further contact with another state of consciousness and which brings to mind an experience of initiation. The image conjured by this definition is very profound and reminds us that the observation of Calatonia is a process of therapy, corresponding to a cascade of transmutation (an expression that Sándor was fond of using to refer to psychical changes that occur from the inside out) of the individual's state of consciousness. To open a door is also to open one's eyes (or to open one's consciousness) up to another form of reality, which can also be representative of a novel perspective. Or simply a new way of "seeing".

The next meaning of the verb *khalaó* to which he refers, "untying the bindings of a waterskin", also suggests numerous interpretations starting with the waterskin itself which, as a bag that stores liquid, is a metaphor for the body. To untie the bindings of a waterskin is to untie the bindings which fasten the body giving rise to freedom of expression through one's body; that which needs to flow is made to flow freely, including the emotions - emotions have always had a pattern of flow. When emotions become trapped the body is bound in place, yet when fingertips subtly touch the tips of one's toes the body loosens and lets go. Sándor spoke of the "neurovegetative commutations" set in motion by emotions being regulated: body warmth, stomach rumbles, palpitations, and so on.

Then comes the "letting go", which indicates a loosening, a release, and unburdening of oneself and taking one's own path. It is an expression of going on one's way, of winning one's freedom. Sandor stated that one should be free to explore the possibilities and rhythms of one's body, "provided you knew what you were doing", to let oneself go responsibly. Campbell (1991), in "The Power of Myth", spoke of following one's own myth, i.e., of following one's happiness; thus, to let go is also to allow the soul path to unfold.

Then, the expression "forgiving one's parents" represents a new covenant with the parental lineage, the lineage from which we must differentiate, in order to grow. However, as we mature and become equally parents, after putting ourselves in the place our parents occupied before us, there comes the need for forgiveness: without forgiveness, we cannot integrate the function of the new role. Through forgiveness, our heart becomes lighter and our resolve becomes clearer and deeper.

Finally, the etymon *khalaó* further indicates "lifting the veils from one's eyes". This meaning is an intriguing one and the derivative of the verb could not have been better chosen. "Lifting the veils" is to open one's eyes to the frontiers of knowledge, to a deeper understanding of it. It is the very definition of *gnosis*, the inner knowing of knowledge which is revealed when one reaches an illuminated state of awareness.

The format of a text and discourse demands limits, precisely because we know that a trajectory of association and amplification has no end. However, a little more about Calatonia and its scope is known, and "why" it is so very important to us. However, now, many years after Sándor's death, how can these techniques be introduced to those who are new to them? After having been so well guided and cared for all this time, having opened the doors and untied the bindings of the waterskin, having found our way and forgiven our parents, and having lifted (almost?) all of the veils from our eyes, we ask: what now?

The world is very different; many walls have been knocked down, patriarchal omnipotence has given way to the feminine, even polarities themselves have become defined in terms of possibility; information and messages are no longer solely the prerogative of the powerful. The relationship between teacher and student has also become more egalitarian, our bodies are less weighed down with societal guilt, although we often feel self-conscious when talking about our body in public and students often have difficulty relaxing when Calatonia is practised on them in class.

The act of touch is no longer as cathartic as it once was; an operative intentionality now governs students' experiences of body-based techniques and they often ask: what are they used for? In what contexts can they be applied? In times past we commented on the sensations which emerged from Calatonia - today we have greater access to colourful neuroimages of emotions as they flow through our neurocircuitry: we have become too cognitivist and a little lazier. Yet in this changing world we resist the subjugation of the sensitive by economic forces and by political power hammered home on social media. And the body, which can remain static for hours in front of a screen to the detriment of the functioning brain, nevertheless manages to dance loosely and to work out in the gym. Although we have untied the bindings and lifted many veils, it seems that we still are very much in need of Calatonia.

The adoption and practice of Calatonia continues to grow in therapy settings in a discreet, albeit safe and consistent way; even if it is not as ground-breaking as it once was, it certainly remains a powerful therapeutic technique. And the unconscious content which can be analysed from its images is still profoundly revealing, despite competition from colourful brain scans which reveal the neurocircuitry of emotion.

Through his reserved and modest demeanour, Sándor seemed to realise that his greatest achievement was to have mobilised an archetype related to knowledge, whose origin he recognised as universal, and over which he never intended to assert ownership. He was much more interested in the aim that his students might integrate this content and that the benefits of Calatonia be made available to all who needed it, so that he could rest in peace. He did not leave us with a "finished work", instead showing us a path which requires and involves personal development, humility and learning. After all, what he least intended was to leave behind a legacy of "Sandorians" ...

References

Campbell, J. (1991). *The Power of Myth*. New York, NY: Anchor Books.

Cortese, F. (2009). *Calatonia and Physiopsychic Integration*. São Paulo, SP: Editora Escuta.

Joint Association of Classical Teachers. (2010). *Aprendendo Grego*. São Paulo, SP: Odysseus.

Kirsch, T. B. (2000). *The Jungians (A Comparative and Historical Perspective)*. London, UK: Routledge.

Machado Filho, P. T. (1994). *Gestos de Cura e seu Simbolismo* (Unpublished master's thesis). University of São Paulo, São Paulo, Brazil.

Petraglia, I. C. (2001). *Edgar Morin, A Educação e a Complexidade do Ser e do Saber*. Petrópolis, RJ: Vozes.

Sándor, P. (1974). *Técnicas de Relaxamento*. São Paulo, SP: Vetor.

3

The Academic Teaching of Calatonia

Rosa Maria Farah

One of the main characteristics of Calatonia is its apparent simplicity. At first glance, the single-mindedness required for the sequence of subtle touches, to the uninitiated, may give the false impression that all that is required is to learn to reproduce certain gestures correctly in order to use the technique.

For this reason, Sándor taught his students based on an experiential process, both as a patient and as a therapist, to contextualise the method of Calatonia as a therapeutic framework. This was his methodology for the groups of students who attended courses in his office, for the students he later taught at PUC-SP, and in the postgraduate courses at the Sedes Sapientiae Institute in São Paulo.

In this way, he physically and psychologically "softened" (sic) and prepared his students to perceive the profound effects of subtle touches, and that experience dissolved the students' "cognitive resistance". Because the students were, from the very start, impacted by the experience with Subtle Touch and Calatonia, they were genuinely curious and intellectually open to learn about the foundations of the method.

With his remarkably centred and focussed personality, the mere presence of Sándor in the classroom created the necessary conditions for an appropriate attitude on the part of the students. This attitude – one of deep respect and receptiveness - was not commonly held by university students at that time (in the early 1970s), as most of the classes were composed of young people who were accustomed to challenging and questioning *a priori* any and all of the teaching that was offered to them.

The predominant mindset in psychology at that time was Cartesian dualism, focussing on the cognitive aspects of learning. In this context, a somatic approach to psychology was still generally regarded as a near-heretical practice, often associated with "unserious" (i.e., unscientific) interventions.

In this setting, Sándor's calm firmness allowed his teachings to be welcomed and appreciated by the students. His firmness was also expressed in the requirement of punctuality and assiduous attendance of his classes. However, once these conditions were established, his courses were an inexhaustible source of knowledge and sustenance to his students.

Sándor established this caring environment more through presence and attitudes than through words, as his verbal instructions were often synthetic and objective. When introducing a new technique in class, he showed the group "how to do it" then added some brief comments. One of his favourites was "this must be done without effusiveness" (sic). With this expression, he conveyed the essential difference between a "friendly touch" and the therapeutic touch: both are attentive and careful, but the latter is not affected by emotionality.

Sándor also emphasised essential teachings about the introduction of touch to the therapeutic relationship, as some aspects of this issue emerged spontaneously during classroom practice. For example, transferential and counter-transferential aspects linked to touching appeared early on in practical classes, facilitating the perception and processing of those aspects by the students.

In parallel, the reading list for the courses ranged from "anatomy sheets" - adapted from Gray's Anatomy for use in class - to Jungian texts that had not yet been published in Portuguese, and which were translated by Sándor.

This was, in general terms, the atmosphere of the groups and courses in which Calatonia was singularly brought to life by its creator. Learning the sequences of subtle touches occurred in a contextualised way, not only as a technique, but as a new therapeutic paradigm and as a psychotherapeutic intervention in psychology.

Contextualising the Presentation of Calatonia

Having passed through the group dynamics and the learning described above, it has since become a continuous challenge to move from an apprenticeship to the position of one who teaches the method of Calatonia. In 1978, a group of Sándor's former students, including myself, took over the coordination of the Somatic Studies nucleus[1] available to students on the undergraduate course in Psychology in the Department of Human Sciences and Health at PUC-SP. Since then, this nucleus - now called "The Body in Psychology" - has gone through different denominations and reformulations in its pedagogical planning. However, Calatonia has always been present as a core component, to be carried out by the students in their clinical internship as a requirement of the course.

A detailed description of the content that makes up the current curriculum of this nucleus is beyond the scope of this article. Thus, I will mention here only some of the general characteristics concerning its structure, with a greater focus on the teaching of Calatonia itself.

Currently, the nucleus is available as an elective component to 5th year Psychology students, as part of their final year of studies over two semesters. The program structure is distributed over twelve hours of weekly activities, including

---
1. Nucleus: teaching unit available to psychology students at PUC-SP. They refer to a set of theoretical and practical course subjects that deal with a particular psychological theme or approach, also including a supervised clinical internship.

theoretical and practical classes in the following subjects: *Basic Principles of Somatic Approaches in Psychology; Somatic Techniques in Psychology: Theory and Practice; Somatic Development; Experiential Techniques*. Students also carry out their supervised clinical internship in which they provide therapy to patients at PUC-SP Clinical School, according to the parameters of their chosen psychological approach.

For the theoretical and practical classes - the core subjects - the whole class meets, composed of groups of 20 to 25 students in each academic year. Internship supervisions are carried out in smaller groups, composed of six or seven students. These activities are conducted by a team currently composed of four teachers; the faculty members in 2016 were Flávia Hime, Irene Gaeta, Leda Perillo Seixas, and Rosa Maria Farah, coordinator.

This ratio of hours per class allows the students to immerse themselves in experiential activities, greatly stimulating the amplification of their own body perception, which is exactly the primary objective of the course. However, due to the course focus on professional preparation, it is important for students to learn each of the different techniques as well as their theoretical bases: both those related to the conceptual bases of the techniques and the theoretical reference of Analytical Psychology.

In this context, Calatonia is taught in *Somatic Techniques in Psychology* but not in the first weeks of class. Although the Somatic Studies nucleus is an elective subject, students may not always be receptive to physical contact. Some students are not psychologically ready to deal with the subjective processes set in motion by the exchange of therapeutic touches with classmates. In addition to this individual factor, it is necessary to consider the need to create mutual trust in a sufficiently welcoming group atmosphere. This way, each student's self-exposure within the group does not become a threat that compromises the participation of the most introverted or sensitive of students due to fear of shaming and vulnerability.

Fortunately, the work conditions described above allow

us to create several preparatory situations that aim to promote an environment that is conducive to the application of subtle touches, from both a practical and ethical standpoint. Thus, the first classes in this subject, *Somatic Techniques in Psychology,* envisage activities that seek to cultivate a group atmosphere of respect, acceptance, moderation and trust. This is also a good time for teachers to observe and to form a rough impression of the students gathered there: their personalities, attitudes, needs and expectations.

Part of this process is the student's individual sketch of "Drawing their Own Body" and the joint observation of these drawings by the class. This activity allows students to establish personal exchanges quite different from those to which they are accustomed in their day-to-day life at university.

Another example is the "Hands Dance" (Farah, 2008): a playful exercise performed in pairs, in which the students' fine tactile perception is stimulated. This dance is usually brought to a close with an activity focussing on integration of the group as a whole.

After both these and other warm-up and group integration activities, the technique of Calatonia is presented to the class around the 7th or 8th week of the course. The students begin to practise using the first sequence established by Sándor: Calatonia to the feet and the head (Sándor, 1982; Farah, 2008 and 2016). After observing a demonstration of the sequence of touches by the teacher, the students form pairs to perform it, switching between giving and receiving touches after completing the sequence. In the subsequent classes, the students will have at least four opportunities to give and receive the Calatonia sequence with different partners. In addition, they also have the chance to make their first personal observations on the subtleties involved in touch-mediated contact, that is, they have the ability to perceive the nuances of touching and being touched by different individuals.

Later, other Subtle Touch sequences such as, "Fractional Decompression", the "Extended Calatonia Sequence" and some variations of touches performed along the spine (Farah, 2008) are progressively introduced. These and other sequences of subtle touches are practised and experienced by the students depending on the issues and needs that arise in the classes, especially when they relate to patient cases in the clinical internship.

At the end of each activity, the teacher always sets aside a time for comments, impressions and observations with the group. These exchanges aim not only to create the opportunity to clarify doubts about the procedures performed, but also - and especially - to provide the chance for awareness and personal processing of the repercussions of the touches.

The exercises are also interspersed with the theoretical underpinnings of the module, in which the specific conceptual foundations of Calatonia are studied. Subjects such as the "neurophysiological functions of the skin", "levels of tactile stimulus", "altered states of consciousness" produced by relaxation and the appearance of "images" in Calatonia, among others, are also part of this module.

At the same time, the other core modules are given concurrently; in *Experiential Techniques,* students continue their experience classes of the other techniques presented in the nucleus; in *Somatic Development,* students follow theoretical-practical classes on developmental issues as they pertain to the needs of the body; in *Basic Principles of Somatic Approaches in Psychology,* students attend theoretical classes on the general principles and foundations of the somatic-based approach in psychology, with emphasis on concepts from Analytical Psychology (Farah, 2008).

At this stage of the course, students are expected to conduct therapy sessions and participate in supervision with a licensed therapist as part of their clinical internship. Thus, our students experience the roles of patient and therapist of the Calatonia sequence.

Student Body-Awareness

We can observe that the set of activities that compose the core modules is quite extensive, even while aimed at an introductory level to Calatonia. However, as previously pointed out, the learning outlined here is not intended to happen at purely cognitive and intellectual levels, but also requires the students to attune at the somatosensory and affective levels.

Learning to be present in one's body and to heighten somatosensory perception can be seen as a way of educating the senses. Intuition and sensation both complement the thought-feeling axis of rational functions, and allow unconscious content that is not always perceived by these rational functions to emerge into consciousness.

In addition, from the very beginning of the academic year it is recommended that students undergo their own psychotherapy process before they start to provide therapy to their patients. At the same time, the students are also asked to provide the faculty with personal history they deem relevant for sharing for the purpose of the course. This includes information about general health conditions, such as surgeries, serious or chronic illnesses, medications or medical treatments, and mental health issues.

Group Work as a Teaching Resource

The set of practical activities described above comprise the principal strategies aiming to fulfil one of the main objectives of the nucleus: the expansion of the students' own somatosensory perception and, as a consequence, an enhanced awareness of their body. In this context, we emphasise a group learning paradigm in our modules, demanding special attention from the teachers when selecting the techniques and exercises used in class.

Under favourable conditions, we observe that the personal development of the students - even in relation to the teaching objectives – is greatly improved, both quantitatively and qualitatively, in a group learning situation.

We recall here the comment made by Sándor when the subject of the active nature of groupwork was brought up in his classes. He expressed its formulation as one of the laws of psychic energy: "The force (of psychic energy) increases, that is, it is potentiated according to a factorial sequence." To better understand this idea, let's look at an illustration of this type of sequence:

1 individual = 1.(multiplied by) 1 = 1
2 individuals = 1.1.2 = 2
3 " = 1.1.2.3 = 6
4 " = 1.1.2.3.4 = 24
5 " = 1.1.2.3.4.5 = 120
6 " = 1.1.2.3.4.5.6 = 720 and so on.

For example, in a group composed of six people - in terms of mobilised psychic energy – there occurs the equivalent of the stimulation provided by 720 people individually.

Sándor also referred to "group syntality": an idiosyncratic atmosphere of groupwork which, if properly cultivated, creates the necessary conditions for the group to offer the support and security conducive to the development of its members. Syntality also refers to the group's personality traits that are nurtured in a particular group combination, in this case, a therapeutic one.

Highlighting the Results

As an illustration of the results obtained throughout the nucleus, we have reproduced below some of the excerpts from the self-assessments made by our students at the end of the 2016 academic year. Additionally, a selected number of drawing pairs have been reproduced, as a "Before and After" snapshot at the beginning and end of the course. We are grateful to our students of the 2016 class who generously agreed to the reproduction of their drawings and excerpts here. Their names have been changed for the purposes of anonymity.

One of the questions in the final self-assessment questionnaire of the nucleus was: "Of the body techniques presented during the year, which was the most significant for you? How? Describe the relevance it holds for you." We reproduce below some excerpts of the answers given by students. It is interesting to observe how contact with the Subtle Touch techniques impacted each student in a unique way.

Claudia

I can't say that it was only Calatonia that was responsible for the changes in me. I believe that all the support of my personal therapy, the other exercises in the nucleus, its organisation, and the teachers helped me greatly as well. But considering the frequency and intensity of my contact with Calatonia, I can see that after entering the core of my body, my personal dynamic and the way I interact with myself and the world have changed a great deal. My defences and complexes have dissolved more, some issues that were not addressed in therapy were finally discussed and this led me to a different perspective on them. I entered into a dynamic which is moved more by extroversion, by expressiveness and expansion towards others, to the midpoint. In contrast to the greater rigidity and withdrawal caused by a strengthening of defences and complexes previously held. (Claudia, November 2016)

Irene

Receiving Calatonia has personally always been very enjoyable, since it allowed me to have access to some memories which are important to me. Professionally, the use of Calatonia with my clinical patient has been very important, as he began to feel more comfortable in the context of therapy and started to bring up some very intimate issues, which did not occur before the procedures. (Irene, November 2016)

Renato
The soft touches to the feet and spine gave me a feeling of balance and support that continued for a few days after their application and that helped me a lot. These techniques also made me see body-based techniques in another light. At the beginning of the nucleus, I was somewhat sceptical. I thought this approach would work more as a support for verbal therapy, but now I realise that body therapy is a therapy in itself. (Renato, November 2016)

Luiz
It is incredible to think that such a complete and powerful technique was developed by someone who had fled the war, and conceived of his work through those who suffered in that period and in his work as an obstetrician. It is as if I have received a very valuable legacy, as if something I had been waiting for over a long time came into my hands and now must be kept and passed on so that others can benefit from this valuable technique. I'm hoping for the day that Calatonia can be found in the dictionary. (Luiz, November 2016)

Highlighting the Evolution of Body Image:
Before and After Pairs of "Drawing your own Body"
Here we highlight some of the pairs of drawings done by some of our students in a "Before and After" snapshot. The first pair of drawings (male and female) was done in March 2016 and the second in November 2016, corresponding to the start and end of the academic year, respectively (Farah, 2008).

Helena

Female Figure 1: March 2016

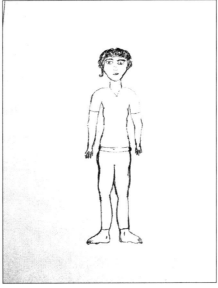

Female Figure 2: November 2016

Helena

Male Figure 1: March 2016

Male Figure 2: November 2016

Marcia

Female Figure 1: March 2016

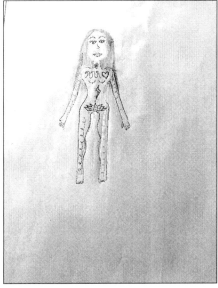

Female Figure 2: November 2016

Marcia

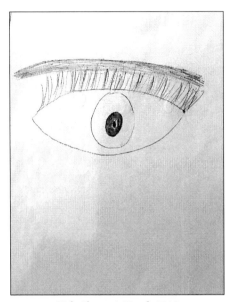

Male Figure 1: March 2016

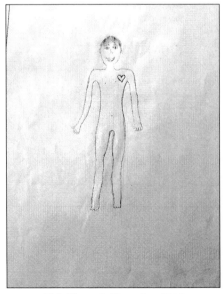

Male Figure 2: November 2016

Renato

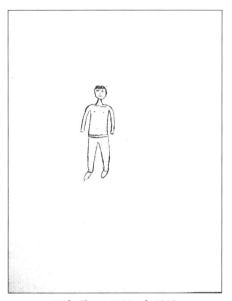

Male Figure 1: March 2016

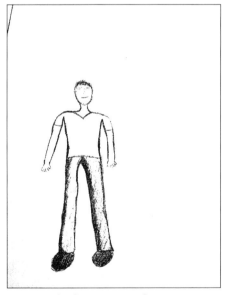

Male Figure 2: November 2016

Renato

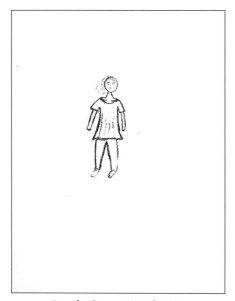

Female Figure 1: March 2016

Female Figure 2: November 2016

Marina

Female Figure 1: March 2016

Female Figure 2: November 2016

Marina

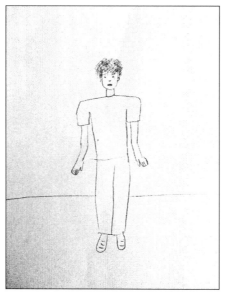

Male Figure 1: March 2016

Male Figure 2: November 2016

Final Considerations

The symbolism and imagery expressed in the drawings illustrate that the authors are in an ongoing process of transformation, even at the year's close. These figures, far from portraying a full and detailed description of their authors, illustrate only flashes of the course these young people are on towards the development of their personal and professional identities. Even so, they demonstrate how tactile stimulation may be central to human development at all stages of life, acting as an important therapeutic resource.

The bond with one's own body can function as a basis for bonding with others. The education of the senses enables maturation from within and is necessary for the integration between body and mind. Somatic techniques in general - and subtle touches in particular - are instruments that facilitate change and growth, bringing liveliness to the senses and allowing for a more conscious and expanded existence.

Especially in the context of a psychologist's training, this form of awareness has proved to be a key resource for their development. We know that not all of our students will go on to become therapists in their future career. Some even state in advance that they intend to pursue other fields or areas in psychology. However, the aim of this nucleus is not limited to training professionals who will necessarily use Calatonia in their daily professional practice. Our goal is a little more ambitious, since we intend to offer them a broader reference for life.

In synthesis, our proposition is a view of psychology which considers 'contact' - and consequently an **attentive presence** - an essential condition for any form of psychological intervention or work. We trust that after the course our students will be able to continue to cultivate and integrate this holistic stance of self-observation, psycho-physical attunement with themselves and others, and the insights from these experiences. Finally, we hope that by furthering their development, this stance will be carried into their relationships in general, whether they be personal or professional ones.

References

Farah, R. M. (2008). *Integração psicofísica – o trabalho corporal e a psicologia de C. G. Jung*. São Paulo, SP: Editora Companhia Ilimitada.
Farah, R. M. (2017). *Calatonia – Subtle Touch in Psychotherapy*. São Paulo, SP: Editora Companhia Ilimitada
Sándor, P. (1982). *Técnicas de relaxamento*. São Paulo, SP: Vetor.

4

Jung and the Body: Using Calatonia in Individual and Group Psychotherapy

Sandra Maria Greger Tavares

The practice of psychotherapy requires the continuous revision of the therapist's theoretical foundations and methods, so as to guarantee a greater degree of efficacy and to adapt to the many different contexts and populations that psychotherapy is designed to address. This chapter discusses individual and group modalities in psychotherapy grounded in a Somatic-Jungian perspective (Sándor, 1982); we reflect further on their specific relevance to mental health demands in the Brazilian public healthcare system.

The Practice of Psychotherapy in Brazil

My work has been guided by an interest in investigating appropriate psychotherapeutic methods to meet the complex demands given the presence of several socioeconomically disadvantaged populations within Brazilian public healthcare (Greger Tavares, Vannuch, & Machado, 2015; Tavares Duran, 1997).

A general pattern that emerges from the mental health resources available to the general public in Brazil, is that meetings between therapist and patient often represent a relationship between two individuals of widely-different socioeconomic backgrounds. Boltanski (1989) refers to this social distance between the user of a public health service and the professional who treats them, particularly between patient and doctor, by emphasising that: "... (members of the working-class) are separated from (a doctor) by the same social distance that separates a middle- or upper-class member from the working-class, especially one who is highly educated and who possesses expert knowledge" (pp. 134-135).

Building a bond of trust in the vacuum caused by the socio-cultural distance between patient and psychotherapist, and developing a program of psychotherapy that is relevant for the daily life of the patient is an arduous task. It requires, first and foremost, respect of and interest in the other individual while avoiding the precipitation and imposition of cultural values and, above all, avoidance of situations which may cause "social humiliation".

Gonçalves Filho (1995) describes the phenomenon of social humiliation as a form of anguish that emerges from social inequality, the injustices of which the poor are acutely aware and mark many aspects of their existence and submission. According to Gonçalves Filho (1995), the poor suffer most severely from the psychological impact of maltreatment and constant implicit reinforcement of their "inferiority". The experience of humiliation is a constant possibility, whether in reality or as some imagined slight, and often leads to the perception of having no rights, of being viewed as dirty or repugnant, of living and speaking as if one were invisible.

Social and cultural differences need to be confronted and explained to one another through communication strategies that make it possible to transcend and not to justify the power relations which frequently occur in the relationship between psychotherapist and patient in the same sociocultural milieu.

While working as a psychologist in the Basic Health Unit (UBS) of the Unified Health System (SUS) in Brazil, I frequently observed that there was a high rate of dropout, with a majority of patients giving up on therapy shortly after initial evaluation, despite the long waiting list for available therapists.

Several factors appear to be associated with this rate of dropout, such as a lack of psychotherapy options and approaches, communication difficulties and difficulties in social interaction between patient and psychotherapist, the stigma associated with mental health disorders, and other factors.

In the context of Brazilian healthcare, the figure of the doctor and the experience of physical sickness still represent the predominant framework within which patients seek mental health assistance, particularly for members of the lower classes. "The Doctor" is the professional most in demand at all UBS centres, and the one who is first consulted when "something is not right". The demand for mental health professionals by the general public is most often a demand for mental health problems to be solved through medical intervention.

The terminology most often employed in this context is one replete with descriptions and explanations of the physical aspects of the individual's mental health, eminently pathological in nature. Nevertheless, once they finally receive a consultation with the doctor, UBS patients often remain in silence or speak very little. They limit themselves only to answering what the "doctor" asks as the doctor's "time is short". Reading between the lines of their silence however, they often reveal intense psychological suffering which, in most cases, is never fully addressed by the doctor.

These are the same patients who are most often referred to the psychologist by the physician when they show physical symptoms of "something" that cannot be diagnosed and much less treated by medical doctors. These same patients then meet with a psychologist because, in their own words, "there's nothing wrong", at least nothing that can be treated by medical knowledge.

Thus, a psychologist begins the patient's treatment by dealing with "nothing", with something that cannot be expressed in words but which is somehow manifested in the body.

By offering a UBS patient the opportunity to be heard, as is the case in a preliminary interview, the subject of the body and its physical manifestations comes up more often than not. These complaints are often expressed as "pains that come and go in the body", "heart palpitations", "roiling of the flesh", "lightheadedness and screws loose", among other "somatic manifestations". These patients also report "episodes of bodily exploitation" (Tavares Duran, 1997), i.e., experiences that leave delible "marks" on the body as a consequence of social exploitation and alienation: symptoms of work-related illnesses, accidents at work, hunger, physical abuse, sexual violence, among others.

The body is continually built and rebuilt through social interaction. What is the most common form that these "corporeal manifestations" take in those patients who have lived through episodes of maltreatment and bodily exploitation? At what stage of their psychosocial trajectory do they occur?

The patients who use the public Unified Health System converge on the body as the repository of a numerous manifestations of unconscious psychic content and styles of social interaction and insertion in the ways they express their living conditions. Can these specific demands be addressed through methods of psychotherapy that predominantly employ verbal interaction, given that these manifestations are most often expressed non-verbally?

Individual Treatment in Somatic Jungian Psychotherapy: The Baker's Case

In order to discuss the development of somatic Jungian psychotherapy in the context of public healthcare, a case of individual psychotherapy is analysed below (Greger Tavares, 1998).

This is the case of Mr. João (pseudonym), who was referred for psychological evaluation at the UBS by a general practitioner because, in his words, "there was nothing wrong" (sic) with him.

Mr. João was born in the Northeast Region of Brazil and migrated to the Southeast at a young age. As a Northeasterner, he carries a cultural baggage from his place of birth that ultimately informs his speech and outlook of the world. As is the case in many countries, the diversity of ethnicities in a country the size of Brazil results in considerable cultural, racial and economic differences between regions[1].

Awareness of this sociocultural background is of utmost importance to a full understanding of the subtleties and regional variations found in the vernacular expressions used by Mr. João, as they reflect the narrator's relationship with cultural values, habits and places - in other words, his cultural identity.

Mr. João, 56, introduced himself as a baker from northeastern Brazil and as a man of faith who followed an evangelical form of Christianity.

When he came to his first session of psychotherapy, Mr. João expected to be received by a doctor to whom, according to his beliefs, "God lends his wisdom", and had no prior expectations of a psychologist and/or psychotherapy.

Several forms of Christianity have become popularised in Brazil, and their dogmas are often diametrically opposed to the secular views and lack of bias held in psychology. Although the importance that religion has in the lives of its adherents cannot be denied, in the clinical practice of psychology we view beliefs as personal and intimate, and not to be judged according to the precepts of psychological science. However in certain religious practices, there is often a narrow scope for understanding the perspectives and practices of psychology such as psychotherapy, and having recourse to them is often seen as a form of "moral weakness".

It was a great challenge for me to even understand this

---

[1]. The Southeast has been historically developed as the center of economic and political power, whereas the Northeast experienced a later process of industrialization and capitalist development. Between the 1960's and 1980's, such disparity led to a significant wave of migration from the Northeast to the Southeast, during which anti-Northeastern sentiments arose in the Southeast. Even though this instance of regional migration abruptly declined as early as the 1990's, prejudicial and vaguely racist views associated with the Northeasterners remain very much in place among the Southeastern population.

man who at first seemed to be from a foreign country. He used unusual words when describing his symptoms, complaining of a "big, bad, churning in the chest", a "roiling of the flesh", and a "nervousness that other doctors couldn't cure". He explained that his body had been thoroughly examined through blood tests, electrocardiograms, and other tests and they had all said that "he had nothing wrong with him". They then sent him to the "head doctor", as he began to call me, to see what I could do. He anxiously hoped that the "doctor" could give him some miraculous remedy and heal him permanently.

It was no use explaining that I was not a physician but a psychologist, much less that I did not prescribe medication. After all, for those who appeared to have the "wisdom of God" these distinctions were mere details; he was interested only in the ability to work miracles and he was certain that I possessed this gift for some reason.

The stories he told me about his life resembled patchwork, sometimes coloured, sometimes colourless, which could form endless quilts if sewn together: Mr. João was born in the hinterland of Bahia. He had so many siblings he couldn't even tell me how many they were. His father died when he was five years old and his mother died when he was twelve. The children were "scattered", and lived provisionally in the houses and "by the good graces" of several relatives. He then decided that he and his siblings should live on their own in the "foundations" that their parents had left them and survive on the crops they had planted but "everything failed" and they "went hungry". He came to São Paulo at the age of 14, along with some of his siblings to "try a life". From that point on it was "just work and suffering". He got married at the age of 31 and had three children. He currently lives in a poor neighbourhood on the outskirts of São Paulo, in a house he built with the help of his children. His profession is that of a baker – "to make our daily bread". He has worked as a baker for thirty years, twenty years of which has been in the same bakery, and he prides himself on having never taken a holiday or even a day off. He feels he has done well in life, because "he serves God through suffering and work".

In the face of a person who suffers from, among other things, a "roiling of the flesh" and who, moreover, considers the complete annulment of his rights and pleasures to be a source of pride, what could make a psychologist be suddenly transformed into "a head doctor"?

As a "head doctor", I expected to come face-to-face with a classic psychic disorder from my extensive training, but what did Mr. João mean by "nervousness"? I decided to investigate further and was surprised when he described his feelings as if his "nerves were stretched out". What now?

We managed to establish a working relationship of trust between us even though we spoke different languages, enough so that we got to know each other little by little and could explore new ways of communication. I invited Mr. João to attend the UBS once a week to "talk", as I could see that some form of psychotherapeutic intervention was necessary in his case, although it was not at first clear how he would respond to what he saw as a peculiar request.

At the beginning of psychotherapy, Mr. João made it very clear that he did not want to change anything in his life and that he was there only to "get rid" of the aforementioned physical symptoms so that he could continue to work at the same pace and fulfil his duties: "to serve God and support my family".

At this point, he spoke at length about his work and religion. He came out with a large degree of personal content diluted through a collective and unilateral form of discourse. He regarded work and religion as "ways to salvation" and believed that "life on Earth is only a test to see who enters the kingdom of God".

Everything he did was aimed at perfection and he only accepted values compatible with "goodness and honesty". He acknowledged the existence of "Evil", yet unilaterally identified this phenomenon with the figure of the devil, of the enemy, and blamed this figure solely for the presence of evil in people of "little faith". "Men of faith", such as he and his family, had the constant obligation to control themselves and resist "Evil".

He recounted the following dream at this part of the process: "I am casting out the demon that has possessed my relatives". I tried to unravel the dynamics of this dream and to point to the unconscious content present in his discourse which compensated for strict regimentation that formed the basis of his existence. From a Jungian perspective (Jung, 1982), it appeared to be an attempt to illuminate aspects of the shadow and to broaden the unilateral nature of his consciousness. I drew attention to the way he projected all conflicts and solutions outwards: "Good" and "Evil" came from the outside, from God and the devil, respectively.

But what were the actual conflicts that Mr. João experienced? Who or what really required compensation and transformation? Was this rigidity and one-sidedness manifested only as characteristics of his external attitude? How could "the baker" understand the language of "the psychologist", given she had serious difficulty understanding the words he used?

My interpretations were inconceivable to Mr. João as, for him, ideas like: "there are things that you cannot control; unknowable and imperfect aspects of human existence" sounded like the "temptations of the devil". Besides not seeing sense in my words, he worried about my attitude and began to try to convert me through full-blown indoctrination, as if he wanted to "save me". In every session he began to read the word of God contained in the Bible he constantly carried under his arm. He also began to intone the "hymns" he had learned in his religious denomination as a form of prayer.

In a way, this "indoctrination" led me to attempt new ways of relating to Mr. João, for example by singing hymns and trying to "see" things from his perspective. I began reading Bible verses to seek a common form of symbolic language and to converse freely on religious subjects with him. In turn, Mr. João was more receptive to my words, trying to understand what I meant and referring to our conversations as "lectures" from then on.

In our "lectures" on the Bible, we talked a lot about the life of Christ. While Mr. João emphasised the perfection and divine attributes of Christ, I made a point of highlighting the critical moments faced by Jesus in his earthly life. When he said that he "feared nothing that is of the earth, for he feared God alone", I reminded him of the passage in which Jesus retired to pray before going to the Calvary hill, and asked the Heavenly Father to "take this cup away from him". I also mentioned the passage in which Jesus forcefully drove the money-lenders out of the Temple, who had defiled the house of God by conducting their business there, as a counterpoint to his assertion that "no man of faith is angry or loses control". I also quoted the phrase attributed to Jesus quoted in the passage where Mary Magdalene - a prostitute - was to be stoned by the people: - "He who is without sin among you, let him cast the first stone at her", in response to Mr. João's view of "the perfection of men of faith".

By way of these "lectures", Mr. João began to refer to the "darker" aspects of his life. He told me that he had been a Catholic but that he had been very "sinful" at that time: "angry, messy, lazy and womanising". He "drank a lot and beat his wife and children". He pointed out that he had become a better person when he got into religion, yet he feared that he would "lose control" if he lost his faith. This went some way to explaining his resistance to facing his shadow in psychotherapy.

At this stage he described the following dream: "A train went off the tracks and turned over and everyone inside it died, including his relatives. He survived, because he was in the last carriage which narrowly escaped the crash".

He reported feeling fearful that the train he took on the subway would derail and lead to a fatal accident, showing signs of great anxiety. He gradually came into contact with the potential for disorganisation and lack of control and gave clear signs of how much this frightened him, while at the same time he began to glimpse possibilities of "surviving" the uncontrollable.

At this point, he began to "complain" about work, claiming that it was due to tiredness. He linked the somatic problems he experienced to overwork. He felt "trapped and stifled" in the bakery. He wished to take a holiday but said he was still "relinquishing" his right to take one under pressure from his boss, contenting himself only with three days off at Christmas when he spent most of his time praying. I made a point of quoting at that juncture that: "God created the world in seven days, yet on the seventh day he rested".

He began to become increasingly aware of the exploitation he suffered at work. He started to criticise his boss; he considered him to be very "demanding" and for the first time called him an "exploiter".

He described another dream he had during this time: "His boss shot him in his back because he also burned people's backs with a lighter".

He became progressively more aware of the aggressive and destructive aspects he had tried to conceal from himself at such cost. Previously unknown symbols revealed themselves as present in the baker's psyche, as though the ingredients which had previously been all mixed together in a dough could now be individually identified.

Mr. João recalled some of the sad stories from his childhood: he had been beaten by adults until he passed out. When he was only three months old, his brothers had unintentionally thrown him onto a fire. As a consequence he had badly burned his hands, leading to the disfigurement of some of his fingers.

He showed his hands to me and described some of the other accidents he had suffered while working as a baker, in which he "lost" one of his fingers and damaged some others in a dough-making machine. He associated the occurrence of so many problems with his hands to a "plot of the devil to cripple him". He said he had played the accordion in church and if his hands had been "crippled" he would not have been able to "pray through music" with such intensity.

From the very beginning, Mr. João had focussed on powerful issues that manifested themselves through his body. As I looked at his hands, I realised that the body could be a powerful tool for expanding our communication. Perhaps there, in the marks he had that carried such a deep history of resentment and exploitation, lay a promising vessel for developing new recipes with the same dough.

For the first time I saw that life pulsated in the form of churning, roiling of the flesh, nervousness and in the memories encoded in his body and especially his hands, precisely those symptoms he had previously described through unusual terms. Instead of trying to decipher what semantic meanings lay behind those words, I wanted to examine more carefully the body which gave rise to them; to understand through touch those hands that even when deformed had performed such feats as making bread and playing the accordion.

At that point, I realised that the somatic Jungian approach developed by Pethö Sándor (1982), the epitome of which we find in Calatonia, could be a significant asset in psychotherapy of this kind and to its inherent mental health demands, not only for Mr. João but also for others with a similar psychosocial profile.

The subtle touch of Calatonia has an intense effect on the regulation of psychophysical tone and the marchalling of global and multidimensional reactions in the body, leading to new forms of physical and social conditioning or reconditioning (Sándor, 1982).

I suggested we apply Calatonia as a method for investigating the root causes of Mr. João's somatic complaints. I explained that we could practise "exercises" so he could get to know his body better. As he did not interpret this proposal as another "temptation of the devil", I began the process of somatic attunement and found that he "gave himself over" to it right from the very first session. Mr. João would close his eyes and relax his body in the chair, attempting to closely follow my instructions when we undertook active methods in which his participation was required.

The act of touching was introduced gradually: we began with the use of body self-observation (Farah, 1995) and relaxation via Schultz Autogenic Training (Schultz, 1991), followed by muscle contraction and relaxation according to Jacobson's Progressive Relaxation technique (Sándor, 1982). After the implementation of these methods, the course of Mr. João's somatic therapy progressed to the application of Calatonia techniques, including subtle touch, rotations and jerks, especially in the region of the arms and hands (Sándor, 1982; Delmanto, 1997).

With the introduction of touch, the dough that had been at rest began to ferment and underwent great transformation: Mr. João reported an initial intensification of somatic symptoms and later described that he was able to "feel and listen to his body from within" during the sessions, especially in his heart and intestine.

He established a relationship between the symptoms of "roiling of the flesh" and "churning", realising that one varied according to the other. He associated worsening of these symptoms with adverse climactic conditions (excessive cold and heat) and with the excessive intake of food or liquids. When his symptoms began to intensify, Mr. João became discouraged but he also allowed himself to rest more often and for longer periods. He again expressed the desire to go on holiday; he wanted to go upstate and enjoy being closer to nature. This time he fulfilled his wish and spent a few days "in the middle of the bush"; relaxing and swimming in the river of his hometown. He felt much better while he was there but when he returned to work, the symptoms worsened and some new ones appeared: he began to feel dizzy and short of breath.

He realised that when he told me "bad things", he felt better, more "lively" because he was able to "unburden" himself. He started to believe that God could forgive him for his sins; he finally admitted that he had some. He reduced his attendance at church and was no longer so "fanatical". He played the accordion at home too, where previously he had exclusively played it at church. He tended to the garden, played with his grandchildren and felt more cheerful. He began to practise some relaxation techniques at home and at the bakery. He said that he really missed "gymnastics", as he called the somatic techniques, when he hadn't practised them in a while.

At the same time he became increasingly irritated with his family at home and with his boss at work. He said that sometimes when they made him angry, inside he wanted to "bite people". During this same period he described the following image when undergoing Calatonia: "He felt that there were hands trying to strangle him and that he should learn to defend himself".

He began to make more demands at the bakery for their working conditions to be improved and their rights to be respected. He began to enjoy the holidays to which he was entitled and also to consider demanding payment for the overtime he had worked and compensation for accidents at work. He thought of retiring - realising that he had worked enough years for him to be able to do so. He decided to apply for retirement and threatened to go to court if his boss did not give him "everything he was entitled to". At the same time, he began to move to self-employment, aiming to complement his income.

At this point he described another dream: "The old house where he lived in Bahia was destroyed by rain, wind and fire, but the earth and the foundations remained, and he built a new house".

He decided to use the knowledge he had gained at the bakery and make custard doughnuts to sell on the street. At first he was a little startled by the novelty of this, but gradually he realised that the possibilities of meeting new people and of walking the streets as an independent salesman "without a boss" gave him a sensation of dignity and freedom he had never experienced before.

He said that people liked his doughnuts so much that he had to ask his children for help in baking them. He decided to use his baker's uniform for sales because it "would make a good impression".

That was the way Mr. João was dressed when he came to the UBS on our last day of psychotherapy which we decided to end by common agreement, "wearing a cap and a white apron, and carrying a basket full of custard doughnuts[2]" – dreams that

---
[2]. TN: custard doughnuts are called "dreams" in Brazilian Portuguese

he had never allowed himself to have.

He gave me a doughnut and at that moment I felt that it was not only Mr. João who had learned to dream. Both baker and psychologist had learned to dream together.

Group Treatment in Somatic Jungian Psychotherapy

My experience in public health care definitively transformed the way I viewed psychic suffering and its psychosocial consequences; I acutely felt that the history of each individual was inscribed on his/her body in a unique, intrinsic and almost totally unconscious way.

But there was still a challenge: was it possible to help these people using specialised and individualised techniques such as variations of Calatonia in the context of public health care, where there was a great demand for psychotherapy?

The high prevalence of psychic disorders in the Brazilian population (Gonçalves et al., 2014) leads to a great demand for mental health care, particularly in lower social classes blighted by poverty and psychosocial vulnerability. In such a context, group sessions of psychotherapy may be a necessity due to the lack of qualified mental health professionals, partly as a consequence of staff reductions in the Basic Treatment services of the SUS (Brazilian Ministry of Health, 2013).

I wondered what results could be expected when applying Calatonia within a group setting of somatic Jungian psychotherapy.

There is a general consensus that group sessions of psychotherapy should not be conducted simply to satisfy logistical limitations (through the reduction of staff hours and payment); the use of a group modality can only be justified as a therapeutic alternative for the care of a specific population if it can meet the real needs of that population.

The results of research carried out in SUS settings (Tavares Duran, 1997) have revealed that the inclusion of patients from different social classes in the same therapy group tends to dissipate the behavioural consequences of social inequality, insofar as it leads the group members, including the therapist, to identify common social and cultural references beyond those of the individual himself and those derived empirically from common knowledge.

It seems, however, that the supposed democratisation of knowledge and power in a group field of psychotherapy is not enough to guarantee the consistent attachment to a group in patients from lower socioeconomic backgrounds. There are also forms of silencing communication even between members of supposedly the same social class.

Following the proposal of a psychotherapy group based on Jungian psychology and Calatonia, SUS patients were found to display several typical defence mechanisms commonly observed in group settings, such as denial, rationalisation and projection. Gradually a more complex and indefinable situation emerged, of which one particularly fruitful characteristic was the intense affective exchanges made between the participants (Tavares Duran, 1997).

The main role of the therapist in a group setting, according to Whitmont (1974), consists of analysing adaptation to the group, so that every individual feels part of something larger than themselves; experiencing conformity as much as uniqueness, cultivating self-sufficiency, learning to tolerate different backgrounds and ideologies, and having presence-of-mind in social situations. Group adaptation appears to lead to greater scope for the individual's projections to be addressed in therapy and the potential for forming genuine relationships.

The use of group psychotherapy in Jungian psychotherapy integrated with somatic methods such as Calatonia enhances the potential for transformation, insofar as both strategies remain sensitive to the idiosyncrasies of the population undergoing therapy (Greger Tavares, 2010).

The somatic experiences depended on the emergent dynamics in each group and in each moment, and were performed in pairs, trios or with all participants at the same time. Somatic experiences were also conducted on a single patient, or on each individual in the group (Greger Tavares, 2010).

Other forms of somatic experience were designed and introduced throughout the process of group psychotherapy at either the therapist's suggestion or from suggestions made by group members. All members had complete freedom to choose to participate or not in the somatic experiences.

With regards to the developmental dynamics of calatonic techniques in the group, some somatic experiences were more individualised and based around the self. For example many involved observing aspects of one's body or self-touch, others were focussed on the bodies of others and involved more and more group elements (Greger Tavares, 2010).

Thus, the act of touch was experienced gradually and occurred according to the sensibilities and needs of the group. The more subtle techniques were introduced after a certain degree of experience with more active and "denser" techniques, such as breathing exercises and movements as well as basic massage movements (Tavares Duran, 1997).

Jung rarely addressed the topic of group therapy in a systematic way. Overall he appears to have focussed on the negative aspects of group therapy, describing their techniques as regressive and massifying. From this perspective, the group represents a predominantly symbiotic and indiscriminate medium. Society, group and mass population are synonymous in meaning to Jung, all defined as an undifferentiated set of individuals. Jung was highly concerned with protecting the individual's integrity in the face of social pressure which drives the individual to conform to the group (Jung, 1961).

Hall (1986) explains that Jung never seems to have experimented with a process of group therapy and appears to have concluded that a group modality of analysis was not a substitute for individual psychotherapy. However, Hall posits that a combination of group and individual therapy may help certain individuals to progress more quickly through the process of personal growth and understanding than through individual therapy alone. According to Hall, group psychotherapy can be a powerful tool for modifying excessively rigid paradigms of negative self-judgement, while helping a person to develop a more realistic sense of self-esteem. My experience in integrating a group modality of Jungian psychotherapy with calatonic techniques has opened up new avenues of approach in my work, as there are several indications of enhanced therapeutic benefits (Greger Tavares, 1999; 2010).

This experience has made me realise that the group itself is an organism with both body and psyche. This unity of being is not merely the projection of an individual's psycho-physical dynamic onto the group field, since the group organism is constellated in a unique form of existence that transcends the sum or magnification of each individual's configuration.

The group field is a third point between the self and the other, between the individual and the collective - that border area in which both conscious and unconscious perceptions, images and sensations converge and simultaneously differentiate to create novel compositions.

Group energy moves in a spiral and always returns to the point of origin, yet it leaves the members of the group in a more developed state on the completion of each loop.

Each member contributes their own set of symbols to the group field, whether body expressions, dreams, images of the individual or the group, or their own somatic and psychic flow. The group as a whole shows psychic and somatic signs of the socioeconomic and cultural conditions that brought the participants together and may therefore help to stimulate the transformation of these initial conditions, by reconfiguring and giving new meaning to each individual's personal stories.

It is often the case in these groups that people learn to pay attention to their own bodies and to seek support when previously they only allowed themselves to feel their body when they became ill or were in pain, not conditions conducive to self-experimentation or self-expression. By giving these people the opportunity to give new meaning to their "body-life" in a group setting through the somatic experiences of Calatonia, I have had the opportunity to observe significant multidimensional transformations in their lives. For example, the perception of the body as a source of pleasure: pleasure in liking oneself, of taking care of one's appearance and health, the exchange of caresses, and a means for overcoming pain.

Through the mediation of psychotherapy groups composed of people struggling to survive – those whose bodies were marked by exploitation at work, by domestic violence, by social exclusion and the lack of basic health care, among other factors – I learned that it is possible to "be reborn from the ashes", especially when we manifest ourselves within the body of a welcoming group that brings our potential to the surface (Greger Tavares, 1999).

When integrated within a welcoming group and treated with love and respect, the inner therapist in each person was capable of being awakened. Thus, each individual became capable of accepting their limitations and flaws and of finding a path to healing when possible, even in the midst of their suffering. In these moments, it seemed possible to touch the skin of the group; like the great mother who nurtures and touches the skin and transforms damaged roots into vibrant life.

Conclusion

The theoretical foundations and effects of subtle touch in Calatonia and other similar body-based techniques have been widely and increasingly reported in the Brazilian and international literature of clinical psychotherapy and in other professional and academic settings (Dias & Reis, 2009; Elizabeth, Papathanassoglou, Meropi, Mpouzica, & Latsia, 2012; Farah, 2017; Gonçalves, Pereira, Ribeiro, & Rios, 2007; Greger Tavares et al., 2015; Jakubiak & Feeney, 2017; Lasaponari, 2011; Nossow & Peniche, 2007; Rios, Dreyfuss-Armando, & Regina, 2012). These studies highlight several quantitative and qualitative results obtained through both empirical research and clinical experience, as well as the progress we have made in our understanding of the neuroscience of touch and psychoneuroimmunology.

The somatic techniques of Jungian Calatonia (Sándor, 1982) may or may not be employed in conjunction with psychotherapy but these techniques are most certainly highly relevant in the context of public health care, insofar as they can increase the patient's conscious awareness of the emergence of unconscious content and can act to restore one's capacity for self-regulation, among other aspects (Blanchard, Rios, & Seixas, 2009; Blanchard, Rios, & Seixas, 2010; Machado, 2012; Tavares, Vanucchi, Machado, & Andrade, 2015).

The subtle touches applied in Calatonia form an intermediate zone between the somatic unconscious of the patient(s) and the therapist (Schwartz-Salant, 1989), who thereby establishes a bipersonal or transpersonal form of resonance (Sándor, 1982), which also allows for variations of pre-verbal transference (Mc Neely, 1992).

The sense of well-being engendered by physical proximity and mediated through subtle touch techniques, which can be performed by the therapist in individual psychotherapy and/or by the patients in group psychotherapy, seems to address the primary and pre-verbal needs of the subject which would otherwise be poorly accessed.

According to Spaccaquerche (2012) and Horta, Minicuci, Fontana and Paschoa (2012), the use of calatonic techniques in the context of psychotherapy leads to an expansion of consciousness as well as a host of significant psychosomatic effects such as a strengthening of the bond of trust between psychotherapist and patient, increased self-regulation and the reconditioning of psychic and muscle tone, greater perceptual integration of body image, a strengthening of self-esteem and greater openness to social interaction.

In the group modality of somatic Jungian psychotherapy, the subtle touches of Calatonia also increase our perception of our psychosocial and cultural drives and influences. These influences can be perceived in the form of somatic manifestations, and can allow the participant to awaken or recover their capacity for creativity and creative potential (Tavares Duran, 1997).

The Subtle Touch techniques are greatly adaptable to different contexts because they can be applied in a simple, low-cost, flexible and individually-tailored fashion. The emphasis can be placed on different aspects, either on a more active or passive approach, on a particular individual or group, or on different modalities of touch - starting from direct touches to the skin on to even subtler touches through puffs of air or sound or even a "touch without touch" guided by one's intention to touch another. Under a lack of institutional constraints, the development of somatic Jungian psychotherapy, especially in a group modality, can contribute to a reduction in the average duration of clinical consultations (significant changes occur around one year of intervention) and to the decrease of indices of treatment avoidance (Greger Tavares, 1999; Tavares Duran, 1997).

Following the reflections and results presented in this chapter on the efficacy of applying somatic Jungian psychotherapy (Sándor, 1982) to both individual therapy (Greger Tavares, 1998) and group settings (Tavares Duran, 1997), there is firm support for the inclusion of both modalities in mental health programs within the Brazilian system of public health care to address the specific demands and needs of patients.

By assigning greater focus to the somatic dimension as a way of accessing the unconscious and understanding it as a fundamental strand in the process of psychosomatic and social transformation (individuation), Calatonia provides a greater degree of self-observation through the subject's enhanced access to the body itself. As such, introducing physical touch into the sacred field of the therapeutic setting of the group or individual allows for the configuration of a protected continent for the psychological and somatic development of any and all individuals involved.

In this way, it becomes possible to transcend the detachment that tends to be present in the approaches of the collective consciousness to the body, which is particularly the case for certain social groups who see the body essentially in an "alienated" form as an instrument for manual labour.

Thus, a patient can awaken a creative and sensitive body that needs to be recognised and cared for and that no longer needs to fall ill, as in the case of the baker. The suffering, sick and alienated body can then reveal itself to be a creative body, turning its pains and scars outwards and unveiling its beauties and joys through the psychic and somatic touches made to others.

References

Blanchard, A. J. R., Seixas, L. P., & Rios, A. M. G. (2010). The Body in Psychotherapy: Calatonia and Subtle Touch Techniques. In R. Jones (Ed.), *Body, Mind, and Healing After Jung: A Space of Questions*. London, UK: Routledge.

Blanchard, A. J. R., Rios, A. M. G., & Seixas, L. P. (2009). O Corpo para Jung. In P. Albertini, & L. V. Freitas (Eds.), *Fundamentos de Psicologia – Jung e Reich: articulando conceitos e praticas* (pp. 65-78). São Paulo, SP: Guanabara Koogan.

Boltanski, L. (1989). *As classes sociais e o corpo*. Rio de Janeiro, RJ: Graal.

Brazilian Ministry of Health – Secretariat of Health Intervention – Mental Health. (2013). *Cadernos de Atenção Básica, 34*. Brasilia, Brazil: Ministry of Health.

Delmanto, S. (1997). *Toques sutis: uma experiência de vida com Pethö Sándor*. São Paulo, SP: Summus Editorial.

Dias, G. P., & Reis, R. A. M. (2009). Plasticidade sináptica: natureza e cultura moldando o Self. *Psicologia: Reflexão e Crítica, 22*(1), 128-135.

Elizabeth, D. E., Papathanassoglou, R. N., Meropi, D. A., Mpouzika, R. N., & Latsia, N. (2012). Interpersonal Touch: physiological effects in critical care. *Biological Research for Nursing, 14*(4), 431–443.

Farah, R. M. (2017). *Calatonia: o toque sutil em psicoterapia*. São Paulo, SP: Companhia Ilimitada.

Farah, R. M. (1995). *Integração psicofísica: o trabalho corporal e a psicologia de C.G. Jung*. São Paulo, SP: Companhia Ilimitada / Robe Editorial.

Gonçalves, D. A., Mari, J. J., Bower, P., Gask, L., Dowrick, C., Tófoli, L. F., ... Fortes, S. (2014). Brazilian multicentre study of common mental disorders in primary care: rates and related social and demographic factors. *Cadernos de Saúde Pública, 30*(3), 623-632.

Gonçalves, M. I. C., Pereira, M. A., Ribeiro, A. J., & Rios, A. M. G. (2007). Subtle touch, calatonia and other somatic interventions with children and adolescents. *International Body Psychotherapy Journal*, 6(2), 33-47.

Gonçalves Filho, J. M. (1995). *Passagem para a Vila Joanisa: uma introdução ao problema da humilhação social* (Unpublished master's thesis). University of São Paulo, São Paulo, Brazil.

Greger Tavares, S. M., Vannuchi, B. P., Machado F. P. T., & Andrade, A. L. M. (2015). Efeitos psicofisiológicos da Calatonia em adultos: um estudo piloto na abordagem quanti-qualitativa. *Jung & Corpo*, 15, 17-33.

Greger Tavares, S. M. (2010). Uma experiência de atendimento psicoterapêutico junguiano em grupo, privilegiando a dimensão corporal, no contexto da saúde pública. *O Mundo da Saúde*, 34, 535-543.

Greger Tavares, S. M. (1999). Estratégias terapêuticas corporais e grupais na perspectiva do método organísmico de Pethö Sándor. *Hermes*, 3(4), 85-103.

Greger Tavares, S. M. (1998). O padeiro que aprendeu a sonhar. *Hermes*, 2(4), 69-80.

Hall, J. (1986). *A experiência junguiana: análise e individuação*. São Paulo, SP: Cultrix.

Horta, E. V. P., Minicuci, M. C., Fontana, O. M., & Paschoa, V. L. F. (2012). *Jung e Sándor: trabalho corporal na psicoterapia analítica*. São Paulo, SP: Vetor.

Jakubiak, B. K., & Feeney, B. C. (2017). Affectionate Touch to Promote Relational, Psychological, and Physical Well-Being in Adulthood: a theoretical model and review of the research. *Journal of Personal and Social Psychology*, 21(3), 228-252.

Jung, C. G. (1982). *O eu e o inconsciente*. Rio de Janeiro, RJ: Vozes.

Jung, C. G. (1961). *O eu desconhecido*. Rio de Janeiro, RJ: Fundo de Cultura.

Lasaponari, E. F. (2011). *A utilização da calatonia no período pós-operatório imediato*. (Unpublished master's thesis). Retrieved from http://www.teses.usp.br/teses/disponiveis/7/7139/tde-21062011-152045/.

Machado Filho, P. T. (2012). Simbolismo das imagens calatônicas. In M. E. Spaccaquerche (Ed.), *Corpo em Jung: estudos em calatonia e práticas integrativas* (pp. 277-290). São Paulo, SP: Vetor.

McNeely, D. (1992). *Tocar: terapia do corpo e Psicologia*. São Paulo, SP: Cultrix.

Nossow, V., & Peniche, A. C. G. (2007). Paciente cirúrgico ambulatorial: Calatonia e ansiedade. *Acta Paulista de Enfermagem*, 20(2), 161-167.

Rios, A. M. G., Dreyfuss-Armando, M., & Regina, A. C. B. (2012). Bases neuropsicológicas do trabalho corporal na psicoterapia. In M. E. Spaccaquerche (Ed.), *Corpo em Jung: estudos em calatonia e práticas integrativas* (pp. 19-38). São Paulo, SP: Vetor.

Sándor, P. (1982). *Técnicas de relaxamento*. São Paulo, SP: Vetor.

Sándor, P. (1982). A Relaxação Progressiva de E. Jacobson. In P. Sándor (Ed.), *Técnicas de Realaxamento* (pp. 56-62). São Paulo, SP: Vetor.

Schultz, J. H. (1991). *Treinamento Autógeno*. São Paulo, SP: Manole.

Schwartz-Salant, N. (1989). *A personalidade limítrofe: visão e cura*. São Paulo, SP: Cultrix.

Spaccaquerche, M. E. (2012). *Corpo em Jung: estudos em Calatonia e práticas integrativas*. São Paulo, SP: Vetor.

Tavares Duran, S. M. G. (1997). *O atendimento psicoterapêutico em grupo aos usuários de uma Unidade Básica de Saúde pelo Método Corporal de P. Sándor: uma interpretação na perspectiva da Psicologia Analítica de C. G. Jung*. (Unpublished master's thesis). University of São Paulo, São Paulo, Brazil.

Whitmont, E. C. (1974). Analysis in a group setting. *Quadrant*, 16, 5-25.

5

Calatonia and Subtle Touch in the Healing of Trauma

Claudia Herbert

This chapter addresses the application of Calatonia and Subtle Touch techniques (Farah, 2017; Sándor, 1982) in the healing of trauma. A definition and some background about the effects of trauma will be given first, followed by an exploration of the scientific rationale and specific principles for the application of Calatonia and Subtle Touch in the healing of trauma.

Traumatic events can have a profound and shattering effect on our healthy functioning in life. Trauma is defined as any situation or event that is experienced as too overwhelming, out of control, threatening or dangerous to be able to be processed and worked through cohesively at the time. Under such circumstances our nervous system dysregulates, conscious awareness fragments and different aspects or parts of the Self are formed to enable us to survive the trauma (van der Hart, Nijenhuis, & Steele, 2006). This split consists of an aspect or several parts of the Self, that help us cope after a trauma to get on with everyday life as it presents itself and of other parts that store the emotional, physiological and sensory impressions of the trauma. This split happens automatically, and is governed by unconscious processes of our autonomic nervous system; thus, different parts are usually only partially and sometimes not at all aware of each other. This is referred to as dissociation. For example, the coping parts hold the masks or roles we present to the outside world, so that we appear to be functioning and apparently 'normal'. These aspects are also referred to as the Apparently Normal Personality/ies or ANP/s (van der Hart et al., 2006). These protective aspects of the Self help us to adapt to what an environment requires us to do to ensure our survival. This enables ongoing survival in what might be an emotionally, physically or spiritually toxic environment under circumstances in which escape does not seem possible, for example, during early developmental stages.

The other aspects that hold the unprocessed emotional, physiological and sensory memories of the trauma, including the coping responses acquired during this event are referred to as Emotional Personalities (EPs; van der Hart et al., 2006). To regulate the potential emotional, physiological and sensory overwhelm held in the memory systems of the EPs, the ANP/s attempt/s to employ various strategies to organise life in a way that keeps these parts dissociated from our conscious awareness, by maintaining a so-called 'dissociative barrier'. For example, the traumatic experience may not be fully remembered or may only be partially recalled; likewise, certain places or issues that might trigger painful memories might also be avoided.

Although these mechanisms have an adaptive survival-based function they carry with them high personal costs. They prevent a person from fully consciously experiencing themselves in life. Moreover, these strategies often do not work perfectly and situations in the here-and-now that may resemble aspects of the past traumatic experience can pierce through the dissociative barrier. This will trigger the EPs, causing distressing flashbacks, re-experiencing of fragments of the past experience and other uncomfortable symptoms.

In clinical practice this means that clients who have experienced trauma often alternate between feeling numb or shutting off from their emotions and body sensations thereby struggling to regulate their feelings, which can result in uncontrollable emotional or sensory overwhelm. Frequently they are hypervigilant, anxious, frightened, easily terrified, under permanent tension and pressure and subsequently find it difficult to relax and let go.

A client's window of tolerance (Ogden, Minton, & Pain, 2006; Siegel, 2010), which describes the zone or range in which clients can comfortably tolerate and regulate their emotions is often very narrow. This results in uncontrollable reactions of hyper- or hypo-arousal in response to perceived triggers relating to the past traumatic experience, making clients' behaviour unpredictable thereby rendering their lives very uncomfortable.

Depending on the nature, severity, longevity, developmental age and resources available at the time of the trauma, clients will vary in their degree of dissociation. If clients have endured repeated, complex trauma they may experience themselves as multiple totally separate identities (DID), which may not be conscious of each other. These identities may carry completely different personalities with different body postures, facial expressions, voices, gender, taste, behaviour and life choices and even different physiological metabolisms. Memories of the traumatic events are very fragmented and often not accessible to the client. Clients may have a distorted sense of reality fluctuating between feeling under constant threat or danger and engaging in risk-taking behaviour, thus compromising their safety. They may find themselves doing things which they later cannot remember having done. Difficulties in concentrating and focussing on tasks is frequently a problem and general memory can be impaired.

The aim of trauma therapy is to enable clients to become increasingly conscious of the traumatic nature and content of their past experiences so that gradually they will be able to remember and process their traumatic experiences in the safety of the 'here-and-now'. This will enable the overwhelming feelings and frozen terror (numbness), as well as unhelpful survival-based coping strategies, acquired by the traumatised parts to loosen their hold. Previously fragmented or inaccessible memories can be processed and, as a consequence, the gradual integration of the various parts of one's identity into a cohesive, whole Self can be achieved. This work is a deeply spiritual, transformational healing process in which clients are facilitated into climbing out of the abyss of their own terror into finding and (re-) discovering their unique, authentic Self, which becomes the healer of the traumatised parts. It is a deep honour for every trauma therapist to be able to bear witness to such a sacred process. Indeed, Peter Levine (2005) referred to the process of trauma healing as one of the four routes by which enlightenment can be attained. The other routes being death, sacred sexuality (tantra) and meditation.

Talking therapy may, to a certain extent, be helpful to a person in understanding their life experiences, the context and nature of their trauma, their underlying coping patterns and the way in which they may have had to dissociate from their unique, authentic Self for survival reasons. However, in order to enable a person to fundamentally shift and transform some of the deeply embedded, trauma-based survival patterns into a pathway for positive growth it requires a much deeper, integrative and holistic approach (Herbert, in preparation). One of the therapeutic challenges is that many of these survival-based coping strategies are controlled by the autonomic nervous system and in the context of the past, traumatic experiences were stored as functionally adaptive by the intricate memory systems of body, mind and Soul. This explains why clients may logically know that their survival-based coping behaviour may no longer serve them in the context of their here-and-now life, but despite this, when triggered, feel out of control and powerless to change this, despite their best intentions. The reason for this is that autonomic processes, especially, when they form part of different dissociated aspects of the Self, cannot be controlled by the rational mind because they are governed by different neurophysiological pathways (Corrigan, 2014; Lanius, Corrigan,

& Paulsen, 2014) from the rational, logical mind system.

For example, one of my clients, Rebecca*, a lady in her 40's who was sexually abused over a prolonged period of time during her childhood and adolescence coped by blocking out her pain and distress with alcohol. She had been struggling with alcohol addiction all of her adult life, despite knowing that it was harmful to her, when she came to me wanting to stop it. Cognitively she fully embraced her intention to stop drinking and could keep this up, until an unexpected trigger in her day-to-day life brought her back to the distressing traumatic experiences. At that point a different part of her took over, governed by autonomic responses and she could not prevent herself from numbing herself to oblivion with alcohol. This had been a never-ending cycle despite her attending established alcohol support groups and several forms of other therapy in the past, including trauma-focussed CBT, EMDR and psychodynamic therapy.

This raises the question as to what might help clients transcend those challenges and transform their unconscious, autonomic responses into conscious choices that can be maintained. Essentially, it requires the 're-wiring' of the underlying pathways that generate the autonomic, survival-based responses, into a system that allows for the realistic appraisal of each here-and-now situation so that appropriate, healthy choices of behaviour, can be made. This proposal of 're-wiring' is based on the understanding that trauma is maintained through complex electro-chemical processes, which are set in motion on a neurobiological level by specific structures of the limbic system in our midbrain region. These include the Thalamus, Amygdala, Hippocampus, Hypothalamus, Periaqueductal Gray (PAG) and others, which respond to a trauma client's external and internal environment in a manner that interprets information as dangerous and unsafe, which in the here-and-now, would be safe to engage in (Herbert, 2017). Thus, essentially, trauma is maintained by a complex, autonomic, neurophysiological signalling system that operates on information from the past, which no longer accurately applies to the here-and-now reality. Therefore, this process of 're-wiring' requires sending novel information to this autonomic signalling system that enables it to experience moments of calm rather than re-triggering the hyper- or hypo-arousal responses.

EMDR (Eye Movement Desensitization and Reprocessing; Shapiro, 1989; Shapiro & Forrest, 2016) therapy as well as TF-CBT (Trauma-Focussed Cognitive Behavioural Therapy; Cohen, Mannarino, & Deblinger, 2006) have been found to be very effective therapies for PTSD (Post-Traumatic Stress Disorder; Seidler & Wagner, 2006). Both are recommended, as the treatment of choice for PTSD by the National Institute for Clinical Excellence in the United Kingdom (NICE, 2005) and the World Health Organisation (WHO, 2013). However, for severely traumatised clients, who can be hypersensitive, both the standard EMDR protocol and TF-CBT need to be especially adapted. Generally, it is agreed that work with survivors of childhood abuse and other forms of chronic traumatisation should be phase-oriented, multimodal, and titrated (Korn, 2009).

This is where Calatonia and Subtle Touch (Sándor, 1982; Farah, 2017) can be brought in as therapeutic methods to support and aid in the healing of trauma. I have now been using Calatonia and Subtle Touch techniques for more than 9 years and many of my clients have found it very helpful as part of their trauma healing journey.

Although Calatonia and Subtle Touch have not yet been scientifically evaluated, findings of several recent research studies might lend a scientific rationale as to why Calatonia and Subtle Touch might have a helpful role in the healing of trauma. Two different nerve receptor systems for touch have been detected. There are the so-called myelinated nerves (LTMs, low-threshold mechanoreceptors) that register touch to the skin. These have an immediate discriminative function, helping to assess the nature of touch so that it can be responded to promptly and appropriately by a person. This system relays our day-to-day touch experiences, for example, if we brush against a piece of furniture and need to adjust our distance this has obvious advantages to our survival. However, there is also another privileged peripheral nerve pathway, a system of so-called C-tactile afferents, which responds to gentle, pleasant tactile stimulation of a social nature (Loeken, Wessberg, Morrison, McGlone, & Olausson, 2009). This nerve system has a very different function (McGlone, Wessberg, & Olausson, 2014). C-tactile afferents are most excited by stroking velocities which resemble the type of slow, tender touch which a mother or father would use to stroke a baby (3cm per second on the skin). It has been found that gentle touch decreases stress activated cortisol production allowing for increased cell development in the hippocampus, positively impacting on short-term and long-term memory function (Miles, Cowan, Glover, Stevenson, & Modi, 2006).

Gentle stroking touch has also been shown to lower blood pressure (Knox & Uvnäs-Moberg, 1998) and increase pain thresholds (Olausson et al., 2008). On a neurobiological level there is evidence that oxytocin, opioids, serotonin and dopamine are released in response to this gentle touch, as expressed via stimulation of CT afferents, leading to a sense of increased psychological well-being, happiness and calm. Interestingly, McGlone and colleagues (2014) have suggested that, in a wider perspective, the CTs may be regarded as an afferent system that is basically concerned with the representation of the Self, rather than being focussed on external events. This would lend support to the reason why Calatonia and Subtle Touch methods might enable clients to experience an inner connection to the Self, which feels pleasant and safe; thus, they do not re-trigger the autonomically-wired trauma-maintaining looping system. We could hypothesise that this may, with continued and repeated use of Calatonia and Subtle Touch, over time, lead to the emergence of new physiological response modes in a client and potential rewiring or weakening of the previously inscribed autonomic trauma-response loops. Another rationale for the application of Subtle Touch techniques as part of specialist trauma therapy relates to the brain activity in traumatised clients.

While trauma has not been processed and integrated, clients frequently find themselves in repeated states of hyper-alertness in response to perceived threat triggers which have been found to activate high frequency Gamma Brain Waves (oscillating up to 100Hz). This leads to the chemical release of excitatory neurotransmitters, such as cortisol, noradrenaline, glutamate and others, putting strain on a person's heart rate, blood pressure, immune system and other metabolic functions. These stress hormones have been proposed to cause glutamate receptors, called AMPA receptors, to become activated on the postsynaptic surface of the lateral amygdala, and due to the chemical environment created by these neurotransmitters, phosphorylates them, which permanently anchors them into place and fixes the content from the trauma as memory in the hippocampus for future reference (Ruden, 2011). These activated AMPA receptors are proposed to be contributing to the ongoing activation of the Amygdala and other limbic structures, keeping a traumatised person locked in their stressful hyperarousal loop. In contrast, soothing strokes and slow, light, gentle touch have been found to induce Delta brain waves (4-8Hz), leading to a meditative, slightly drowsy, sleepy state (Kim et al., 2007). Delta brain waves are also associated with Stage 3 and 4 of our sleep phases and have been linked to the release of calming neurotransmitters, such as Serotonin, GABA (Gamma Aminobutyric Acid) and Oxytocin. The release of these calming neurotransmitters has a positive, restorative and pleasurable effect on a person. Moreover, it has been proposed (Clem & Huganir, 2010; Kim et al., 2007) that these calming neurotransmitters create a calcium rich environment which enables the production of an enzyme that enables the de-potentiation of these activated AMPA receptors in the lateral Amygdala; thus stopping the stressful hyperarousal loop. According to this hypothesis, soothing touch can be used for the de-coding of trauma, as also utilised in the Havening Technique (Ruden, 2011). Although more specific research is required for Calatonia and Subtle Touch, it might be proposed that any therapeutic method that enables a client to experience a subjectively felt alternative to their survival-driven autonomic responses, warrants genuine consideration in the treatment of trauma.

With clients suffering from complex developmental trauma certain aspects need to be considered when using Calatonia and Subtle Touch. Firstly, many clients have had past experiences of either aversive touch or total isolation and abandonment (no touch) or both, which will have had detrimental effects on them. The prospect of touch for these clients is therefore frequently a traumatic trigger in itself, which will take them out of their window of tolerance into either a hyper- or hypo-arousal loop. Therapeutic touch in trauma must be approached very carefully and it is a matter of appropriate timing as to when this can be safely introduced. I have worked with some very complex trauma clients whom it has taken several years of in-depth, specialist trauma therapy (Herbert, 2019), which predominantly focussed on intense safety-building, grounding, stabilisation, resourcing, attachment repair and also, their getting to know their internal organising system, before they were able to contemplate the possibility of any form of touch.

It requires comprehensive, ongoing assessment by the treating trauma therapist before deciding whether touch may be appropriate and in what manner it could most helpfully be introduced that would not re-trigger past trauma memories or negative arousal loops in a client. This is of utmost importance because, unless the administration of Calatonia and Subtle Touch feels safe for a client, it will become yet another trigger, and will not achieve its desired effect of re-wiring previously acquired, (and now unhelpful), response loops. Sometimes, when Calatonia is tried and a client does not yet seem to feel comfortable with this form of touch, it is far better to honour and validate this client's feelings at that point rather than push on. This way, trust can be established, and therefore it is possible to come back to Calatonia at a later stage in therapy when the client may feel ready.

Secondly, it is very important for the trauma therapist to

be familiar with and recognise dissociative responses in their clients and carefully assess when and how these might operate in each of their clients. For example, clients who were physically and/or sexually abused as children, often had to acquire complex dissociative response structures for their survival, that enabled them to be compliant with their perpetrator (frequently a parent, close family member or friend of the family) in order to survive or receive any form of attention or what was perceived as love. They may have had to allow themselves to be touched and maybe even show some form of pleasure, depending on the nature of their traumatic circumstances. These clients may host several different dissociated personality parts, some that took on the role of allowing themselves to be touched and be compliant with the perpetrator; other parts that felt terrified of being touched and other parts that hated and detested being touched. When working with such clients, it is important that their internal organising system is explored, and the personality parts made conscious to both the client and therapist before any work with direct touch is attempted. It is important to remember in this context that the trauma memories and response patterns which the different personality parts hold are timeless and encoded in their original context. This means that these dissociated parts (although now personality parts of the client in an adult body) are still holding the emotional and sensual information of how it felt to them at the time of the abuse (which is likely to have been when they were in a much younger body). Once the internal organising system has been understood (which can take many months or years of specialist trauma therapy) it is important to involve the relevant parts in determining and controlling how they want to be touched and where, in order to provide a safe, healing touch experience.

    This, together with other specific trauma processing techniques, can enable the release and rescripting of past encoded patterns. It cannot be stressed enough that touch must always be administered in a way that feels safe to the client now. An essential part of trauma therapy includes a collaborative working relationship between therapist and client. One which feels solid and empowering enough for clients to be able to express and share their needs with their therapist and for therapists to feel grounded and centred within themselves to be able to hear and deeply attune to their clients' needs and maintain safe and healthy boundaries. Even for clients who have experienced less complex trauma it is important for the therapist to have an awareness of possible dissociative responses in the client when considering introducing and administering Calatonia and Subtle Touch. Indicators for dissociation, may be, for example, changes in breathing pattern, voice, eye movement, tracking and gaze; agitation; restlessness; changes in body posture; changes in muscle tone; repetitive micro movement patterns; spacing out; numbing in particular parts of the body and many others. Such reactions need to be addressed by the therapist and mutual exploration of the potential trigger/s and stabilisation techniques, to enable the client to re-ground and come back into their window of tolerance. If the client is already familiar with Calatonia or Subtle Touch, elements of this could be included as part of the stabilisation and grounding process.

Thirdly, the timing as to when and how Calatonia and Subtle Touch may be used as part of trauma therapy needs to be carefully tailored to each client's individual needs. As a broad observation I have found that the more complex and severe the trauma and the more fragmented the client's personality, the longer it will take until the application of Calatonia and Subtle Touch will feel safe enough to be helpful for a client. I have observed that once trauma clients are able to receive touch that Calatonia is often a very helpful first step into touch experiences. One of the benefits of Calatonia is that it follows a prescribed set of movements which over time becomes predictable to clients.

This can feel very reassuring and containing, especially to clients for whom touch has been very unsafe and unpredictable in the past. For many clients when their feet are touched this may not hold as many triggers as if they were touched on another part of their body. However, this cannot be assumed and must be gently explored with each client. For example, one of my clients, Victoria[1], who suffered DID (Dissociative Identity Disorder) as a consequence of severe institutional abuse, was unable to tolerate any form of touch. After several years of specialist trauma therapy, this client allowed me to show her the sequence of Calatonia touches first on one of my hands. She then tried out this sequence on one of her own hands. Gradually, this client was able, under her own control, to allow me to touch both of her hands, later her feet and eventually, became very comfortable with lying down fully clothed, but with her socks off, on top of a massage couch, enjoying the whole Calatonia sequence, including on her head. She also frequently reported seeing colours, hearing sounds, and feeling that she was being helped by a divine presence, all of which she experienced as very soothing, deeply relaxing and healing.

    Touch in Calatonia is performed in such a subtle, light and consciously attuned manner that most clients have not been able to experience such quality of touch ever in their life before. Clients are often surprised at how deeply relaxing and nourishing Calatonia feels once they are able to allow themselves to experience it. I tend to meet with many of my trauma clients for a 2-hour long treatment session (Herbert, 2006) and have found it helpful for most of my clients to weave Calatonia into the latter part of their trauma treatment session on a regular basis. Calatonia seems to beautifully complement and integrate the more active trauma processing methods (such as EMDR, TF-CBT, Havening technique (Ruden, 2011) or Comprehensive Resource Model (CRM; Schwarz & Corrigan, 2016), imagery re-scripting, and/or shadow-transformation work) which, with many of my clients, will take place in the earlier parts of their treatment session. Once clients are comfortable with receiving Calatonia, I may also use it at the beginning of a trauma treatment session to help ground, resource and stabilise a dysregulated client in order to facilitate other subsequent

---

1. All names have been changed to preserve the anonymity of the individuals.

work during that session.

Subtle Touch techniques can be introduced once a trauma client feels safe and familiar with Calatonia and comfortable about being touched by their therapist. It can then be used to work on particular areas of the body where the energy is blocked thereby preventing clients from "feeling" themselves. Subtle Touch techniques can be used to clear blocks in the physical as well as in the energy bodies (subtle body) of a client and it can be helpful for grounding, stabilising and self-regulation. Applying Calatonia and Subtle Touch to the healing of trauma requires the trauma therapist to carefully attune to the therapeutic process and to the client's needs at all times. Comprehensive training in and experience of working with trauma are equally necessary. In order to meet clients at this level of skill, therapists will have needed to have undergone their own trauma healing work, including body-focussed therapy.

In summary, working with trauma is complex and requires the gradual processing of adverse past experiences and the eventual integration of aspects or parts of the Self that have been dissociated in order to ensure survival at the time. Such integration can only happen if different internal and external conditions in a client's body and mind, as well as, in the actual reality of their here-and-now life are created. It is proposed that Calatonia and Subtle Touch, if skilfully and correctly applied with trauma clients, can be very helpful in the healing of trauma. I have used Calatonia and Subtle Touch across the whole spectrum of traumatic experiences, from very early and prolonged developmental abuse trauma, including with clients who have suffered from Dissociative Identity Disorder (DID), as well as, multiple and single incident traumas. It requires skilful tailoring and interweaving of these approaches into each client's individual process of trauma therapy.

Without thorough scientific investigation, it is difficult to discern which specific aspects of trauma therapy have led to the healing in a client and what part Calatonia and Subtle Touch have played in this. However, clinical observation suggests that Calatonia and Subtle Touch are able to induce a depth and level of relaxation, which many trauma clients have not been able to access before. This would suggest that on a neurophysiological level, Calatonia and Subtle Touch enable the body to establish new connections in the central nervous system which counteract the psychophysiological symptoms of stress, tension or trauma-related hyperarousal. This neural integration should lead to a broadening of a client's window of tolerance and emotional comfort zone. Clinical observation suggests that clients become more receptive to trauma processing, as they are learning to self-regulate and are less easily triggered by reminders of their trauma. Calatonia and Subtle Touch seem to be able to down-regulate clients' brain wave activities and enable clients to access feelings of positivity, calm, well-being and internal balance. Some of my clients have been able to enter into deep transcendent states of bliss during their Calatonia session, during which they report seeing colours, images or feeling sensations, which usually have a very peaceful, restorative and calming effect on them.

While more specific, targeted research is needed, clinical experience suggests that the integration of Calatonia and Subtle Touch into specialist trauma therapy can play an important role in bridging the gap between body- and mind-oriented approaches. Thus, supporting and enabling a deep and profound trauma healing process which works towards the eventual embodiment of a person's authentic Self.

References

Cohen, J. A., Mannarino, A. P., & Deblinger, E. (2006). *Treating Trauma and Traumatic Grief in Children and Adolescents*. New York, NY: The Guilford Press.

Clem, R. L., & Huganir, R. L. (2010). Calcium-Permeable AMPA Receptor Dynamics Mediate Fear Memory Erasure. *Science*, 330(6007),1108-1112.

Corrigan, F. M. (2014). Defense Responses: Frozen, Suppressed, Truncated, Obstructed and Malfunctioning. In U. F. Lanius, F. M. Corrigan, & S. L. Paulsen (Eds.), *Neurobiology and Treatment of Traumatic Dissociation Towards an Embodied Self*. New York, NY: Springer Publishing Company.

Farah, R. (2017). *Calatonia: Subtle Touch in Psychotherapy*. São Paulo, SP: Companhia Ilimitada.

Herbert, C. (2019). *From the Experience of Trauma to Positive Growth*. Manuscript in preparation.

Herbert, C. (2017). *Overcoming Traumatic Stress – A self-help guide using cognitive behavioural techniques*. London, UK: Robinson, Little Brown Book Group.

Herbert, C. (2006). Healing from Complex Trauma: An integrative 3-systems' approach. In J. Corrigal, H. Payne, & H. Wilkinson (Eds.), *About a Body: Working with the embodied mind in psychotherapy*. New York, NY: Routledge, Taylor Francis Group.

Kim, J., Lee, S., Park, K., Hong, I., Song, B., Son, G., ... Choi, S. (2007). Amygdala depotentiation and fear extinction. *Proceedings of the National Academy of Sciences of the United States of America*, 52(104), 20955-20960.

Knox, S. S., & Uvnäs-Moberg, K. (1998). Social isolation and cardiovascular disease: An atherosclerotic pathway? *Psychoneuroendocrinology*, 23(8), 877-890.

Korn, D. L. (2009). EMDR and the treatment of complex PTSD: A Review. *Journal of EMDR Practice and Research*, 3(4), 271.

Lanius, U. F., Corrigan, F. M., & Paulsen, S. L. (2014). *Neurobiology and Treatment of Traumatic Dissociation Towards an Embodied*

Self. New York, NY: Springer Publishing Company.

Levine, P. A. (2005). *Healing Trauma: A pioneering program for restoring the wisdom of your body*. Boulder, CO: Sounds True.

Loeken, L., Wessberg, J., Morrison, I., McGlone, F., & Olausson, H. (2009). Coding of pleasant touch by unmyelinated afferents in humans, *Nature Neuroscience*, 12(5), 547-548. doi: 10.1038/nn.2312.

McGlone, F., Wessberg, J., & Olausson, H. (2014). Discriminative and Affective Touch: Sensing and Feeling. *Neuron*, 82(4), 737-755.

Miles, R., Cowan, F., Glover, V., Stevenson, J., & Modi, N. (2006). A controlled trial of skin-to-skin contact in extremely preterm infants. *Early Human Development*, 82, 447–455.

National Institute for Health and Care Excellence (2005, update expected Dec. 2018). *Posttraumatic Stress Disorder (PTSD): The Treatment of PTSD in adults and children*. London, UK: NICE Guidelines (CG26).

Olausson, H., Cole, J., Rylander, K., McGlone, F., Lamarre, Y., Wallin, B. G., ... Vallbo, A. (2008). Functional role of unmyelinated tactile afferents in human hairy skin: sympathetic response and perceptual localization. *Experimental Brain Research*, 184, 135–140.

Ogden, P., Minton, K., & Pain, C. (2006). *Trauma and the Body: A Sensory Motor Approach to Therapy*. New York, NY: W.W. Norton.

Ruden, R. (2011). *When the Past is Always Present*. Psychosocial Stress Series. New York, NY: Routledge.

Sándor, P. (1982). *Técnicas de Relaxamento*. São Paulo, SP: Editora Vetor.

Schwarz, L., & Corrigan, F. (2016). *The Comprehensive Resource Model (CRM): Effective Techniques for the Treatment of Complex PTSD*. London, UK: Routledge.

Seidler, G. H., & Wagner, F. E. (2006). Comparing the efficacy of EMDR and trauma-focused cognitive-behavioral therapy in the treatment of PTSD: A meta-analytic study. *Psychological Medicine*, 36(11), 1515–22.

Shapiro, F. (1989). Eye movement desensitization: A new treatment for post-traumatic stress disorder. *Journal of Behavior Therapy and Experimental Psychiatry, 20*(3), 211-217.

Shapiro, F., & Forrest, M. S. (2016). EMDR. *The Breakthrough Therapy for Overcoming Anxiety, Stress, and Trauma*. New York, NY: Basic Books.

Siegel, D. J. (2010). *The Mindful Therapist: A clinician's guide to mindsight and neural integration*. New York, NY: W.W. Norton.

van der Hart, O., Nijenhuis, E. R. S., & Steele, K. (2006). *The Haunted Self: Structural Dissociation and the Treatment of Chronic Traumatization*. New York, NY: W.W. Norton.

World Health Organization (2013). *Guidelines for the management of conditions that are specifically related to stress*. Geneva, CH: WHO.

6

Subtle Touch in Child Psychotherapy: An Alchemical Perspective

Maria Irene Crespo Gonçalves

> *"Know all the theories, master all the techniques,*
> *but as you touch a human soul be just another human soul."*
> Carl G. Jung

Child therapy is an art based on play, in which the mystery of the child psyche becomes manifest: at the same time as the child creates and interacts with the outside world, they access their inner world. Play is the motor axis of childhood life; regardless of ethnicity or culture, children always express themselves through games. The educational psychologist Maria Amélia Pereira "Peo" (2013) refers to the act of playing as:

> This doing and being of childhood is in truth an entry way to the practice of freedom. This way, the boundary between the inner and outer worlds is woven in a spontaneous and creative manner, integrating physical, emotional, mental and spiritual bodies of knowledge. (Pereira, 2013, p. 48)

In the history of child therapy, Melanie Klein (Mitchell & Friedman, 1994) was the first to use toys and games in child psychoanalysis at the beginning of the 20th century. Soon afterwards, Margareth Lowenfeld created the "World Technique" (1929) in which children arranged scenes from a pre-defined set of toys in a small box of sand, with the result generally illustrating certain archetypical configurations which help to amplify the comprehension of child conflicts (Mitchell & Friedman, 1994). Based on this technique and her experience of playing with her own children, Dora Kalff (1980) systematised this process by linking it to Jungian theory. The result was the *Sandplay* technique, which is now used not only with children but with adults as well: this method proved to be an excellent instrument for reestablishing the creative flow of the psyche through play. Kalff saw the psyche as possessing an inherent tendency to cure itself, with the therapist acting in such a way as to prepare the path for this tendency to take hold through the establishment of a safe and protected space. Thus, the therapist cultivates a state of unconditional acceptance: by observing without judgement and by allowing their observations to guide them.

In the second half of the 20th century, psychotherapy based on Jungian practice gained a new method developed by Pethö Sándor (1974), who incorporated body-based techniques into his practice as a therapist. He developed Calatonia and a great number of other Subtle Touch sequences which facilitated psychophysical integration. He encouraged and stimulated his students, who treated children, to utilise and adapt Subtle Touch for child psychotherapy in a welcoming and playful environment, integrating the child's body perception with psychotherapy.

His teachings emphasise the foundation of therapy as a bidirectional resonance between therapist and patient. He added that:

Any therapeutic approach to human beings will always

impact them in their totality, causing reorganisations and exchanges within the most diverse spheres of existence. Such spheres will manifest or irrupt at times at the psychophysical or biopsychic level, and sometimes at a soul or spiritual level. Any reductive or limiting attitude from the therapist's part to these forms of expression will greatly disturb the spontaneous multidimensional responses of the patient's organism and will harm the therapeutic alliance. (Sandór, 1974, p. 5)

Consequently, the role of the therapist is of vital importance in this process. In child therapy, the therapist is a continent in which the child anchors its psyche and explores without fear as long as a safe and protected environment is cultivated.

The child interacts with the world through the body; for us to communicate with children it is essential that our body be actively present. One can say that it is through the practice of psychotherapy that children awaken therapists to this fact.

The case of a 6-year-old boy illustrates this point. He was hyperactive and immature, wholly dependent on adults to be able to perfom tasks both at home and at school. He also had learning difficulties due to his inability to concentrate. In therapy sessions he was very dynamic and imaginative: one day he wanted to play a hero mounted on a horse, and spontaneously jumped onto the therapist's back. She accepted the game and they "rode" around the room, while he wielded his sword, conquering lands and winning battles. By anchoring himself to the therapist's body, he became a hero and took steps on a path to male consciousness. Several sessions included this same role-play. The therapist observed that this role-play activated and facilitated his neuromotor and learning development: he became better organised and more attentive in his classes at school, and showed greater autonomy when completing homework.

Sándor used to encourage us when we had an unusual idea, to "do, observe, and tell me about it afterwards". Here we see a parallel with the basic assumptions found in Sandplay, where the therapist must assume an attitude of observing without judging whilst being guided by the observations themselves, believing that there is a fundamental direction of the psyche towards wholeness and healing. I can say that this position guided my work, making it more creative and enriching. Thus, the body-based techniques learned in Sandor's method were adapted and developed for interactions with children and their perceived necessities, in a dynamic similar to the dyadic regulation process between mother and child (Neumann, 1991; Fosha, 2001; Schore, 2000).

In this way the therapist's body is placed within the context of therapy: by rolling around, skipping, playing ball games, singing, dancing, sword fighting, dressing up as a witch, queen or fairy, and painting one's face or hand. Also, by touching and being touched. Often children want to repeat a Subtle Touch sequence on the therapist after receiving it. This is often the pattern of interaction between child and therapist, where both are touched in body and soul.

It is important to emphasise the importance of parents establishing a relationship of trust with the therapist in child therapy. It is often necessary to clarify the type of approach to be taken in therapy and the theoretical basis on which it is based. Jointly, the child's family can be informed about this form of non-verbal communication, with children often asking the therapist to teach their parents the techniques so they can do them at home or even in the session. An adopted eight-year-old girl asked to do a sequence of Subtle Touch on her mother after receiving it on her back. With the consent of the therapist, she called her into the room and asked if she wanted to receive a massage. Her mother lay down and she enthusiastically repeated the sequence of touches she had just received: she massaged her spine by kneading and sliding her hands. She even spontaneously added a step to the sequence; while sliding her hands she realised that her long hair was brushing against her mother's back so she keenly increased her head movements so that more of her hair swept against her mother's back. This experience gave them both great contentment and the girl wanted to repeat it at home with her sisters and father. Thus, Subtle Touch strengthened the bond between the parents and their adoptive daughter.

Subtle Touch with Children in Foster Care

Body-based techniques are also effective when used in therapy with children in foster care. These forms of intervention have been developed in institutions that receive children and adolescents sentenced for juvenile delinquency by the justice system. They can also be used in homes or wards for younger children, who are taken in due to parental negligence or abuse or simply because they have been abandoned. Subtle Touch sequences were observed to contribute to transforming residues of violence and helplessness into an attitude of receptiveness and hope, insofar as they allow for the constellation of the positive aspect of the maternal archetype, and aid in the dissolution of traumatic experiences, thus stimulating psychological and motor development.

The boys in group interventions were initially extremely agitated and resistant to the proposed activities. The playful environment indulged them so that they were encouraged to pour out all of the energy normally kept in by the restraints to which they were subjected, in a very chaotic way. After strengthening their bond with the therapist, they were able to transmute feelings of rebellion, distrust and rivalry, into cooperation and trust. This process resulted in resignification of their emotional experiences. From then on, the participants showed interest in activities such as blind man's bluff and ball games, which provided the establishment of a "field" conducive to body-based techniques. The boys were then able to participate in group techniques such as wall dancing, group drumming, shaking one's upper and lower limbs, the living mattress game, Jacobson's progressive relaxation and Michaux's relaxation technique[1].

If an individual's agitated behaviour persisted during

---
1. See "Description of Techniques" at the end of the chapter.

their participation in these activities, the therapist gave the individual a simple touch on the shoulder which had an easing or calming effect, allowing them to continue to be included in the group activity. This individual attention from the therapist, even in a group context, strengthens the ego due to the experience of "being cared for". It is in this precise moment that the person is able to recover their individual identity, in contrast to the feeling of being annihilated as an individual by the institution.

In some cases, individual attention was also given when it was felt to be needed, which allowed Calatonia and spinal vibrations to be applied with intense repercussions on the redirection of psychic energy. One case of an 11-year-old boy who was extremely aggressive, dubbed "El Matador", illustrates the transformational effect of Calatonia. At the end of each sequence of Calatonia, he often spontaneously drew a picture of a boat on the sea. After two months of individual treatment, he drew the boat as if attached to a pier. Consequently, his aggressiveness gave way to a path of improved social adaptation.

The children were also observed to begin expanding their social repertoire, with gestures which were qualitatively different from prior previous gestures which had generally been of an aggressive and malicious nature.

The purpose of the proposed intervention was to develop body awareness, respect for one's own body and for the bodies of others, which also led to qualitative improvements in their interpersonal relationships. These initial results and improvements validated the use of body-based techniques in the eyes of the institutions, which were hitherto perceived by many of the administrators and social workers as dubious or sexually-oriented.

The qualitative measure of human-figure drawings has proven useful for illustrating the benefits of body-based techniques. According to Farah (2008), asking participants to draw a human figure before and after therapy sessions which included a body-based technique allows the therapist to obtain information about any potential changes which may be caused by the technique used, in terms of the projective expression of a body image. Therefore, this measure makes it possible to gauge the development of body image over the course of the therapy process. To illustrate a potential course of development, I have included the drawings of a 12-year-old boy who drew a naked man and a woman in the first image (Fig. 1) in which he emphasised the genitals, with greater emphasis on the female figure. After a month of therapy, he drew a couple in the second image (Fig. 2) who were now dressed and holding hands, with smiling faces and more anatomically correct proportions between their heads, torsos, hands and limbs, explicitly revealing the reorganisation of his psychic energy and sexual libido. Following therapy with Subtle Touch sequences, he had a greater awareness of the other body parts, reducing his fixation on the genitals and sexual content.

Figure 1

Figure 2

In foster care homes for children from 0 to 5 years of age, there is increasing interest and responsiveness in employing body-based techniques as much for the educators as for the children. Interventions with children are often made in the form of group sessions of Calatonia; when a sequence of touches is made to one child, usually, the other children come closer and soon after, repeat the sequence on their friends. The children quickly learn the subtlety of the touches. They often prefer to make the touches with feathers or drops of water on the body which they spread out with a brush, or with short puffs of air mainly made to the abdomen around the belly button.

These forms of interventions may also include Shantala[2], spinal vibrations and/or other movements made to the spine or joints of the body. It is possible to make Subtle Touch sequences with babies even when they are asleep, by subtly contouring the entire body to the sound of lullabies. Shortly after the first

---
2. An Indian massage technique for babies (Leboyer, 1998).

sessions of Shantala, sleep disturbances have been observed to subside, with children becoming more cheerful.

In this way, children are able to experience different modalities of bodily stimulation: from Shantala to subtle touches made with puffs of air or feathers. The application of a Subtle Touch sequence, when made in a warm and welcoming environment, allows for the dissolution of abandonment issues and helps to constellate the positive aspect of the maternal archetype, fostering psychoaffective and motor development. When the hole left by the absence of one's biological mother is occupied by other people who nurture, contain and protect the child, and, above all, form affective attachments, this facilitates individual development (Neumann, 1991).

Current neuroscience studies reveal that the baby's first interactions with their mother, even when they are nurtured in suboptimal environmental conditions such as prisons, stimulate their neurological and affective development more than if they are separated from their mothers at birth and raised in an institution even with a highly qualified nursemaid. Neuroscientists have found evidence that the child's brain is shaped from these initial interpersonal experiences. After the child's birth, the mother begins to predominantly use her right cerebral hemisphere when interacting with her child; entering in tune with a new-born baby who also shows a right-hemispheric dominance in their early development. This rightwards tuning stimulates the formation of distinct neural networks associated with social cognition in the child's brain, and prepares for the onset of left hemisphere development at around 18 months of age, with the emergence of language. Problems that occur in this initial phase can lead to disturbances in the integration of the two hemispheres, which start to function autonomously (Cozolino, 2002).

In response to the importance of this mother-child bond, "Francisco's Home" was founded in 2007, welcoming mothers and their babies. This was the third institution in which work was carried out especially for former homeless women. One of them was a 20-year-old mother of a 4-month-old baby, who was rejecting this new phase of her life. She was conflicted between taking care of her child and going back to the street and relapsing into drug use. She oscillated between moments of care and breastfeeding, and moments of harshness, sometimes beating her son when he cried incessantly. The work conducted with the mother consisted of kneading and sliding movements over her whole body, touches along the spine, and polarity balancing alternated with Calatonia. At the same time Shantala and spinal vibrations were applied to the baby: first by the therapist and later by the mother. The experience of playing with her child and of being touched made her perceive and introject a different form of touch from those she had previously experienced. She began to have more patience when faced with her son's basic needs, and also started taking better care of herself and rearranging her living environment.

This type of treatment centre avoids the separation of mother and child, welcoming them instead. This environment also facilitates the emergence of maternal instincts, strengthening the mother's bond with their child. Once this bond has been established, it is possible to observe both the mothers' psychic and social structuring. Over time, it has been observed that these children are physically healthier compared to children who are separated from their mothers and cared for in shelters.

Body-based Techniques and Alchemical Processes

In order to broaden our understanding of the underpinnings of body-based techniques, we have recourse to the parallel made by Edinger (2006) between alchemical symbolism and psychodynamic processes.

When left free to explore, children express a natural interest in playing with the elements of nature, especially water and fire. Through these natural elements they mobilise the elements in their own body, as the body is constituted of these substances. According to alchemy, all physical objects in the world are a combination in different proportions of the four elements that originate from the "*materia prima*". According to Edinger (2006), the four-pillared structure of the "*materia prima*" which represents the four elements in opposite pairs - earth and air, fire and water - corresponds to the creation of the ego. Similarly, the ego emerges from an undifferentiated unconscious through a process of differentiation of the four functions: sensation and intuition, thought and feeling.

In alchemy, the elements are related to alchemical processes: the earth refers to *coagulatio*; water refers to *solutio*; fire refers to *calcinatio*; and air refers to *sublimatio*.

Earth - Coagulatio

Games played with earth and clay correspond to the process of *coagulatio*. In almost all cultures earth is identified as the matrix or continent of life, and linked to the symbolism of "Mother Earth", to fertility and to nourishment. The experience of tilling the earth in order to plant a seed and waiting for it to germinate connects the child with a cyclical notion of time and the stages of growth. This experience can be linked to an initial process of individual psychic development, to the emergence of the ego from its original state of oneness with the psyche. Jung states that:

> In the child, consciousness emerges from the depths of unconscious psychic life, initially forming small islands, which gradually gather together into a 'continent', to form coherent consciousness" (Jung, 1983, p. 195).

This is clearly a process of *coagulatio*, in which things turn into earth. By equating earth with the body, we can compare the development of consciousness to the development of a physical ego, which is formed from self-experience of the body and by the coagulation of all affective experiences. Montagu (1988) refers to the importance of touch for the psycho-affective development of the baby. According to Montagu (1988), early deprivation of contact in infancy entails consequences for later development as an infant who is deprived of touch later becomes an individual who is not only physically clumsy in his or her relationships with others, but also doesn't know how to react to others on a psychological and behavioural level.

It is therefore from the body and especially the skin, the surface that delimits the relation between the body and the external world, that the child experiences sensations which will serve as the foundations of his or her individuality, coagulating into significant experiences of the body and psyche.

The primary relationship with the mother is not only the basis of the child's relationship with their own body, but also the basis of their relationship with other people. At birth, the child has a sensory system with innumerable cutaneous nerve endings that lie dormant and the activation of this apparatus of the peripheral nervous system occurs through touch. By virtue of its closeness to life in the outside world, the skin is also a social organ (Linden, 2015).

Neumann, who devoted much of his work to child development, also emphasises the importance of touch in the mother-baby relationship, noting some of its psychodynamic aspects:

> In the phase of unitary reality, babies already begin to distinguish between what they are and what is external to their body, and to replace dispersed elements of the cosmos within their own borders. Thus, the earliest awareness of a distinct individuality can, by necessity, be said to occur through the skin, the surface that delimits the body from the outside world. (Neumann, 1991, p. 34)

Edinger (2006) states that the initial process of individual psychic development refers to the emergence of the ego from the experience of the child and conscious awareness of innate archetypal images, which "materialise" into concrete, that is, personalised forms.

The individual only perceives those aspects of the archetypes found in personal relationships, that is, the part of the archetype that the parents' personality is able to activate, mediate and incorporate will be the same part which the child can more easily incorporate and build in his/her own personality"(Edinger, 2006, p. 115).

Neumann refers to this process when defining secondary personalisation:

> The principle [of secondary personalisation] states that man has a persistent tendency to perceive primary and transpersonal content as secondary and personal content, and to reduce them to personal factors. Personalisation is directly linked to the growth of ego, consciousness and individuality . . . (Neumann, as cited in Edinger, 2006, p. 116)

According to Neumann (as cited in Edinger, 2006), it is consequently through this secondary personalisation of the transpersonal that the ego emerges from the flow of transpersonal and collective events, made solid and stronger based on a consistent increase of its own (egoic) importance and personality.

The personal relationships in childhood coagulate archetypes, but can also distort and restrain them if these personal experiences are negative. If, for example, the child has a very destructive and traumatic experience, he may find it difficult to accept and withstand positive parental experiences. The child's negative perception of parental archetypes will remain simply because this was how its initial image coagulated in his or her psyche, and thus, it represents an element of safety and protection, however negative it may be. This accounts for the fact that even when children are adopted by emotionally responsive foster parents, they cannot always reciprocate the love they receive and in many cases may countertransferentially manifest the reliving of rejection. We find this same dynamic at work in institutions. A 7-year-old girl who was adopted when she was a 3-year-old, after living in a shelter, still sketched self-portraits of her body with a circle in her belly, symbolically representing a void (Fig. 3). After a year of psychotherapy with a body-based approach, this image gave way to a more cheerful figure (Fig. 4), with colourful clothes in a beautiful landscape and a predominance of earthy brown colours.

Figure 3: at 5 years 10 months old.

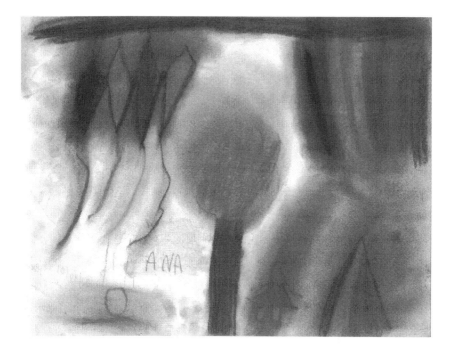

Figure 4: at 6 years 10 months old.

Edinger (2006) states that in cases where a child loses a parental figure at an early age and where an adequate substitution cannot be found, "*a kind of hole*" remains in the psyche. This hole is an important archetypal image which retains a primordial and limitless power to threaten the ego and can negatively affect future personal relations.

On the other hand, there are children who are able to form an important relationship with a secondary figure in their childhood, such as a relative, a caregiver, an adoptive mother or even a therapist, in spite of the severe deprivation they suffered at the beginning of their lives. Thus, the child is able to develop resilience through her interactions with an adult who is able to genuinely relate to her and mediate between the child and the personalised archetypal image of a parent.

In psychotherapy sessions, children often come into contact with their individuality through the symbolic expression of an affective charge linked to their own body image, such as a clay figurine or by tracing the contours of their own body on paper. These art techniques help the child to delimit their body and become more aware of their somatic sensations. Thus, from a creative activity we can create an affective resonance field, which leads to greater confidence necessary for the utilisation of other subtler body-based techniques.

As such, we attribute to *coagulatio* all the techniques that delimit the body with a "firm" touch: massages, clay and mud wraps, or surrounding the body with balls, bamboo, damp cloths, etc. These techniques establish a connection with the body that occupies a distinct place in time and space, with its own limits, with its own rhythm. This connection facilitates relationships with others and with the external world.

Water - Solutio

Water holds great fascination for children, especially children of up to five years of age. Perhaps because it is the first element which children encounter in life when still in the maternal womb, it remains connected to the first phase of the child's development and evokes sensations of acceptance, sensitivity and affection.

In many cultures, water is considered the essence of life made manifest, "its symbolic meaning refers to three basic themes: the origin of life, the means for purification and as a regenerative substance" (Pereira, 2013, p. 117).

There are countless recreational activities that are based on our interaction with water: colouring water with paints or dyes; making *papier-mâché* or paste; experimenting with different states of water, such as ice or steam; and creating contrivances with hoses or tubes to channel water. These games allow for the experiences of fluidity and containment, a particularly productive form of education for children who show symptoms of enuresis or affective disorders.

When interacting with water, children may start to recognise tactile sensations that trigger different affective states. For example, it is very common for children to brush the paintbrush against their own skin when painting, because of the pleasant sensation that is produced. Another pleasurable sensation is to let drops of water fall onto one's skin; which led to the development of the droplets technique created by Maria Amélia Pereira (Peo) at the children's school Casa Redonda (Pereira, 2013).

This technique and these wrapping games, such as packing or balancing children in nets, give rise to feelings related to warmth and comfort as well as cleanliness and purification, some of the aspects associated with the alchemical process of *solutio*. In psychological terms, it re-awakens an experience of being within, of delving back into the womb and consequently the unconscious, to return once more in a more differentiated state of mind through the strengthening of the ego (Edinger, 2006).

In clinical practice, these techniques have been observed to promote relaxation and purification, and to help dissolve residues of rejection and abandonment. They can also help to release stress and tension that have become embedded in the body, and to lead to greater ease in expressing one's feelings as well as to enhanced self-communication and communication with others.

Fire - Calcinatio

Activities with fire are those most often requested by children from 7 to 10 years old. This phase marks the end of childhood, a phase in which many transformations occur both in the child's body and in his/her social environment. It may be because fire is the element that produces the most intense transformations in matter, that it arouses so much fascination during this period. Children become little alchemists, attentive to the transformations that occur in objects when they are subjected to heat or fire: those that harden, those that melt, food cooking or cakes baking in the oven.

Experiments with fire require attention and care, which develops one's self-control, acceptance of limits, and control of impulsive gestures. Such is the fascination which fire exerts, that normally hyperactive children will remain seated for the entirety of a therapy session, simply observing the wax drops from a candle falling and solidifying in water. Through this activity they can produce beautiful medallions covering the entire surface of water in a glass or bowl, using glitter and drops from different coloured candles to decorate them.

The alchemical process linked to fire is *calcinatio*. It acts *upon* the black matter *nigredo* turning it white, and thus purifying it. At the psychological level, Edinger (2006) relates this process to the purification of psychic elements linked to desires which the ego is not ready to cope with, and which therefore generate frustration, intolerance and obsession. Writing these thoughts on paper or drawing monsters that appear in dreams and then burning them in a small bonfire, also help the child to symbolically transform these elements of the psyche.

Body-based techniques that help to activate the element of fire are those that provoke friction (like rubbing and *cafuné*[3]) and those that generate sounds (such as drumming or snapping one's fingers). Sándor mentioned in his classes that buzzing sounds, made behind another's ears for example, purify one's mental state by eliminating irrelevant ideas, obsessive content and irritability.

Air - Sublimatio

Children encounter the element of air mainly through puffing or blowing. Because taking breath is the first exchange the newborn makes with the world, this element is linked to the origin of life.

Blowing on the flame of a candle or blowing soap bubbles, filling balloons, and playing flutes and whistles, all allow the child to experience this element. More indirectly, making kites, paper airplanes, parachutes and weathervanes also helps to develop the manual skills and geometric accuracy necessary for the object to move in or through the air.

---

3. TN: This is a common Brazilian term for the action of running the fingers of one hand in an expanding circle over the scalp of another person (likely from the Quimbundu *kafu'nu*: to plant or bury). See Description of Techniques for more details.

Experiencing the air on swings or simply running, leads to a sense of elation and relaxation. The interaction with the element of air activates the imagination, frequently leading to motifs of wings or capes. Therefore, children often seek identification with a hero from mythology or comic books. They incorporate this hero into their play, which helps to strengthen their ego.

The body-based techniques that activate the element of air are mainly those that work through breathing, such as learning how to breathe through vocalisation or exercises with sound. There are also those that move air over the body without touching it, from hand movements to using fans, feathers, or pieces of cloth. The element of air can also be evoked by swinging children around by their wrists; this action places them in a state of complete surrender in which everything is in motion, leading to an experience beyond gravity and to a new and wholly different experience of their body in space.

Air corresponds to the alchemical process of *sublimatio*, whose main aspect is that of elevation, "the sublimated leaves the earth and is transported to heaven ... a fixed body becomes volatile: that which lies below is lifted up" (Edinger, 2006, p. 135). In psychological terms, *sublimatio* corresponds to an elevation in consciousness. When one stands at a distance from certain psychic states, it becomes possible to look at them from 'above'; thus, one is able to differentiate them and soften their impact. As children do not yet possess the resources for this form of conscious elaboration, they experience this process bodily; by releasing tension acquired from the environment in which they exist and by simply realising that what once troubled them no longer bothers them as it once did.

The Quintessence - Coniunctio

In this category we begin to approach Calatonia and the other forms of Subtle Touch that activate the primordial force, the quintessence, from which the other four elements arose.

According to ancient teachings, the fingers are associated

with the elements: the middle finger with earth, the index finger with water, the ring finger with fire, the little finger with air, and the thumb with the quintessence which lauds over and unites all of the other elements (Roob, 2006). Sándor taught us that Calatonia works by subtly stimulating the toes following the prescribed sequence so that all the elements are activated, inducing a mental and spiritual reorganisation that ranges from the denser to the subtler.

The application of more subtle techniques results in a state of surrender in which the child experiences a time outside of time. One often observes that at these moments the child's gaze seems distant, as if an internal expansion were occurring in parallel (Pereira, 2013). Other times, the child has a little nap during the application. The story of a 10-year-old girl exemplifies this process. After receiving Calatonia, she made the following comment while pointing upwards and then towards her own body: "Daddy came from Heaven to see if everything was alright here". We can thus infer that the subtle touch sequence allowed her consciousness to open up onto an area that Jung (1985) called the numinous, strengthening one's connection to that organising centre, the Self (Gonçalves, 2012).

Thus, the child begins to come into direct connection with her/his soul. According to an alchemical text quoted by Edinger (2006), the body "perfects itself" through its ongoing spiritualisation, alluding to the alchemical process of *conunctio* in which the union of purified opposites occurs in a similar way to that of the union of the body with the spirit.

In conclusion, this study in alchemical categories is based on the observation of predominantly body-based techniques within the practice of psychotherapy, but it is important to emphasise that touch acts on all levels of existence: physical, emotional, mental and spiritual. Just as elements mingle and compensate for one another, body-based techniques can act predominantly on one plane, but reverberate on others. Therefore, "the attentive and subtle care of the body seems to bring human beings closer to their soul" (Machado, 2013, p. 13).

Psychotherapy, which explores the elements, works through the body, and is anchored in the emotional resonance between the child and the therapist, offers fertile ground for development. Neuroscience shows that the affective attunement to their environment allows a child to experiment with new transformations in established patterns of perception, emotion and action (Cozolino, 2010).

And, in the words of Gitta Mallasz (1907-1992):

> Only that which is experienced survives. Only that which we experience in the deepest fibres of our being makes us evolve as human beings. Knowledge or understanding alone are not capable of bringing us forward. Only that which is experienced can be shared with others. It is only through that which we have experienced that we can act upon the world that surrounds us. If you transform yourself, matter is also forced to transform itself. (Mallasz, as cited by Pereira, 2013, p. 125)

Description of Techniques

Group Drumming: One child lies down on his/her stomach, the others sit around him/her and drum and slide their hands over the body of the one lying down.

Cafuné: The therapist performs friction movements with their fingertips over the child's scalp (Delmanto, 1997).

Living Mattress game: Four children get down on their hands and knees, placed two by two; another child lies on their back on top of them. The four children alternate between moving their bodies up and down and back and forth in a wavy pattern, imitating a moving mattress.

Wall Dancing: The children lie on their backs on the floor, close to a wall, and lift their legs up and rest their heels against the wall. They move their pelvis, legs and feet freely, dancing in time to different musical rhythms.

Polarity Balancing: Simultaneous taps made to the elbow and knee, alternating between the right and left side of the body.

Jacobson's Progressive Relaxation: The children lie down on their backs and follow verbal instructions made to guide them through six distinct steps: contraction and relaxation of the arms, of the legs, deep breathing, relaxation of the forehead, the eyes, and the muscles linked to the vocal cords (Sándor, 1974).

Michaux Relaxation Method: The child lies down on his/her back and the therapist gently bends and/or inclines their elbows, knees, head and neck (Ferreira, 1974).

Shaking the Limbs: The child lies down on his/her back and the therapist (or other child) raises their arms, enough so that their head falls backwards freely. They then alternate between pushing and pulling the child's arms. The same procedure is then repeated with the child's legs.

Droplet Technique: A pipette is used to squeeze droplets onto the child's skin, which are then moved across their skin by blowing air or drawing them with a paintbrush. Technique developed by Maria Amélia Pereira, at the Centre for Casa Redonda Studies (Pereira, 2013).

Spinal Vibrations: Vibratory touches are made to the spinal vertebrae in an upwards direction, in time with the child's respiration.

References

Araujo, C. A. (2012). Psicologia Analítica. In F. B. Assumpção & E. Kuczynski (Eds.), *Tratado de Psiquiatria da Infância e da Adolescência*. São Paulo, SP: Ed. Atheneu.

Cozolino, L. (2002). *The Neuroscience of Psychotherapy: Building and Rebuilding the Human Brain*. New York, NY: WW Norton & Company.

Cozolino, L. (2010). *The Neuroscience of Psychotherapy: healing the social brain*. New York, NY: WW Norton & Company.

Delmanto, S. (1997). *Toques Sutis*. São Paulo, SP: Summus Editorial.

Edinger, E. F. (2006). *Anatomia da Psique, O simbolismo Alquímico na Psicoterapia*. São Paulo, SP: Editora Cultrix.

Farah, R. M. (2008). *Integração Psicofísica*. São Paulo, SP: Companhia Ilimitada.

Ferreira, L. M. (1974). Relaxamento em crianças com o método de L. Michaux. In P. Sandór (Ed.), *Técnicas de Relaxamento*, p. 36 - 43. São Paulo, SP: Editora Vetor.

Gonçalves, M. I. C. (2012). Toques sutis em crianças institucionalizadas. In M. E. Spaccaquerche (Ed.), *Corpo em Jung: estudos em calatonia e práticas integrativas*. São Paulo, SP: Editora Vetor.

Jung, C. G. (1983). *Desenvolvimento da Personalidade*. Petrópolis, RJ: Vozes.

Kalff, D. M. (1980). *Sandplay, a Psychotherapeutic Approach to the Psyche*. Santa Monica, CA: Sigo Press.

Leboyer, F. (1998). *Shantala*. São Paulo, SP: Editora Ground.

Linden, D. J. (2015). *Touch: The Science of Hand, Heart, and Mind*. New York, NY: Viking.

Neumann, E. (1991). *A Criança*. São Paulo, SP: Editora Cultrix.

Machado Filho, P. T. (2013). Preface. In M. A. Pereira (Ed.), *Casa Redonda: uma experiência em educação*. São Paulo, SP: Editora Livre.

Mitchell, R. R., & Friedman, H. S. (1994). *Sandplay: Past, Present & Future*. New York, NY: Routledge.

Montagu, A. (1998). *Tocar - O Significado Humano da Pele*. São Paulo,

SP: Summus Editorial.
Roob, A. (2006). *O museu hermético: Alquimia & Misticismo.* Cologne, DE: Taschen.
Sándor, P. (1974). *Técnicas de relaxamento.* São Paulo, SP: Editora Vetor.
Schore, A. N. (2000). Effects of a secure attachment relationship on right brain development, affect regulation and infant mental health. *Infant Mental Health Journal, 22,* 7-66.

7

Subtle Touch in Deep Pedagogy

Céline Lorthiois

Deep Pedagogy

The approach of Deep Pedagogy was developed over the course of individual therapy sessions with children presenting emotional problems and learning difficulties, individual therapy sessions with adults, and group sessions with children and adolescents. This teaching method was originally inspired and continues to be inspired by interactions with enthusiastic parents and professionals, as much by their constant and sincere queries.

Today, Deep Pedagogy is taught on continuing education courses intended for professionals who work with children in schools and many other educational or therapeutic settings. The total duration of the course is 156 hours, usually distributed into 39 weekly classes of 4 hours each.

Deep Pedagogy can be applied in any context where a relaxed environment may be sustained (institutional, recreational, family, etc.). The site of its master plan is *Atelier Fazer e Ser* (Studio for Doing and Being), an extracurricular centre for children between 3 and 14 years of age, conducive to self-knowledge and the exercise of creativity in which the children participate in small-group activities, and each one can receive individual attention from the educators.

Deep Pedagogy takes a holistic approach to child development, accounting for the interaction between body, mind, creativity and dreams. It entails including the soul of the student in the educational process, since it is from the soul that "the enthusiasm, the inspiration and the feeling of life in its fullness come"[1] (Jung, 1987, p. 58) and, "if the soul exists, it is present in all of life's circumstances"[2] (Jung, 1963, p. 13). That is to say, it is a question of bringing the soul in from the obscurity in which it has languished and admitting that the inclusion of the *spiritual* in educational spaces has a pedagogical, prophylactic and therapeutic scope.

Jung's thinking is the theoretical basis of Deep Pedagogy, although it is informed by many other authors and has widely-referenced theoretical underpinnings.

Life forms the curriculum for this pedagogy and in practice it involves playing and games, as well as arts and crafts and other expressive techniques which use different materials such as clay, wood, natural fibres and raw materials, paper, paint, plaster, paraffin, etc.; or, seen from a different angle, water, fire, earth and air. The practice of Deep Pedagogy also includes circle dances from the Sacred Circle Dance movement based at Findhorn, Scotland, which hosts both traditional and contemporary folk dances from many cultures. In addition, Deep Pedagogy integrates free movement and improvisatory games with props, accompanied by music, as well as several body-based techniques.

The main body-based technique used is Pethö Sándor's array of relaxation techniques broadly known as Subtle Touch, which includes the technique of Calatonia. In Subtle Touch, the subject receives a series of touches in a passive receptive state,

---

1. (Author's translation)
2. (Author's translation)

generally in a prone or supine position; the majority of touches are extremely light, and are made to specific points on the body according to the chosen technique: the soles of the feet, the back, legs, abdomen or other regions of the body. The touches take the form of small circles, strokes, using gentle contact or pressure, or puffs of air.

This somatic approach opens up possibilities for progress, balance and health by facilitating access to unconscious content. It complements our modern unilateral preoccupation in developing our intellectual and technical abilities. Through carefully-placed touches in body-based techniques, of which we will see more later; through artistic expression, produced by arts and crafts; and through dance and body movement, "the unconscious is externalised and made manifest. Henceforth it can be perceived through distancing oneself from it and can eventually be integrated into consciousness, thereby facilitating the flow of dialogue between these two states" (Seixas, Rios, & Blanchard, 2009, p. 69).

The Body in Deep Pedagogy

Including the body in education relies on having the freedom to move around. This is in sharp contrast to many school environments as students today are required to remain seated and are often immobile at their desks for long periods. The use of certain tools for the benefit of the body, such as Pethö Sándor's somatic method, has a multimodal effect on physical, emotional, cognitive and spiritual levels (Delmanto, 1997; Farah, 2008).

There is something humble and true in these techniques, which often affect us so deeply that it is difficult to put their impact into words.

Above all, this body-based approach consists of a sophisticated dialogue between two bodies and relies on immense mutual respect. This dialogue is further refined through the connections which a body makes with other vital aspects within the individual that impact mood, intellectual performance, soul states and creativity. Those who conduct and receive these techniques know how frequently the sequence of touches leads us to discover a different world, to change our state of consciousness, and to enter a space rendered in colours which stem from a broader reality. Furthermore, in Education, this somatic work assumes that a human life is 'written', first of all, *through a living body on earth.*

The utilisation of Subtle Touch forms the basis of a healthy education, in which touch presents the body - life's shell - in a non-reductive form to children. It affords children the chance to get to know and experience their body from the inside, and not merely by naming its parts or learning anatomy. In addition, children who receive body work generally replicate their experience in their games by repeating the sequence on dolls or their peers; or, they spontaneously ask for the sequence later on and subsequently show well-being and poise, which is indicative that the experience was positive and enjoyable for them.

The following example illustrates this type of reaction to Subtle Touch in children. A boy diagnosed with ADHD used to be unable to concentrate for more than a few minutes on any activity. After receiving "The Astronaut" technique (see a description of this technique at the end) and several sequences of touches to the feet, he began to develop self-initiated activities and was able to remain concentrated, patient and satisfied for long periods of time. He appeared to have found the motivation to do whatever was relevant to his inner tempo with no prodding or suggestion from the teacher. He had entered his own internal space and discovered both his desires and that which he needed to achieve them.

The Etymology of Calatonia

Calatonia was named by its founder Pethö Sándor from the many meanings of the Ancient Greek word *khalaó*, which among other things means *relaxation* and *forgiving one's parents* (Sándor, 1982, p. 92). There follow some considerations of this last meaning.

When parents relate the pain they feel when they realise how many mistakes they made in their child's upbringing, Calatonia reveals the power of one of its meanings, *forgiving one's parents*. When used to refer to the pain they feel, this meaning soothes and relieves their suffering.

Beyond the suggestion that *forgiving one's parents* is the archetypal disposition of the son or daughter, and that each child invariably has something or even a lot to forgive of their procreators, this meaning leads us to reflect on the fact that it is probably inevitable that parents will make mistakes. That, despite all of their efforts to avoid mistakes and to try and strike the right balance, being a father or being a mother entails making mistakes as they are raising their child. This meaning also suggests that parents can forgive themselves for their own mistakes, in the same way they can forgive or already have forgiven their own parents, and in the same way that their children will be capable of forgiving them. Likewise, this definition suggests that forgiving one's own parents is to forgive all parents, to forgive humanity itself; and at the same time to share the suffering of all children and of all parents, throughout generations. Thus, *forgiving one's parents* offers us a way out from the pain of perpetrated errors or of offences received, heals our wounds and allows us to continue on our way. Jung theorised: "in this way ... great suffering is placed within a larger context, and this makes it bearable. In this situation there is a beneficial effect which emanates from archetypes"[3] (Jung, 1987, p. 323).

And here Calatonia – as much in its somatic effects as in the verbal exchange to be had over one of its meanings – allows the individual's pain, which is often crushing or paralysing, to be transformed into a connection with a collective endeavour, an endeavour of redemption which is placed upon humanity's path towards consciousness.

---

3. (Author's translation)

Pathways to Matter

At the beginning of a child's journey towards consciousness, they learn to navigate a world of sensations while receiving sustenance from the Earth, from Matter. This word corresponds to the Latin *materia*, which is in turn derived from *mater* meaning 'mother'. On mother and matter, Jung explains that for the baby, the object is the mother, the 'mater', the world; in the initial indiscrimination everything is 'mother'. It does not appear separate from what surrounds it, hence the world is 'mater', 'matter' (Jung, C. G. 1983, 277). This holds true for humanity's childhood as a whole, or for the beginning of the development of human consciousness.

Nature, the great mother, gives greater sustenance to the child than the child's real biological mother; this greater sustenance allows the child to move away from his/her biological mother and forms the foundation for their development. Mother Nature's sustenance enables the child to "separate in order to grow" (Rufo, 2007).

Both the world of nature and of man-made materials extracted from nature invite the child to fall in love with them. Nature and playing with matter allows the child to lay down roots in the earth. This is not always something which is obvious because the inner landscapes in the first years of life, a phase when children have not yet developed consciousness, can continue to captivate them, (Jung, 2011, p. 195), whilst "for them the essential question is that of adaptation to the environment. It is necessary to undo their attachment to the original unconscious as its persistence is a powerful obstacle to the development of consciousness, which they need above all else"[4] (Jung, 1977, p. 96).

For this process to take place, the educator must discourage inappropriate habits – such as overprotectiveness, excessive caution and obsessive hygiene - so that a child can find their kingdom, that of simple, natural, crude matter, which primitive man used for taking hold of the Universe. Through anachro-

---

4. (Author's translation)

nistic modes of 'taking hold' of the world, the child takes root. A child learns actively with their hands, with their touch, with their whole body, with their mind, with their imagination, before moving on to more advanced methods of acquiring knowledge and perhaps, later, to making their own contribution to the extent of Humanity's knowledge and consciousness. In other words, when a child is able to interact regularly with the natural world, they have an inexorable need to re-create the primordial stages of Humanity's knowledge. In this early phase of learning about the world the child actually 'remembers', in the same way the embryo and foetus are 'reminded' of the stages of man's phylogenetic development to form the child's body.

Similarly, Marie-Louise Von Franz concluded: "man's curiosity, which led him to experiment with substances, has always been based on the idea that he could indirectly discover more about the Divine" (1998, p. 18). And, nowadays, when children mix different elements and play with them, are they not constructing themselves as spiritual beings? And when children playfully recreate the world, are they not contributing to the edification of their personality through this activity of a demiurge? Demiurge here is understood in the sense of an artisan who fashioned the world from pre-existing matter (from the Greek *demos*: country, people; and *ergon*: work, action).

Hence play represents the child recreating humanity's journey on this planet. It would be wise not to shorten this stage, as the child is, in a sense, resuming that which came before (Dubois et al., 2007). Jung states:

> In the course of its development, the foetus retells, to speak of, and alludes to, its phylogenetic evolution. In the same way, the soul of the child accomplishes "the tasks of humanity which preceded us". The child lives in a pre-rational and, above all, pre-scientific world, the world of a humanity that existed before us. It is in this world that our roots are plunged, and it is through these roots that children grow. *Their early maturation drives them away from*

*these wells; their lack of maturity binds them.*⁵
(Jung, 1977, p. 258).

It is in this sense that Deep Pedagogy considers knowledge not to be an end in itself, but as an inevitable consequence of a well-lived childhood.

Play, contact with the natural elements, arts and crafts, dancing and Subtle Touch are ways for children to come into contact with the ebb and flow of humanity. These methods symbolically gather the human family around the children and invite them to make their own mark on the planet, while demanding accurate awareness from the educator of their own role in this process.

The Role of the Educator in Deep Pedagogy

"One must forge the child's body with body-based techniques," as professor Pethö Sándor said in class. One must also forge the educator's body in experience with Subtle Touch, as these sequences strengthen the body and awaken beautiful sensations, beautiful images, beautiful thoughts and beautiful questions. They seem able to bring forth ideas and intuitions of what can be done and how to do it in many situations, even in the absence of a favourable environment.

Jung warns about the unmet needs of educators:

> As for young people who have chosen pedagogy as a profession, it must be assumed that they themselves have been educated. But ... they generally had the same faulty education as the children whom they must educate .... Our whole educational problem has a faulty approach: it sees only the child who must be educated and fails to consider the lack of education in the adult educator. (1981, p. 180)

---

5. Emphasis added (Author's translation).

For this reason, educators attending the course on Deep Pedagogy go through a process of self-learning which is facilitated and supplemented by both theoretical content and practical classes, through which they familiarise themselves with various tools. In Deep Pedagogy, educators are not only instructed, they are also the object of care, aiming to restore, maintain and increase their well-being. The teacher is the key piece in the educational process of students and the bastion of best pedagogical practice. Thus, an enlightened educator will be able to listen to a child's dream because they have learned to consider their own dreams, to encourage enthusiasm because they are full of wonder at life themselves, and to 'read' their students because they are engaged in the process of self-discovery every day.

The tools proposed by Deep Pedagogy - Subtle Touch, dance, play and work with various materials - request the presence of the body in the educational process: the touching body, the moving body, the playing body, the body that builds and expresses itself. "The soul predates the living body so that its images can breathe," said Jung (1963, p. 26), revealing a frequent double omission in our work as educators. Jung insisted that we must "return to earth, to the body", to the senses, to our oneness; thus, ceasing to be just a 'stream of unconscious life', like a river in which nothing happens because nobody is witnessing it. The body, he added, "is the here and now; when one is really in the here and now, one is in the body" (Jung, 1960, pp. 300-301).

But what does "being in the body" mean? Al-Chung-Liang Huang (1973, p. 240) refers to "the feeling of oneself very, very much here: this is one's point of reference; this is one's stability. This is the life force that gives one balance. This is the home you carry with you wherever you are".

The practices mentioned above, in so far as they involve the body, can elicit this presence in the here and now.

Teaching and Learning of Subtle Touch in Deep Pedagogy Training Courses

In this process, the dimension of teaching is melded with that of therapy (Farah, 2008, p. 31). During the teaching-learning sessions of Subtle Touch, participants on the course go through the experience of conducting and receiving the sequences of touches. This experience of being the recipient of Subtle Touch gives the educator an immediate understanding that they can be transformed through care and they themselves are the first practical example of this transformation. In other words, when we talk about body-based techniques in education we tend to think of the child as an object of care, but in Deep Pedagogy the primary focus of care are the adults around the child: the teacher, the therapist, the mother, the father (the students on the Deep Pedagogy courses are made up of architects, artists, dancers, journalists, teachers, educational professionals, psychologists, occupational therapists who are often mothers or fathers themselves). They make up the child's landscape and are the witnesses of the child's experiences, of their very existence.

Subtle Touch Integrated into Children's Games

It is to be noted that among the benefits of going through the experience of learning, applying and receiving bodywork as an educator, is the possibility of appreciating the exquisite level of the touches appearing in children's games, which, without a proper understanding, would be considered only rough, banal and of little pedagogical use. Once the educators open themselves up to understanding the effect of specific playful gestures, they will know how to identify them, respect them and accommodate their expression. Indeed, children spontaneously brush and touch their own body and the bodies of their peers; they manipulate physical substances with their hands; they lie on the grass for many hours when they have access to an outdoor setting (the composer Pyotr Ilyich Tchaikovsky himself spent much of his time lying down on the ground to 'feel' his native Russia); they tread through clay barefoot; they wisely give themselves over to games involving the body (for example wrapping themselves in sheets in which they pretend to be caterpillars waiting to leave the cocoon); they invert their usual upright posture, allowing the top of their head to rest against the floor, or they sit facing each other and lower and touch both of their heads together, or put their bare feet together so their soles match up with the soles of another child and 'pedal' together in the air. These playful touches are natural facilitators of child development, even without having this purpose, and for this reason, they deserve the status of "subtle". For example, the sensations detected by the skin receptors activated by these games inform the central nervous system both of the subject's internal conditions as well as of their external environment. Children use the resources in their somatosensory system to subtly learn about themselves, about others and about the world! It is by using their body that they refine it. And it is through practising on this physical plane that connections with other planes are established, as seen above.

The Use of Subtle Touch in Different Environments
By learning Subtle Touch, teaching students are able to apply this method to the various environments in which they work.

On the course there have been many wonderful reports of the use of Subtle Touch in often improbable environments: a physics teacher who taught classes of teenage students who varied from total unruliness to delinquency, after many feelings of impotence and despair, dared to suggest a technique to one of her classes. She performed a sequence of facial touches to the central axis of the nose (see a description of this technique at the end) on a boy who had a long history of delinquency, and who had walked by her desk when arriving late to class. Once the boy had accepted this, the classroom went very quiet whereas the noise had previously been constant and none of the students listened, making it impossible for their teachers to teach them anything.

One girl asked, "what just happened? The class has never

been so quiet!"

With this simple sequence of touches, the teacher profoundly affected an entire class and gave everyone the experience of containment through silence, for at least a few moments. Surprisingly after this experience, the boy, who was previously unreachable, that is, had not bonded with the teacher, befriended her and accepted some of her suggestions. Subtle Touch allowed for the establishment of a positive bond. Here, we can see the profound capacity that it holds for the reorganisation of attachment and bonding.

This teacher felt the need for sequences that could be performed when the students were standing up or sitting down, as these were the only positions that were possible in the school where she taught. In addition to the two sequences previously mentioned, she was taught sequences consisting of tapping, sliding, 'piano fingering' touches, as well as experimenting with sequences of a few touches with sound - for example, using the rain stick - that often have a profound impact on participants.

Elsewhere, in a classroom teeming with some 35 five-year-olds, an educator introduced a sequence called "the Astronaut". The children quieted down and concentrated, all participating in an extensive choreography performed in groups of five children, in which four children carefully moved the limbs of a fifth classmate who was lying on the floor – this fifth child, the receiver, was deeply immersed in that form of play.

Another educator applied the same technique to three-year-olds and found that those who appeared to be more introverted tended to direct the work, controlling the movement of their limbs without giving in completely. On the other hand, the children who appeared to be more extroverted surrendered themselves more easily and confidently to the "therapists". This observation seems to point to the fact that introverts accept suggestions more readily from their inner universe, while extroverts readily accept suggestions from the external world. In this sequence, the adult's full acceptance of the child expressing their personality style will allow her to experience a deep feeling of being in the here and now.

A different sequence, "stones in the hair scattered around the head" (see a description of this technique at the end) was successfully implemented in a mental health outpatient clinic with extremely agitated children. The children calmed down significantly and were able to participate in more organised activities, which were previously unworkable because of the agitation.

In certain schools or other educational settings however, physical contact is not always encouraged or possible. Occasionally, body-based techniques with children are prohibited with the claim that such experiences could encourage them to become too permissive. It is indeed true that people who are only briefly instructed in the different modalities of Subtle Touch, without having had enough time or guidance to develop an ethical stance, can inadvertently leave boundaries unclear or undefined. In any case, when the touches and motions in Subtle Touch are made purely mechanically, they do not communicate to the child the notion that his/her body is deserving of respect and that it should not be touched in just any way, nor by just anyone.

The awareness of a "third point" (Blanchard, Rios, & Seixas, 2010) contributes to the development of the above-mentioned ethical stance. Pethö Sándor describes this third point during Subtle Touch, as the process whereby the person receiving the stimulation and the person giving it are handed over on an equal footing to a process of transformation. In this dialectical process we consider the presence of a third factor, a non-individual field of the soul, where the creative experience takes place, mediating and transcending duality.

In other words, the ethical stance that the application of Subtle Touch requires is not a superficial, distracted or frivolous one, but one that needs to be learned and implemented carefully.

Body-Based Techniques Created by Children

When children receive careful sequences of touches, their respect for the body comes naturally. Introducing Subtle

Touch in a pedagogical environment, while taking a clear ethical stance, appears to give the children permission to formulate an appropriate repertoire of physical contact. They then begin to exchange touches that have not been taught by the adult, taking an absorbed and focussed attitude and applying careful touches to their peers, usually when they play at being a doctor, nurse or hairdresser.

The Effects and Consequences of Some Techniques

Applying body-based techniques in a didactic setting where the participants do not know each other can provide other interesting answers. In a conference on body-based techniques, for example, The Astronaut technique was proposed. This work was carried out by body therapists. One woman made the following comment: "I thought: my legs must be really heavy, rigid ... but I wasn't worried, I didn't care, I don't know anyone here, so I can just enjoy it!" And one young man added: "when they started I thought: nobody knows me, I'm really just going to enjoy it!"

That is, in a group where people do not know each other and are invited into the structured physical contact of Subtle Touch, people eventually allow themselves to retreat healthily and playfully from their *persona*. This allows them to experience Subtle Touch without shyness or formality and facilitates the expression of another dimension of being.

In general, this physical contact awakens a varied range of sensations in the individuals receiving it:

- Sensations of water; of being underwater; of floating; of being flotsam in water; of being an amoeba in water;
- Sensations of being inside a ball; of floating through space; of mind expansion;
- Sensations of not being in control; of surrender; of having one's body divided into four semi-autonomous parts followed by a sensation of wholeness;
- Sensations of joy; of pleasure; of wanting to dance, to laugh or to cry;

- Pleasant sensations of cold or of heat;
- Sensations of being a baby again; of being a baby in water; of being cared for; of receiving loving attention; visions of the subject's mother singing to them as a baby;
- Sensations of wanting more; of the brevity of this physical contact;
- Sensations of strangeness; of having never experienced anything similar before; of having found something they had been waiting for; of thoughts coming to mind but not mundane ones;
- Unusual and intense perception of the spine;

Those who conduct the sequence report experiencing: greater compassion or empathy; well-being when following the sequence; relaxation when applying the sequence.

The basic sequence of Calatonia (Sándor, 1982), the sequence of breaths made to "the interspaces between the fingers" (see description at the end) and the touches made to "the interspaces between the toes" (see description at the end) provide other such images and sensations. These include:
- Images of foetuses, flowers, a rose, and pleasant colours;
- Sensations of water around one's head; of stepping into mud;
- Sensations of experiencing something completely different; of lightness; of hovering above the surface on which they are lying; of entering another universe;
- Sensations of swaying from side to side; of one's chest bursting or being unburdened.

It is through the sensations which Subtle Touch propitiates that nature can be found in oneself. When nature is so cruelly lacking in many large cities, experiencing elements such as water, earth, fire (heat), air (lightness), flowers and colours allow us to access feelings of regression and joy, and to surrender to the sublime.

Subtle Touch also offers opportunities to reclaim one's inner space, to discover one's inner riches, and to eventually cease one's search for external riches, as one finds value in oneself. There is often a beautiful rapture to the countenances of the individuals who conduct these sequences. It is clear that the experience of Subtle Touch can be as positive for the giver as it is for the receiver and can facilitate the acceptance of one's role as either giver or receiver.

The Effects of Subtle Touch on Educators

The individual pedagogical support to educators who are engaged in a process of self-learning allows us to record other positive effects from the Subtle Touch technique.

One educator on the Deep Pedagogy course reported that Calatonia helped her to cope with what had previously been unbearable: in this case all thirty-five children in her classroom shouting, pulling on her clothes and constantly demanding attention. Her ability to withstand these conditions increased significantly and she was able to teach the class with a calm demeanour and presence and found that her prospects of providing adequate and focussed responses had multiplied. She also reported observing a green colour when receiving Calatonia that healed her pain and reappeared at other times when she felt particularly de-energised and lonely. One day, together with this green colour, she experienced a very intense feeling that "someone really loves me!" A similar experience is described in E. Maitland's mystical experience (Jung, 2003, p. 33): "I was able to focus my consciousness on the target desired: an ineffable white light arose, it was the duality of the Father and Son proving that it is love and will, male and female, father and mother".

Another educator, experiencing an acute phase of a chronic illness that left her with an extremely sore body, felt as if she were in a foetal position on receiving Calatonia and the sequence of touches felt like a warm and comforting cuddle.

Among many other wonderful stories, there is that of an educator who was afraid of doing a headstand in Capoeira, the Brazilian martial art. This difficulty seemed to stem from a fear of inverting his upright posture and thereby subverting the primacy accorded to the 'head', to the mind and to the intellect, as this individual was particularly focussed on the mental plane. At the same time, she was going through a remarkable set of coincidences involving her head: she had bruised her face in an accidental fall and she had badly strained the muscles in her neck, leading her to feel torn and ruptured. At the same time, she dreamed of her father violently beating her on the head with a plate and ordering her to have dinner with a young man who was, in her own words "handsome, flippant, jokey, very immature". She also dreamed that blood continued to flow from her head, which felt very sore (perhaps losing some vital fluid?). She frequently stated that she could not stop thinking: "all I can do is think!"

In the first sessions of Calatonia, she perceived a force that reorganised her and left her body feeling more cohesive. In a later session, she reported a dream in which her hand caressed her neck which caused her to feel a great deal of pleasure through what appeared to be a reconnection of the head to the body via the neck, and consequently likely a realignment from the intellectual sphere to a more global and organic perspective.

Pethö Sándor said that Subtle Touch is a set of unusual stimuli, as mentioned earlier, capable of creating openings on all levels of our being: on the physical, intellectual, emotional and spiritual planes. That is, through careful, differentiated, and sometimes surprising touches, the body can explore the paths conducive to personal development.

Description of Techniques

The Astronaut: the subject lies down on her/his back with 4 therapists each seated in front of one of the subject's limbs. Simultaneously, each of the 4 therapists holds the one limb, of the subject, that is in front of them and moves it gently and playfully.

Touches to the central axis of the nose: the subject stands with their arms loose. With the lower edge of the right index finger, the therapist slowly and gently applies a sequence of touches along the midline of the nose, beginning at its tip and ending on the depression below the forehead. This sequence is immediately repeated with the left index finger. This double sequence can be repeated without interruption. Duration: from 1 minute to 1 ½ minutes (Delmanto, 1997, p. 225).

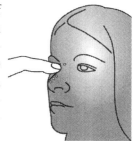

Stones in the hair scattered around the head: the subject lies down on their back with their hair laid out around their head. The therapist places a stone under a lock of hair and gently knocks it with another stone. This process is repeated 6 times at different positions around the head.

The interspaces between the fingers: the subject is seated in an armchair with their hands resting on the knees or on the chair arms. They can also sit on a couch with their legs crossed and with their hands on their knees. The therapist blows 7 times in each interspace between the fingers of the subject. Each breath should be strong yet precise, corresponding to a full exhale. When breathing in, the therapist should take care to avert their face, in order not to affect the subject's energetic field. This sequence can be conducted by two therapists at the same time, one on the right and the other on the left, or it can be performed individually first on one side and then on the other (Delmanto, 1997, pp. 200-201).

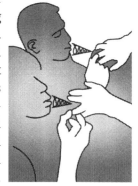

The interspaces between the toes: the subject lies down on their back with their arms laid alongside their body and with their eyes closed. The therapist sits facing the subject's feet. The therapist delicately places their fingertip on the interspace between the patient's toes. The therapist should use the corresponding finger to touch each interspace, i.e., use the little fingers to work on the base of the patient's fifth toes and so on. The touch is bilateral, the pressure is gentle. The duration of each touch: from 45 seconds to 1 minute (Delmanto, 1997, pp. 70-71).

References

Blanchard, A. R., Rios, A. M. G., & Seixas, L. P. (2010). The Body in Psychotherapy: Calatonia and Subtle Touch Techniques. In Raya Jones (Ed.), *Body, Mind, and Healing After Jung: A Space of Questions* (pp. 228-249). London, UK: Routledge.

Delmanto, S. (1997). *Toques Sutis – uma experiência de vida com o trabalho de Pethö Sándor*, 1. ed. São Paulo, SP: Summus.

Dubois, J., Mitterand, H., & Dauzat, A. (2007). *Dictionnaire étymologique & historique du français*. Paris, FR: Larousse.

Farah, R. M. (2008). *Integração Psicofísica - O trabalho corporal e a psicologia de C. G. Jung*. São Paulo, SP: Companhia Ilimitada.

Huang, A. C-L. (1973). *Expansão e Recolhimento – A essência do T'ai-Chi*. São Paulo, SP: Summus.

Jung, C. G. (1960). Seminários dados entre 30 de outubro/5 de novembro 1930. *The Visions Seminars*, Spring. Tradução apostilada de Sándor, P. (1982).

Jung, C. G. (1963). *L'âme et la vie*. Paris, FR: Buchet/Chastel.

Jung, C. G. (1977). *Psychologie et Éducation*. Paris, FR: Buchet/Chastel.

Jung, C. G. (1981). *O Desenvolvimento da Personlidade*. São Paulo, SP: Vozes.

Jung, C. G. (1983). *Métamorphoses de l'Âme et ses Symboles*. Genève, CH: Librairie de l'Université Georg & Cie.

Jung, C. G. (1987). *L'homme à la découverte de son âme*. Nouv. ed. Paris, FR: Albin Michel.

Jung, C. G. (2003). *Estudos Alquímicos*. Petrópolis, RJ: Vozes.

Jung, C. G. (2011). *Seminários sobre sonhos de crianças - Sobre o método da interpretação dos sonhos – Interpretação psicológica de sonhos de crianças*. Petrópolis, RJ: Vozes.

Lorthiois, C. (2007). Pedagogia Profunda. Por quê? Para quê? Como? *Hermes*, 12, pp. 96-105.

Lorthiois, C. (2008). *Exercícios de Pedagogia Profunda – Uma inclusão da Alma na Educação*. São Paulo, SP: Paulus.

Lorthiois, C. (2012). Os toques sutis na educação – Um re-ligar do corpo com a cabeça, in M. E. Spaccaquerche (Ed.), *Corpo* em Jung (pp. 105-116). São Paulo, SP: Vetor.

Sándor, P. (1982). *Técnicas de Relaxamento*. São Paulo, SP: Vetor.

Rufo, M. (2007). *Détache-moi! Se séparer pour grandir*. 1. ed. Paris, FR: LGF/Le Livre de Poche.

Seixas, L. M. P., Rios, A. M. G., & Blanchard, A. R. (2009). O Corpo para Jung. In P. Albertini, & L. V. Freitas (Eds.), *Jung e Reich – Articulando conceitos e práticas* (pp. 65-78). Rio de Janeiro, RJ: Guanabara Koogan.

von Franz, M.-L. (1998). *A Alquimia e a Imaginação Ativa*. São Paulo, SP: Cultrix.

8

Calatonia & Art:
Expressing Trauma Through Images

Irene Gaeta

Alice

This chapter presents a case study describing the experience and aftermath of early trauma, and the use of Calatonia followed by art-therapy to access, reorganise and integrate pre-verbal memories. It highlights the case of a patient, 'Alice' (fictitious name), who was born during a difficult and traumatic birth experience. One of a set of twins at birth, Alice's sibling died during her mother's labour. Losing one child and gaining another at the same time produced a unique emotional context: her mother mourned the loss of one child while learning to care for Alice, her surviving daughter. Consequently, this presented many attachment difficulties to the relationship between mother and daughter.

Attachment (Bowlby, 1958; Landa & Duschinsky, 2013) is fundamental not only for emotional development throughout the life span, but for the establishment of one's sense of self (mental representations of the self) and the ability to relate to others, particularly in terms of expectations about how others behave in relationships. At the basis of these patterns, or "internal working models", lies the parental complexes (Jung, 2001, v.9/I), the stored experiences about the bond between infant and mother or parental figures. This dynamic impacts the development of the personality more potently during the child's pre-verbal phase (Knox, 2003; Schore, 2011).

Problems that develop at a pre-verbal phase, such as the intrauterine and early infancy stages, may block further harmonious development (Schore, 2011). In adult life, these issues may only surface through images or physical sensations, as they refer to a stage of development prior to verbal communication.

Thus, the body takes on the role of manifesting conflicts of psychogenic origin, which can strain the organism (Williams, Conway, & Cohen, 2007). These stresses of psychogenic origin accumulate in the body and can potentially be released in physical symptoms such as tics, tremors, coughing, stuttering, headaches, seizures, catharsis, crying and other physical manifestations (Berry, Varese, & Bucci, 2017; Williams et al., 2007). These tensions generally refer to undeveloped potential, unresolved conflict, and content, which has not been integrated into consciousness. In these cases, somatic psychotherapy can be of great help.

Calatonia

When individuals find themselves in a situation in which they see no way out, psychological tension is generated. While the conflict cannot be resolved satisfactorily, energy is blocked and returns to the unconscious, where it mobilises resources to overcome the tension and resolve the conflict.

The nature of gentle touch in Calatonia allows for a multisensory and multidimensional experience, which integrates emotional and cognitive processes, and sensory memories (Gaeta, 2005, 2010). These processes establish a communication between the somatic unconscious and the individual's awareness, from which isolated images, or sequence of images or scenes emerge (Arcuri, 2005, 2006), which are meaningful as a psychological experience, in the same way a dream is (Jung, 1995). Insofar as it places the individual in a state of relaxation, Calatonia allows access to unconscious fantasies while one remains awake, thus, facilitating a creative dialogue between the conscious and the unconscious through the interaction between the body and the psyche (Seixas, Rios, & Blanchard, 2009).

The emergence of this content is fostered also by the fact that the somatic techniques are conducted within the trusting boundaries of a therapeutic relationship in which the individual feels safe, cared for and known (Dales & Jerry, 2008; Fosha, Siegel, & Solomon, 2009; Mancia, 2006). In this way, Calatonia offers a context in which the therapist mediates the process in dyadic (affective-somatic) regulation with the patient (Seixas et al., 2009).

In this more contemplative or observant state, one's awareness can witness emotions, images, sensations or thoughts, to which no attention had previously been given. After the Calatonia session, these contents can be addressed in psychotherapy and may often find concrete expression in the form of drawing or painting; thus, helping the patient to re-engage consciousness with the inner world – now in a more proactive manner (Carvalho, 1995).

In this process of observing one's internal reality (as described above), the tension between the body and the psyche is lessened, leading to greater physical, emotional and mental balance and consequently, decreased anxiety.

Sándor (1982) suggests that the patient's reports after receiving Calatonia should be accepted without judgement or interpretation. This way, the patient can stay with the emerging images and sensations from the dialogue established between their consciousness and the somatic unconscious.

Damasio (1999) attests to the importance of this dialogue:

> The entire construction of knowledge, from simple to complex, from non-verbal imagistic to verbal literacy, depends on the ability to map what happens over time, in-

side our organism, around our organism, to and with our organism, one thing followed by another, causing another endlessly. (Damasio, 1999, p. 188)

The Neuropsychology of Expressive Therapy

From the perspective of neuropsychology (Arcuri & Horschutz, 2012), expressive techniques in psychotherapy focus on both the non-verbal imagistic as well as the somatic medium, accessing the primitive area of the brain called the amygdala (Greek for *almond*, in reference to its shape). The amygdala is a set of nuclei situated above the brainstem and is distributed bilaterally, with a unit in each cerebral hemisphere within the anterior-inferior region of the temporal lobe. Arcuri & Horschutz (2012) point out that the amygdala maintains extensive connections with the hypothalamus and the rest of the limbic system. These connections play an important role in the mediation and control of higher-order emotional activities, such as friendship, love and affection, the outward manifestations of mood, and especially emotional states of fear, anger, and aggression.

The amygdala is fundamental for the organism's self-preservation, as it is the centre for identification of threat, leading to responses of fear and anxiety. It records the olfactory and tactile memories associated with sensations, emotions, and traumas experienced from the intra-uterine stage onwards, as it is a part of the limbic system formed in the first forty days of gestation.

Therapy techniques that allow access to memories formed prior to symbolic language which can be translated first into images, then into emotions and finally into language stimulate the reconstitution and the reconstruction of the individual's psychological integrity. In short, they allow the individual to become aware of that which could not be expressed directly through speech.

The area corresponding to the motor production of speech, called Broca's area (Bohsali et al., 2015), develops only later during the maturation of the individual's central nervous system.

Newborn babies record information primarily through non-declarative, implicit memory (Williams et al., 2007), thus, there is no way to verbally express such primordial memories. A similar process happens with traumatic experiences (Kalsched, 1996) that cause excitation of the right hemisphere, recording the experience in implicit memory where the affective state and not the event itself is remembered (Schore, 2011).

Increased activation of emotion-related regions in the right hemisphere (Schore, 2011) leads to the dominance of aversive emotional regions over approach-related emotional regions in the left hemisphere, which is also the dominant hemisphere for speech production and where Broca's area is most active. This may be a contributing factor to traumatised patients' inability to verbalise traumatic experiences.

A traumatic scene is recorded in images or sensations that are repeated throughout the person's life as implicit memories, where the event is not located in a specific place or time and therefore occurs continuously (Siegel, 1999), generating an excitatory state typical of trauma.

With each new experience, endorphins are released by the pituitary gland and hypothalamus which produce a state of analgesia and a sense of well-being, calming down the individual but leading to maladaptive conditioning. As such, a compulsion towards internal repetition of the trauma is created, so that the organism continues to release an endogenous form of morphine. This makes the individual feel better temporarily just as if they had an addiction of some kind.

In Jungian terms (Jung, 2001), the individual identifies with a negative numinous side of the psyche, with a negative aspect of the archetype of the Self, which is overpowering and potentially destructive, requiring the therapist to help the patient to break this vicious cycle (Kalsched, 1996).

In these cases, Calatonia, accompanied by art therapy (creative expression), can help the patient to relax, which will reduce stress and anxiety, and positively unlock images and sensations that exert a certain fascination or power over the psyche (Gaeta, 2010).

Expressive Arts and Analytical Psychology

Jung (1986) regarded imagination as one of the main functions of the psyche: a direct expression of vital activity and a unique form of psychological energy manifested in consciousness. Thus, we should pay attention to the language of the psyche - fantasy - by means of which man can embark on a process of symbolisation that broadens one's outer experience.

Jung (1986) suggested that his patients paint what was in their dreams so that they could open up a dialogue with the symbolic material and make it part of concrete reality. This allowed them to gain some perspective on this internal narrative and, with some experience and a dose of sensibility, to reach a deep understanding of images drawn or painted.

He (Jung, 1985) reminds us of the fact that in certain circumstances such images have a considerable therapeutic effect on their creator, as these images often represent a bold attempt to see and unite seemingly irreconcilable opposites and prevail against seemingly insurmountable inner divisions.

According to Jung (1985), a simple attempt made in this direction holds curative properties, as the patients begin to perceive that painting a picture can free them from a deplorable psychic state. This result encourages them to express themselves every time their condition worsens. For Jung (1985), this is the first step towards self-agency, self-care, and psychological maturity, through the patient's own creativity: "The patient need no longer depend on their dreams or on the physician's knowledge, as by painting himself onto a canvas - as it were - he plasters himself" (p. 46).

He clarifies that identical processes occur with the hand that guides the pencil or the brush, with the feet which perform the steps of a dance, with sight and hearing, with words and with thought - they have an intention of their own - led by unconscious contents that seek to take form and reveal their meaning (Jung, 1991).

The image and its meaning are identical and as the former takes on a more defined form, the latter becomes clearer. Hence, the form that is presented does not need interpretation because it suffices to describe its own meaning. While science and philosophy purport to explain the world, this is not the purpose of music, poetry or painting. Art, by giving up on explaining the world, allows us to tolerate the unexplained world and to transform its strangeness into appeal and interest.

The Process

Alice began her treatment in 2003 at the age of 60. She was happy to say that she was free to do everything she had always wanted to do, because she had retired.

In our first session, Alice cried as she told me about the loss of her daughter. I understood little of what she was saying but decided to just listen and accept whatever she said. I explained about working with art and somatic work in therapy. She chose to do Calatonia at the start of our sessions and responded well to it, in her words, "it felt like a kind of affection. I really felt it in the throat area, I saw a violet-coloured light coming out of my throat – it was very beautiful. I also felt a sensation of relief in my stomach. You know, I'm taking antidepressants, I have sinusitis, and I'm also taking Omeprazole for my stomach".

I invited her to draw what she had experienced, and she said she would prefer to do it at home. Alice brought the picture to our second session (Fig.1).

The neck is the anatomical connection between the head and the rest of the body and symbolises the link between the material (body) and the abstract or divine (head), and appeared to be a source of tension for Alice. It is through this passage, the neck, that exchanges are made possible: food, air and especially language and verbalisation of bodily feelings.

Figure 1. Alice painted this picture about her experience of seeing violet light coming out of her throat, surrounded by a vibrant yellow.

Grof (1987) states that blockages in the throat indicate important unresolved issues in the individual's life history. According to him, these issues are usually related to traumatic memories of situations that threatened the individual's oxygen supply, extreme verbal or oral aggression, emotional deprivation, etc.

Alice said that the very meaning of the word 'depression' gave her a clear sense of what she might be experiencing about the death of her daughter. From an energetic point of view, depression means a decrease in the flow of life energy.

In the Hindu tradition, the centre of the larynx is referred to as the Visuddha chakra, described as having a white colour with sixteen purple or smoke-coloured petals, whose symbolic meaning is associated with creativity and self-expression (Varenne, 1977).

From an Eastern perspective (Varenne, 1977), each person possesses an energy field (aura) permeated by diverse feelings. Within this theory, which we use here to broaden our exploration of human phenomena that would otherwise be discarded, the individual aura is an image of all that the person feels and has already felt (Gaeta, 2005). It is a moving image, not a static one, as it reflects fulfilled potential and missed opportunities, as well as the dynamics of the present moment. The colours of the field indicate both the quality and intensity of the person's feelings.

Alice described a violet colour and felt relief in her stomach, unable to verbalise what was happening in her inner world. Here lies the importance of combining Calatonia and the expressive arts, that is, Calatonia brings the patient's awareness to their inner experience of themselves and the expressive arts facilitate the manifestation of it in its own terms.

For Pain and Jarreau (1996), the body is also a place of emotional resonance and the emotions felt in the body seek expression through movement and sensations, respectively transformable into gestures and colours. Through artistic activities, the earliest vestiges of memory will find appeal in an amorphous material, in which the richness of kinaesthetic and visual sensations, allied to the creative impulse, allow for the emergence of emotion (Pain & Jarreau, 1996).

Alice chose to start the second session with Calatonia, and afterwards, she reported feeling her "arms opening up". Until that moment she had not noticed the tension in her body as if she were wearing a medieval armour that prevented her from moving her arms. This rigid posture was, as it were, a protection against crushing feelings of mourning and suffering.

Little by little, Alice spoke about her childhood. She had looked after her younger sisters, so much so that her youngest sister considered her to be 'mum'. Alice told me about her boyfriends and how she had also cared for them. She was engaged to one of them, whom she greatly helped by encouraging him in his studies and work, only to be abandoned by him when he achieved success and then went and married another woman.

She spoke about how she met her husband, a priest who was leaving the clergy. At that time, she was busy setting up a library at the school where they worked, and he taught her how to do so. He was cultured and taught her things she valued.

They got married and after a long period of time she fell

pregnant, but unfortunately, the baby died soon after being born. The same night she lost the baby, she adopted a baby boy and managed to breastfeed him. Later, they adopted a girl who developed several neurological impairments and died a few years later despite all their efforts to care for her.

After several Calatonia sessions, Alice felt her arms slowly moving as if they wanted to open up, changing her previous posture. Upon reaching a state of deep relaxation, she had a vision in which the image of a newborn baby was handed over to an outstretched hand. "As I told you", she said, "my mother was pregnant with twins, and my sister died while I survived. I always joked that I was born tired because I had to fight to live".

I was struck by the ease with which she described this experience of surviving within the womb, which she had never mentioned before. I wondered if her mother had had severe postpartum depression, and I realised that Alice and I had something in common.

Before my birth, my mother had lost a baby in childbirth and became pregnant with me soon thereafter. When I was born, I used my dead brother's baby clothes. My mother used to tell me that, as a baby, I cried so much that she let me sleep in one of the downstairs rooms to avoid hearing me cry. I, too, had a depressed mother, and our shared history enabled me to have a greater understanding of both her feelings and my own, and to be able to distinguish between them.

Following the vision of a newborn baby being passed over to waiting hands, Alice went on to speak about her childhood. The fact that she had experienced death so close to her being born may have given her a sense of victory and defeat at the same time. This feeling of survivor's guilt permeated her whole life. She never outgrew her sense of guilt and regarded everything that went wrong with the people close to her (son, husband, niece, etc.) as her own fault.

Alice portrayed the experiences she had during Calatonia by painting a mandala (Horschutz, 2010) that resembled a mother's womb with two foetuses (Figure 2):

Look at this yellow, it wants warmth, comfort, but at the same time it wants it, it doesn't let itself become involved; this blue looks like a spermatozoid, life in the womb again. To me, this here looks like conception, it looks like two foetuses here, bringing something to the boil, I don't know, it seems to provoke a reaction and these are the colours that appeared during Calatonia and that seem to always dance around. Sometimes it appears like ascension, sometimes a sensation which comes after noticing the tension in my chest. Breathing becomes easier and more energised, with more light. It's a rebirth. I always see yellow and violet colours. (Alice, 2004)

I want to write about this sensation:

Sea of emotions
Wanting to depart
Yet staying
Going beyond
And, upon returning
To search for a scar
That needs to be
Thrown, into the ocean
So, its waters
May clean it and take it away
Then, the sky and the blue
Will find each other
And smile and embrace one another
Alice's account of her feelings continued:

The first picture speaks of conception and of evolution and of life; the two foetuses are closer to the exit - all this brings things to the boil - it has movement. In Calatonia, these are the colours that come and go, that are always dancing around. Sometimes there's something

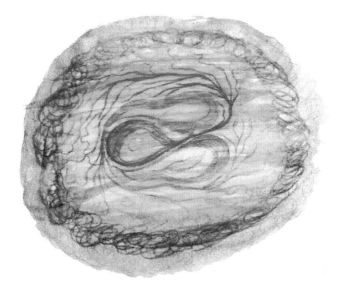

Figure 2

emotional, a sensation in the chest which feels tight and then it's as if the stomach is tense, which then travels up to the chest and begins to open up, and it becomes easier to breathe and is more energised. There is more energy, more light. (Alice, 2004)

After the subsequent session of Calatonia, Alice reported:

The other picture seems to be linked to nature, with a lot of circular movement, of coming and going. There's a mouth in the centre. I think I want to say something about taking ownership of things so that I can free myself. At the same time, getting things out there makes me realise how I've been searching for a release. (Alice, 2004)

In one session, Alice spoke about how her young adult son could not establish himself professionally. He had quit law school after the first three years. Subsequently, he passed his college entrance exam again to study history but missed the registration date. Without consciously realising it, Alice had allowed her son to remain a child by giving in to his whims or by giving him money so that he didn't feel the need to establish himself in any particular line of work.

Alice realised that her naive kindness and the inability to say 'no' distressed her. The way she communicated was difficult to understand, her stories were fragments of experiences, pieces of thought, mixed with feelings that had not been expressed before. In attempting to understand her I would have to think in a non-linear form, that is, I would have to let her express herself in whatever way she felt was possible and gradually weave these fragments into a meaningful form – a form of reasoning capable of embracing her uniqueness. Whenever she changed the subject, I tried to be attentive without interfering.

When Alice spoke of release she meant physical relief, but also release from her dysfunctional relationship patterns, such as spoiling her loved ones and placing herself in an overly servile position.

After two years of psychotherapy, Alice felt better physically and emotionally. She said that initially she felt very sad, depressed, distressed, and short of breath. She suffered from gastritis, labyrinthitis, sinusitis, and took medication such as Omeprazole and other anti-inflammatory drugs.

She reported that at the beginning of therapy, she couldn't even turn her neck sideways, but with time she stopped taking the medication for sinusitis and gastritis. In her own words:

> The interesting thing is that when I receive Calatonia, especially when you place your hands on my ankles, I feel a lot of energy coming up through my legs and affecting the stomach itself, and it seems to energise that area, as if I were receiving something and it often goes up through the chest. I felt an energy that rose and stopped in the larynx. The larynx lit up, I noticed an intense violet colour, with orange in the middle, and lights went up like

a whirlwind. I think that as the lights seemed to move I transformed them into a mandala, which I cut out and made into a wind chime. And I played around with it, making it three-dimensional. I gave it a lot of movement (Fig. 3). (Alice, 2004)

Figure 3. Three-dimensional mandala

Those who struggle to be born and face death at the time of birth may be comparable to a hero who struggles in search of consciousness and a life fully lived. In the heroic saga, the individual must continue to engage in a challenging environment for redemption of their inner universe, collecting images that facilitate this process (Giegerich, 2005).

"This picture has a tree with many roots underneath it. I think these roots are my need to stay firmly on the ground. To feel safe in the things I do, and, in life (Fig. 4)".

Figure 4. The roots of the tree.

The pictures, sculptures, and gestures seemed to have given Alice a way of reliving the experiences she had at birth and infancy. As she elaborated on these experiences a healing process unfolded as she was released from the bonds and oppressions of her internal and interpersonal relationships. In allowing oneself to create something, a person manifests a part of themselves - how they see, think, feel, and act - in a dynamic and integrative manner.

The combination of Calatonia with art in Alice's therapy played a most important role in accessing a process of imagination that was healing, one that connected, selected, interpreted, and transformed her inner world (Gaeta, 2006).

References

Arcuri, I., & Horschutz, R. (2012). Calatonia e Mandalas: Recursos Corporais e Artísticos na Prática Clinica. In M. E. Spaccaquerche (Ed.), *Corpo em Jung – Estudos em Calatonia e Práticas Integrativas*. São Paulo, SP: Vetor Editora Psicopedagógica.

Berry, K., Varese, F., & Bucci, S. (2017). Cognitive attachment model of voices: Evidence base and future implications. *Frontiers in Psychiatry*, 8(111). DOI: 10.3389/fpsyt.2017.00111

Bohsali, A. A., Triplett, W., Sudhyadhom, A., Gullett, J. M., McGregor, K., FitzGerald, D. B., ... Crosson, B. (2015). Broca's area - Thalamic connectivity. *Brain and Language*, 141, 80–88. https://doi.org/10.1016/j.bandl.2014.12.001

Bowlby, J. (1958). The nature of the child's tie to his mother. *International Journal of Psycho-Analysis*, 39, 350-373.

Carvalho, M. M. M. J. (1995). *A Arte Cura?* Campinas, SP: Editorial Psy II.

Dales, S., & Jerry, P. (2008). Attachment, affect regulation and mutual synchrony in adult psychotherapy. *American Journal of Psychotherapy*. 62(3):283-312

Damasio, A. (1999). *The Feeling of What Happens: Body and Emotion in the Making of Consciousness*. Boston, MA: Houghton Mifflin Harcourt.

Fosha, D., Siegel, D. J., & Solomon, M. F. (2009). The healing power of emotion: affective neuroscience, development, and clinical practice. *The Norton Series on Interpersonal Neurobiology*, 1, 349.

Gaeta, I. (2005). Psicologia Transpessoal, Arteterapia e Calatonia. *Revista Hermes*, 10, 101-111.

Gaeta, I. (2006). *Arteterapia: Um Novo Campo do Conhecimento*. São Paulo, SP: Vetor Editora Psicopedagógica.

Gaeta, I. (2010). *Psicoterapia Junguiana – Novos caminhos na clínica – O uso de mandalas e Calatonia*. São Paulo, SP: Vetor Editora Psicopedagógica.

Giegerich, W. (2005). The ego-psychological fallacy: A note on "the birth of the meaning out of a symbol". *Journal of Jung-*

ian Theory and Practice, 7(2), 53-60.
Grof, S. (1987). *Além do Cérebro*. São Paulo, SP: McGraw-Hill.
Horschutz, R. W. (2010). *O Símbolo da Mandala no Sandplay* (Unpublished thesis). Retrieved from International Society for Sandplay Therapy database.
Jung, C. G. (1985). O espírito na arte e na ciência. In *Obras Completas de C. G. Jung* (v.15). Petrópolis, RJ: Vozes.
Jung, C. G. (1986). Símbolos da Transformação. In *Obras Completas de C. G. Jung* (v.5). Petrópolis, RJ: Vozes.
Jung, C. G. (1991). A Natureza da Psique. In *Obras Completas de C. G. Jung* (v.8/II). Petrópolis, RJ: Vozes.
Jung, C. G. (1995). Psicologia do Inconsciente. In *Obras Completas de C. G. Jung* (v.7/I). Petrópolis, RJ: Vozes.
Jung, C. G. (2001). Aion: estudos sobre o simbolismo de Si-mesmo. In *Obras Completas de C. G. Jung* (v.9/II). Petrópolis, RJ: Vozes.
Jung, C. G. (2001). Os arquétipos e o inconsciente coletivo. In *Obras Completas de C. G. Jung* (v.9/I). Petrópolis, RJ: Vozes.
Jung, C. G. (2002). A Energia Psíquica. In *Obras Completas de C. G. Jung* (v.8/I). Petrópolis, RJ: Vozes.
Jung, C. G. (2007). Eu e o Inconsciente. In *Obras Completas de C. G. Jung* (v.7/II). Petrópolis, RJ: Vozes.
Kalsched, D. (1996). *The Inner World of Trauma*. Hove, UK: Brunner-Routledge.
Kirsch, T. B. (2000). *The Jungians (A Comparative and Historical Perspective)*. London, UK: Routledge.
Knox, J. (2003). *Archetype, Attachment, Analysis: Jungian psychology and the emergent mind*. London, UK: Routledge.
Landa, S., & Duschinsky, R. (2013). Crittenden's dynamic-maturational model of attachment and adaptation. *Review of General Psychology*, 17(3), 326–338. https://doi.org/10.1037/a0032102
Mancia, M. (2006). Implicit memory and early unrepressed unconscious: Their role in the therapeutic process (How the neurosciences can contribute to psychoanalysis). *International Journal of Psychoanalysis*, 87(1), 83-103 https://doi.

org/10.1516/D43P-8UPN-X576-A8V0

Pain, S., & Jarreau, G. (1996). *Teoria e Técnica da Arte-terapia: A compreensão do sujeito*. Porto Alegre, RS: Artes Médicas.

Sándor, P. (1982). *Técnicas de Relaxamento*. São Paulo, SP: Vetor.

Schore, A. (2011). The right brain implicit self lies at the core of psychoanalysis. *Psychoanalytic Dialogues, 21*, 75-100.

Seixas, L. P., Rios, A. M. R., & Blanchard, A. R. (2009). O Corpo em Jung. In P. Albertini, & L. Freitas (Eds). *Fundamentos de Psicologia – Jung e Reich: Articulando Conceitos e Práticas*. São Paulo, SP: Guanabara Koogan.

Siegel, D. (1999). *The Developing Mind*. New York, NY: Guilford Press.

Varenne, J. (1977). *Yoga and the Hindu Tradition*. Chicago, IL: University of Chicago Press.

Williams, H. L., Conway, M. A., & Cohen, G. (2008). Autobiographical Memory. In G. Cohen, & M.A. Conway (Eds.), *Memory in the Real World* (pp. 21-90). London, UK: Psychology Press.

9

Pethö Sándor's Method in the Treatment of Schizophrenia

Leda Maria Perillo Seixas

This chapter will briefly review the progress in our understanding of schizophrenia, its causes and treatments, as well as address the use of the body-based techniques developed by Pethö Sándor (1974) in the treatment of patients with schizophrenia, and as a potential resource to be harnessed in Jungian psychotherapy. Before introducing Sándor's method in the context of schizophrenia, it is important to cover, albeit succinctly, the theories about this disorder in order to understand the contexts in which somatic psychotherapy can be successfully employed.

Schizophrenia has been widely studied for several decades, as it is a severe psychic disorder occurring chronically in adolescence, characterised by affective changes in thinking and behaviour that can cause a series of difficulties not only for the individual but for their relatives as well.

Kraepelin (1856-1926) described a state of mental disorder, based on medical observations, which includes symptoms of hallucinations, deficits in reasoning and affect, difficulty maintaining attention, and catatonia. This syndrome had previously been given the name of *dementia praecox*, due to its occurrence at a young age. Kraepelin further distinguished three forms of early dementia: hebephrenic, paranoid, and catatonic dementia. Bleuler (1857-1939) went on to coin the term schizophrenia (from the Ancient Greek *skhizein*, division, and *phren*, mind) to describe the same phenomenon, focussing on the dissociation or fragmentation of the individual's mental processes. Jung (1875-1961) worked under Bleuler in the Burghölzli as his first assistant and noted several important psychic aspects in the dynamic of schizophrenia that will be presented below.

Many attempts have been made to treat schizophrenia: hydrotherapy, bleeding, sleep therapy, electroconvulsive therapy, medication with pentylenetetrazol, insulin and lithium, or lobotomy.

Until 1950 the treatment for schizophrenia consisted of admitting the patient to a psychiatric hospital where some of the treatments mentioned above were frequently employed. With the discovery of typical antipsychotics (neuroleptics) and the use of chlorpromazine for schizophrenia, patients began to show a marked improvement in symptoms and were able to return to social life.

Typical antipsychotics often take days or weeks to produce results and often have side effects such as motor disorders, difficulty coordinating and performing voluntary movements, dystonia, stiffness, tremors, bradykinesia (slow movement), immobility of facial expression, gait alteration, difficulty keeping one's legs still (the patient "walks" while remaining in place), stereotyped facial movements (lip suction, tongue movements), choreiform movements of the arms and legs, dry mouth and skin, tachycardia, constipation and urinary retention. More recently, atypical antipsychotics such as clozapine, risperidone and amisulpride have been used, which are more effective in the treatment of chronic schizophrenia by preventing symptom relapse (Silva, 2006). While pharmacological treatments reduce the symptoms of schizophrenia, they do not cure the underlying disease. The best results are often obtained through a combination of psychotropic drugs, psychotherapy and occupational therapy involving creative activities such as painting, sculpture and dance.

Characteristics of Schizophrenia

Early signs may appear in adolescence or early adulthood and may also manifest abruptly. These signs include a lack of energy, initiative or interest, depression, social isolation, inappropriate behaviour, poor hygiene and appearance, poor academic achievement, and a loss of income at work.

Approximately 90% of patients with schizophrenia have positive (i.e., hallucinations, paranoia, delusions) and negative (i.e., apathy, lack of emotion, poor or non-existent social functioning) symptoms including cognitive impairment (disorganised speech and thought) and inappropriate behaviours. Current studies indicate that the types of hallucinations these patients experience vary, with 15% experiencing visual hallucinations, 50% auditory hallucinations (hearing voices), and 5% tactile hallucinations (Silva, 2006). These statistics reveal the importance of working with touch in schizophrenia, as it has been shown to be one of the sensory modalities that is least affected in the disorder; thus, it is instrumental as a counterweight to the other senses. The multisensory integration we can achieve through touch also helps to guide our visual and auditory processes, by recalibrating one's perception of reality.

Disorders of thought and/or delusions can be recognised through changes in speech and vocabulary, both in the structure and content of speech, which can sometimes lead to incoherence, with pressured or cluttered speech, poverty of speech, or tonal monotony due to flattened levels of affect. Patients with schizophrenia often obtain lower scores in cognitive tests, with neuropsychological deficits in tests of complex conceptual reasoning, psychomotor speed, learning and memory, problem solving and especially attention. Inattention or an inability to attend to stimuli for a sustained period of time is the most common characteristic of schizophrenia.

Behavioural disorders in schizophrenia frequently take the form of a heightened state of anxiety or agitation, an inability to follow routines of behaviour, and a lack of inhibition or impulsivity. Patients may also engage in stereotyped forms of behaviour such as automatic gestures, mannerisms, grimaces or body positions, as well as increased pessimism and echopraxia – the repetition or imitation of movements. Catatonia is no longer considered characteristic of schizophrenia.

Affective disorders in schizophrenia typically reflect an underlying flattened affect, one of the most common characteristics of schizophrenia, as well as anhedonia, the inability to feel pleasure in general be it eating, drink, music or nature, and extreme apathy, a complete lack of interest and drive in the world around them. Anhedonia and apathy are also common in patients with depression (Silva, 2006).

Aetiology of Schizophrenia

The causes of schizophrenia are still unclear, but a growing consensus attributes its emergence to an interaction between upbringing, neuropsychology and biological factors such as genetics. According to some genetic studies, an individual with a first-degree relative with schizophrenia has a significantly greater chance of developing the disease later in life.

One of the most widely-accepted hypotheses of schizophrenia is based on the hyper functional central dopamine system, although other neurotransmitter systems such as nitric oxide are also involved in the brain abnormalities observed in schizophrenia. The use of psychostimulant substances such as amphetamines and cocaine, for example, increases the production of dopamine and produces psychic changes similar to schizophrenia.

There are also studies that identify contributing factors to the onset of schizophrenia at early stages of life prior to or soon after birth, such as foetal malnutrition that can lead to impairments in brain development. In neurodevelopmental terms, maternal conditions such as diabetes, chronic lung disease, anaemia or starvation can also alter the foetus' development, predisposing it to the later onset of schizophrenia. Other important contributing factors include preterm birth (occurring before 33 weeks of pregnancy) and complications in labour, which can cause damage to the hippocampus and cerebral cortex due to lack of oxygen, although these factors account for only a small percentage of cases.

Current studies based on the use of cranial tomography have detected signs of cerebral atrophy in schizophrenic patients, as well as a widening of the cerebral ventricles and increased cortical sulci. The areas most affected by these structural changes are located in the medial part of the temporal lobes, frontal cortex, thalamus, basal ganglia and corpus callosum, which may contribute to some of the cognitive and affective deficits observed in schizophrenia.

Studies using structural magnetic resonance imaging have confirmed volumetric reductions of cortical tissue, specifically in the left medial temporal lobe. Other temporal areas such as the upper temporal gyrus, involved in language production, also show state-dependent changes in cortical volume.

Last but not least, psychological theories of schizophrenia are based on the history of dysfunctional family relationships as well as interpersonal communication with ulterior meanings seeming to be frequent factors in individuals with schizophrenia. A psychological history of maternal hostility, rejection and neglect also seems to influence the onset of the disease.

Other factors that may trigger the onset of the disease are excessive emotional demands on the part of family members and psychosocial changes such as the loss of a loved one or difficulties in housing, work or school.

Treatment

As mentioned previously, several pharmacological treatments have been developed for schizophrenia based on the administration of several drugs, with results that often alleviate the symptoms but do not cure the underlying causes of the disease. Drug treatment can be combined with psychotherapy as a therapeutic support for the individual to cope with their reintegration into society, which is one of the core objectives of psychotherapy. Without a doubt, psychotherapy is an essential part in the treatment of schizophrenia.

Before 1970, schools of psychotherapy were based on psychodynamic theories that considered schizophrenia to be caused by pathogenic patterns of behaviour or communication in the individual's family. The great majority of articles in the literature on psychotherapeutic treatment for psychosis identify cognitive-behavioural therapy as the approach most likely to produce an improvement in outcome among patients with schizophrenia.

We wish to highlight another approach that also produces some very promising results: body-based techniques utilising Subtle Touch sequences such as Calatonia (Sándor, 1974).

It is important to emphasise that a body-based approach should be considered an auxiliary tool in the clinical armamentarium of schizophrenia and not as the only form of treatment. Patients should be properly assessed and treated by a psychiatrist and all therapy techniques should be carefully chosen according to the patient's clinical profile.

Jungian Theory in Calatonia

Calatonia is one of the many body-based techniques developed by Pethö Sándor, but it also represents an approach to psychotherapy with an inherent set of assumptions: the unity of body and psyche, their capacity for self-regulation, and a belief that every individual has an objective of self-fulfilment within them, as C. G. Jung (1990) proposed.

The psyche, like the body, is a system endowed with self-regulation: its harmonious functioning depends on a balance between each of its components, for example, blood circulation depends on the efficient function of the heart, lungs, veins and arteries. Likewise, in the case of the psyche we can refer to a balance between consciousness, the unconscious and the body, as well as with the environment and the individual's flow of psychic energy (libido) towards introversion and extraversion. For Jung, the libido is a desire or impulse that cannot be restrained, and which defines our emotional states and physical needs such as hunger, thirst, sleep, and sexuality. It is an energetic value that can be transmitted to any area but is not linked to any particular instinct (Jung, 2007).

When consciousness is deployed unilaterally, i.e., when one disregards unconscious content important to individual development, the Self "provides" a dream which allows the content therein to be integrated. In cases of more pronounced unilateralism, compensatory mechanisms can be experienced as more unpleasant through the creation of disruptive symptoms of consciousness: many psychological disorders have their origin in the loss of this spontaneous capacity for self-regulation. But it is important to note, once again, that Jung considers these symptoms to be an opportunity to re-establish a more harmonious form of psychic organisation, geared towards the personal fulfilment of the individual (Jung, 1990).

For Jung (1984a), the organisation of the psyche occurs through what he called "affectively toned" complexes which constitute the royal road to the unconscious. A complex of "feeling-toned contents" (Jung, 1984a, p. 27), is a grouping of ideas with an emotional charge in the unconscious, which disrupt normal psychic processes and compel unconscious content to be consciously recognised or integrated. While searching for new connections between the unity of body and mind in Analytical Psychology and cognitive concepts of memory, Jean Knox (1999) equates the Jungian complex with the concept of implicit memory, i.e., those memories that were recorded before speech development and which remain inaccessible to conscious awareness.

A complex carries the "feeling of the whole" in all its constituent parts: every time a cue (an action, word, etc.) triggers a certain complex, the "whole" resonates. This whole is constituted by way of a nucleus (a signifier of meaning) which is outside of conscious control or will, and which forms the basis for the association of early personal characteristics and experiences originating from the environment. When one's innate disposition collides with an uncorrected reality, an emotional charge is created that causes the complex to begin to disrupt conscious functions by breaking the unity of consciousness, often causing an additional identity to form within the individual (a partial psyche).

Complexes have different degrees of autonomy. The ego is just one of several complexes in the psyche. As other complexes encounter the ego they enter conscious awareness. Some, however, remain for long periods in the depths of the psyche, awaiting a suitable situation that allows for conscious manifestation: they remain out of sight yet infiltrate daily life to prepare for future transformation.

A complex that is "recognised" is more likely to be integrated into consciousness than those that remain totally unconscious, in which even the symptoms it produces are not consciously registered. The further away from consciousness the complex lies, the more likely it is to be clothed in archaic-mythological terms – drawing ever nearer to schizophrenic fragmentation. "Recognised" complexes lose this numinous-mythological character, they become personalised and fall into a process of conscious adaptation, releasing the emotional energy that was retained in the unconscious.

Complexes are living proof of the psyche's capacity for dissociation, which is at the root of the belief in multiple souls inhabiting a single individual and may also explain the mediumistic manifestations common to schizophrenia. An autonomous complex can lead a life of its own in the depths of the psyche, able to acquire its own voice and personalities (as in psychosis), perceived by consciousness as "non-self".

Intellectual recognition is not enough to integrate the complex: only that which is experienced emotionally can lead to its release from the unconscious. A complex is composed not merely of *meaning* but of *value* as well; as such the body must necessarily be included in this process. Röhricht (2015) points to the body as the centre of sensory and affective experiences and which serves not only as the basis of our relationships to the world, but also as the field for the individual to experience the conflict, threat or traumatic aspects inherent in his/her connection to the world.

A complex is itself a structural element of the psyche, and for that very reason can only be considered a healthy part of psychic functioning. That which manifests itself through the collective unconscious cannot be considered "abnormal" as it represents the basis on which our psyche is organised, without either conflict or division. That which is abnormal comes from the personal unconscious as that is where unconscious content was associated with an individual's conflict and underwent a transformation (or deformation), acquiring a personal imprimatur distinct from its original form.

It is often necessary to differentiate the personal aspects of the complex from its collective elements, so as to free oneself from the problems in one's relationship with our personal father and to perceive that we must become separate from our father without feeling guilty for wanting this separation – the latter is the collective aspect. When, however, our conscious mind ignores or represses its archetypal foundations, the libido employed in this process activates the collective aspect of our psyche, leading it to become emotionally charged and to break off from the whole. In these cases, the individual runs the risk of experiencing a neurotic and/or schizophrenic split.

The entry of unconscious content into consciousness may lead the individual to develop a neurosis or psychosis, depending on the state of their ego. If one's consciousness is very unilateral or fragile it will cling to its usual mode of functioning, in which it is at risk of collapsing in a manner that will be proportional to its rigidity. If one's ego is open to the contributions of the unconscious, it can gain a level of transcendence to enable it to self-regulate between its own demands and those of the environment and those which the Self wishes to integrate. If one's consciousness becomes closed off, compensation ceases to occur, and one's unconscious is led to attempt to destroy the unilateral nature of consciousness in order to re-establish a balance between conscious and unconscious demands.

The Practice of Calatonia

Body-based techniques in psychotherapy work to stimulate the appearance of images from the unconscious, and as such these techniques must be chosen judiciously to ensure that the material that emerges is later worked through with the patient verbally or through the use of expressive techniques such as drawing, painting, sculpture, etc. Recording these images in a concrete way has a therapeutic effect, as it gives "body" to the ghosts that haunt us as individuals, allowing us to exert some kind of control over these elements.

In my master's thesis (Seixas, 1989), I wrote a case study of a patient with schizophrenia whom I had treated using Pethö Sándor's approach. Described briefly, this patient, a young woman, came to therapy and said absolutely nothing during the first interview. As she did not want to talk, I explained the technique of Calatonia and asked if she was willing to try it, and to my surprise, she took off her shoes and lay down.

This pattern of silence was repeated for the next fifteen sessions, until one day, she came to therapy with a smile on her face and began to tell her story. I conducted a regular set of relaxation techniques and suggested that she draw what she saw when in a state of relaxation. She began to draw the images that appeared in her head; pictures of animals and flying saucers that appeared to her in her room at night, and she began to realise the difference between what was real and the hallucinations she experienced.

The fact that she could share these images with me helped her establish a dialogue with them and, slowly, they ceased to be so threatening. Therapy lasted for four years, at which point she asked to be discharged, because she felt that each person had to "carry their own cross" and she now felt capable of doing so.

A complex becomes pathological when consciousness becomes unilateral and is unable to access specific content which may hold a painful emotional charge, either because

it is incompatible with the subject's environment or through the subject's continuing denial. This leads to the content being repressed and remaining at an unconscious level, resulting in an increase in the weight of the complex. This process can go so far as to give complexes such a degree of autonomy that they stand out from the unconscious and may appear in personified form through dreams, forming what Jung called "partial psyches" (Jung, 1984a, p. 32). In psychosis, these complexes take the form of "voices" which seek to guide the subject's behaviour. In serious pathological disorders, the subject often has enormous difficulty in adapting towards what they are being impelled to do by their instincts.

According to Jung (1984a), in common usage the word "instinct" is employed to designate behaviour which originates from a need which is indistinct as knowledge of its purpose or motivation is lacking. Instinctive action should therefore constitute an unconscious process – but it is not. The most striking features of instinctive behaviour are regularity, compulsiveness and commonality/universality, such as the commonly-held belief that elephants are afraid of mice. Accordingly, when someone is afraid of chickens we recognise this fear as a phobia and not as an instinct, as fear of chickens is not a universal form of behaviour in the same way that fear of snakes or spiders is.

The impulse to fear chickens is unconscious, as are obsessive thoughts and ideas, whims, impulsive emotions, and states of depression and anxiety. Instincts are hereditary and not learned through experience.

Rationalising instincts is a way of taming some of them to the point where they seem to disappear. However, the disproportionate way in which we sometimes react points precisely to the opposite: it is precisely because an unconscious process has been unleashed within us that we act in an exaggerated fashion, often against our will.

Human nature can set psychological processes in motion which disguise our instincts under the guise of rational motives and transform archetypes into rational concepts (Jung, 1984a).

The difficulties faced by an individual in response to his/her instincts are partly due to their specific attributes and partly due to environmental influences that make it impossible for the individual to lead a life that wholly satisfies their instincts. Because of this conflict between the parameters of consciousness, internal needs and their environment, the individual's ego becomes fragmented and incapable of aligning all the information it receives into a coherent whole, leading it to produce a set of discourse and behaviour which is meaningless for all those around the individual. Due to the limitations of this chapter, the symbolic significance of hallucinations or delusions will not be addressed, although they are important for understanding the patient's process of psychotherapy (Fierz, 1997).

The conscious mind may suddenly find itself invaded by strange ideas that fragment the internal cohesion of the personality, often originating in the deeper layers of the unconscious and intrinsically close to mythological motives. We can assume that this invasion occurs so as to re-establish a balance between the demands of the environment (or of the subject's consciousness) and its innate attributions. This process constitutes, in other words, a search for healing, which requires the integration of content previously rejected by the conscious mind.

Jung (1990) points out the similarity between these fragments and dreams, albeit emphasising that dreams are produced during sleep, whereas in schizophrenia they appear in a state of wakefulness and are perceived as real.

These fragments of ideas enter consciousness accompanied by a strong affective tone, resulting in several bodily sensations such as sweating, tachycardia, tremors in the knees, etc., which may in turn cause the individual to associate ideas and/or fantasies with the emotional states they experienced previously, or to be fearful of future events that the ego cannot control. Consciousness is also invaded by countless associative variations on the same theme which, while enhancing the individual's perception, also make it impossible for then to organise their conscious mind.

The individual is fascinated by this content but feels as if he/she is treading on quicksand: there is no solidity to this experience, no conscious structure which renders us capable of discriminating between reality and fantasy; we feel dangerously isolated from the world around us as we constantly strive to maintain the internal coherence of our own ideas.

Jung stated that psychotic ideas remain beyond egoic control and may threaten to engulf the individual in his own system. In such cases, the unconscious takes control of personality and generates confusion and insanity, since it does not represent a whole other organised personality, but the "decentralised congeries of psychic processes" (Jung, 2001, p. 271). He believed that patients with schizophrenia could be treated and cured by psychological means but noted that more severe cases have rather narrow limitations (Jung, 1990). With access to new psychiatric drugs however, it is possible to increase the success rate of psychotherapy.

The psychotherapeutic approach towards schizophrenia has several distinct characteristics. First, the patient is not always in a position to talk: sometimes their reasoning is compromised, disconnected, exacerbated or absent of emotion. Their perception may also be altered, i.e., they may experience delusions or hallucinations, psychomotor disturbances, etc.

Physical contact is important for improving rapport and can help to increase trust between therapist and patient, a key condition for the success of any therapy. The application of body-based techniques may mobilise certain complexes and may provide information about the patient's unconscious content through the manifestation of images or other sensations. Thus, the therapist should carefully listen to any reported sensations after each session since, in addition to the "bipersonal resonance" between patient and therapist, the "variety of material that emerges provides the basis for dialogue in terms of biographical exploration, a broad and stratified survey of the current situation and subsequent planning or preparation for the next steps in therapy" (Sándor, 1974, p. 100).

Another important feature of Sándor's techniques is that they do not require the patient to do anything other than "let go", "move away from a state of anger, fury, or violence", "open a door" (Sándor, 1974, p. 92). The patient is asked to give themselves over to the process by relying on the fact that relaxation of the body will positively impact the individual's self-regulation, both physically and psychologically. The lack of top-down direction allows the subject to evolve as a whole, by integrating the irrational aspects of their process: in this way we can all reach down deeper and experience a more intense shift towards readjustment.

Sándor's somatic therapy has proven to be a method of inestimable value precisely by enabling this amplification of verbal expression through the inclusion of the body within the near-infinite range of sensations which can be experienced in psychotherapy and which are often impossible to express in a verbal form.

In Sándor's method, one begins from Jung's assumption that "mind and body are presumably a pair of opposites and, as such, the expression of a single entity . . . According to an ancient belief, man arose from the coming together of a soul and a body" (Jung, 1984b, pp. 267-268). In this view, including the body in therapy seems fundamental.

In schizophrenia the normal mechanisms for adaptation to reality no longer function and have been replaced by other mechanisms from the more primitive layers of the unconscious. This finding argues for the use of body-based therapy in this instance; as human beings, our first form of consciousness is corporeal.

Skin plays a fundamental role here: as the largest organ of the human body, it represents the first form of organisation, which allows us to differentiate between ourselves and the world. The skin and nervous system originate from the same structure in embryonic development. For this reason, stimulation of the skin through soft and novel forms of touch is capable of directly modulating the central nervous system. A subtle touch sequence is often a new experience for the patient as soft touches are rarely part of one's behavioural repertoire. This type of stimulation generates new neural networks associated with a therapeutic context.

Body-based techniques also help to ameliorate the patient's body image and the conscious awareness of inhabiting their body, leading to an enhanced awareness of the reality of the here and now, which is generally absent in individuals experiencing psychosis.

However, the greatest gain from somatic psychotherapy in schizophrenia is the emotional support which is made available to the patient: a strong therapist-patient bond is created, fostering the confidence necessary for the recovery of emotional stability.

Jung points out that "the sense of touch and the bodily sensations are sufficient to make consciousness possible" (Jung, 1984b, p. 266). This phrase recalls the famous case of Helen Keller, the blind and deaf-mute girl who, while not psychotic, was completely unable to adapt to and interact with her environment. It is important to emphasise here that often it is only through the body that it is possible for the individual to develop a form of consciousness that can adapt to the world around them.

The body responds best when approached through its own language, i.e., the language of touch and sensation. In the case of psychotic patients, touch should be smooth, subtle and non-invasive, as in these cases the body may hold unpleasant associations and painful memories of prior physical experiences. Due to the enormous associative capacity of schizophrenia, physical contact with patients must be limited to tried-and-tested techniques, in order to avoid any imaginings or misinterpretation on the part of the patient.

At the very beginning of my professional life, I met Guto[1], a 16-year-old boy diagnosed with disorganised schizophrenia who had been admitted to a psychiatric hospital for children.

---
1. All names have been changed to preserve the anonymity of the individuals.

He wandered the hospital corridors all day and night, murmuring meaningless words. One day he tied a sheet around his neck, wearing his underwear over his trousers and, while the nurses were otherwise occupied he climbed up onto the window bars, but then fell down and lay sprawled on the floor. He was severely injured and was confined to bed for a few days. At this juncture I was assigned as his therapist. It was easy to understand his desire to be a superman and to fly "up, up and away!" But the interesting thing was that because he couldn't move, I was able to apply a sequence of touches to his joints. He became less agitated over the course of a few days and when he was able to walk again, he waited for my arrival in the hospital courtyard and shouted "Cinderella, Cinderella!" when he saw me. He started to tell me that there were two worlds and that he constantly travelled from one to another, but what he really wanted was for the two to become one. The medium of touch helped him to feel the concrete presence of another person (myself, the therapist in this case), and served as a clear waypoint within his personal life story. Unfortunately, shortly thereafter due to budgetary cuts in the mental health service I was unable to continue his treatment or follow up on his case. However, this short experience revealed the importance of physical contact in establishing a reciprocal form of relationship with him and a subtle improvement in his speech.

Due to the emotional instability of some patients, they may exhibit physically aggressive behaviour. In these cases, it is advisable to count on the support of other mental health professionals who can help to calm down or even physically restrain the patient.

Reinaldo had also been hospitalised and often started hostile altercations with staff or other patients, under the influence of another patient who displayed characteristics of psychopathy. One day I was conducting a body-based technique with some other patients in a room upstairs, when I heard shouting and aggressive noises coming from downstairs. We heard the banging and loud footsteps approaching, and suddenly Reinaldo opened the door to the room and threatened to break a window with his head, so he could jump out. As on a previous occasion he had set fire to the Occupational Therapy room, I judged him capable of such an act and suggested that he lie down so that we (the other patients and I) could conduct the technique we were practising on him. To my surprise Reinaldo agreed, and we applied a sequence of touches to the knuckles of the hand. I sat on one side and another patient sat on his other side, while another patient touched his head, and another touched his feet. At the end of the sequence, Reinaldo stood up and said that it was just as well we had "held him back", because he really had meant to jump out of the window.

In another instance, it had been critical to have the nursing staff in the mental health clinic on hand to help restrain another patient who had tried to strangle me (Blanchard, Seixas, & Rios, 2010; Seixas, 1989). Since there are no rules or certainties regarding the behaviour of psychotic patients, it is critical that the therapist be attentive and open to their intuition – with the confidence to face their own fears. In dealing with these patients, any hesitation or deviation from the truth on the part of the therapist is immediately perceived; as such, it is advisable for the therapist not to play the hero as the patient can very easily knock them off their high horse.

Another caveat when employing body-based techniques with these patients is to take great care when choosing which techniques to apply. For example, a patient with symptoms of paranoia will react more positively to the experience if they are allowed to keep their eyes open and to interact with the therapist during the sequence, instead of lying down with their eyes closed and receiving a more passive technique such as Calatonia or fractional decompression. The body-based approach to psychotherapy should respect the patient's limits and preferably act as a complement to more conventional forms of therapy by providing the components which the patient lacks to maintain psychic balance.

Patients with paraphilia or other sexual dysfunctions

need to be approached extremely carefully by avoiding any possible sexual connotations with physical touch to prevent triggering sexual fantasies. The same caution is recommended in cases of patients who have suffered sexual abuse or other forms of physical violence. Here, taking a stance of respect for the patient's body is key. Hugs, patting, stroking and other forms of physical affection should be avoided.

Marcelo, aged twenty-three, had sought therapy because he did not want to leave his bedroom. He had broken all of the bathroom faucets in his house without explaining why or how. When I sought to understand the circumstances surrounding this story, he reported that he masturbated excessively and had once had a fantasy of killing his parents. He had broken the taps on a day when he had wanted to wash himself clean to get these impulses and ideas out of himself. Marcelo had never had sex and had not kissed a girl. Despite his good looks, he felt he was awkward and ugly, and he was afraid of being rejected by girls. In childhood he had been the butt of many cruel jokes because he had had protruding ears, which had only been corrected through surgery when he was nineteen. He had also suffered from nocturnal enuresis until he was twelve, which had made him feel ashamed and uncomfortable when sleeping at friends' houses and further affected his ability to socialise. His parents, while acting with the best of intentions, had opted to keep him overprotected and consequently he failed to develop coping and self-sufficiency mechanisms. One day, after applying a relaxation technique I asked him to draw a life-size impression of his body. To that end, I pinned a long roll of paper to the wall, corresponding to his height and width. He drew an outline on the paper that even he could see was the size of a 12-year-old boy. From that point on, the body-based techniques we practised concentrated on the awareness of his body as an adult; it was important for him to realise that he had grown up, and that he now had other resources available to him for facing the world. After about a year of body-integrated therapy, Marcelo was capable of going back to university, of going out to clubs with his sisters and of getting his driving licence. He was no longer tormented by thoughts of murdering his parents and he no longer felt guilty every time he masturbated.

The treatment of patients with severe psychological disorders within a non-institutional setting should always be supervised by a qualified psychiatrist who can oversee the patient's medication, and by the moral and emotional support of the patient's family. Novice psychotherapists treating these patients should also be assisted by an experienced supervisor. Under these circumstances, the application of body-based techniques can have some very positive results.

Estela was 64 years old at the time of therapy and lived on her own in another Brazilian State. She was a widow and her adult children lived in different places scattered throughout the country. One day, her neighbours telephoned her daughter because they had not seen Estela for several days. Her daughter found her in bed, stained and covered in urine and faeces. Her body was extremely thin and dehydrated, and she spoke in halting, disconnected patterns of speech. Her daughter drove her to São Paulo and took her to the mental health clinic after seeking medical assistance. At first, her daughter participated in the sessions, and the initial evaluation was made through her. Estela did not communicate either verbally or non-verbally; she sat on the edge of the bed, folding and unfolding the hem of her clothing. One day I asked her to lie down so I could help her relax – I then applied Calatonia. In the next session she went in and immediately lay down on the bed. Little by little, Estela began to tell me her story. She became interested in other activities, made new friends and started to come to therapy without her daughter. After a year and a half, she said she was going to give her daughter some rest for a while because she wanted to spend some time at the beach by going to live with another of her children. The way in which to reach Estela had undoubtedly been through a body-based approach.

An important observation to be made about body-based approaches in therapy, is that a novel form of psychophysiological conditioning necessarily implies a certain rituality which in itself often has therapeutic benefits. This sense of ritual is evoked through darkening the room where possible, covering the bed or divan with clean sheets (and blankets when it is cold), and by setting a quiet environment. The therapist then asks the patient to remove any rings, watches, tight belts, etc., and leaves the room to allow them some privacy. The therapist comes back, applies the selected sequence of touches, guides the patient through the process of recovering their habitual state of awareness, and leaves the room again so that the patient can get up, ground themselves, put their shoes back on and sit down. The guidance consists of verbal instructions such as moving one's fingers and toes, taking a deep breath, stretching and getting up very slowly. These instructions aim to prevent the patient from becoming dizzy or disorientated after being in relaxation. The therapist then comes back into the room and asks the patient for any observations they may have made. In some situations, the therapist may even ask for a drawing that illustrates any images that may have appeared during the somatic work.

This sense of ritual is important because the path to the unconscious (in both body and psyche) inherently holds a numinous aspect (Armando, 2006), full of the "perils of the soul". Jung says that when the unconscious touches us, we become unconscious of ourselves and are invaded by uncontrolled affect and emotions. This represents the "peril" that the primitive part of us recognises instinctively because it lies so close to its own domain – for in this environment:

> ... consciousness breaks down under [uncontrolled emotions] and gives way to possession. All man's strivings have therefore been directed towards the consolidation of consciousness. This was the purpose of rite and dogma; they were dams and walls to keep back the dangers of the unconscious, the 'perils of the soul'.
> (Jung, 2001, p. 32)

Primitive rites consist accordingly in the exorcizing of spirits, the lifting of spells, the averting of the evil omen, propitiation, purification, and the production of helpful occurrences.

Sándor's subtle and non-invasive body-based approach allows the ego to get to know the body and its sensations, to moderate dangerous levels of tension and stress and to acknowledge the moment of doing nothing – to simply observe by recognising the limits of one's ability to act. This is only the first – but very important – step on the path to remoulding one's consciousness once it has been fragmented by psychosis. This form of intervention, utilising the reconstruction of the body/psyche relationship helps to decrease the symptoms of psychosis by improving the patient's ability to relate to others, reintegrating them into a more adaptive form of life.

References

Armando, M. D. (2006). *Calatonia e Religiosidade*. Unpublished Master's thesis, Pontifical Catholic University of São Paulo, São Paulo, Brazil.

Blanchard, A. R., Seixas, L. P., & Rios, A. M. G. (2010). The body in psychotherapy: Calatonia and subtle touch techniques. In R. A. Jones (Ed.), *Body, Mind and Healing after Jung: A space of questions*. Abingdon, UK: Routledge.

Fierz, H. (1997). *Psiquiatria Junguiana*. São Paulo, SP: Paulus.

Jung, C. G. (1984a). *A Natureza da Psique (Vol. VIII/2)*. Petrópolis, RJ: Vozes.

Jung, C. G. (1984b). *Sincronicidade (Vol. VIII/3)*. Petrópolis, RJ: Vozes.

Jung, C. G. (1990). *Psicogênese das Doenças Mentais (Vol. III)*. Petrópolis, RJ: Vozes.

Jung, C. G. (2001). *Os Arquétipos e o Inconsciente Coletivo (Vol. IX/1)*. Petrópolis, RJ: Vozes.

Jung, C. G. (2007). *Símbolos da Transformação (Vol. V)*. Petrópolis, RJ: Vozes.

Knox, J. (1999). The relevance of attachment theory to a contemporary Jungian view of the internal world: internal working models, implicit memory and internal objects. *Journal of Analytical Psychology*, 44(4), 511-552.

Röhricht, F. (2015). Body psychotherapy for the treatment of severe mental disorders – an overview. *Body, Movement and Dance in Psychotherapy*, 10(1), 51-67.

Sándor, P. (1974). *Técnicas de Relaxamento*. São Paulo, SP: Vetor.

Seixas, L. M. P. (1989). *O Caso de Nina: um atendimento na esquizofrenia dentro da visão junguiana*. Unpublished master's thesis, Pontifical Catholic University of São Paulo, Brazil.

Silva, R. C. B. (2006). Esquizofrenia: uma revisão. *Psicologia USP*, 17(4), 263-285.

10

The Psyche in Pethö Sándor's Method

Anita Ribeiro Blanchard

> "The oak tree is the purpose that the matter of the acorn serves".
> Aristotle, Lavine, 2011, p. 71

> "I believe we have been robbed of our true biography –
> that destiny written in the acorn – and we go to therapy to recover it".
> Hillman, 1996, p. 5

The objective of this chapter is to highlight some Jungian concepts, fundamental to the Subtle Touch and Calatonia method, for readers and psychotherapists who are interested in somatic integration, interventions for trauma, psychosomatic dysfunctions, access to pre-verbal memory and psychological well-being, but who are unfamiliar with Jung's theory. I also hope the chapter will be useful for professionals in education, healthcare, and preventive and behavioural medicine, even if they do not necessarily use Jungian therapeutic resources. Sándor's method (1974) can be used in conjunction with any other theory or lens of subjectivity in psychotherapy, although the method was originally structured within the epistemology of

Jungian psychology (Farah, 2017; Horta, Minicuci, Fontana, & Paschoa, 2012; Rios, Seixas, & Blanchard, 2010; Seixas, Rios, & Blanchard, 2009).

Amid the stresses of a war-torn environment, Sándor's method helped restore well-being in traumatised individuals, no matter what their external circumstances were. He used gentle bodywork to promote healing and regulated states and developed this method guided by his medical knowledge but essentially, by perceiving and/or asking patients how they felt during the application of these techniques. For example, he would ask how they felt different qualities of touch and pressure, or how they experienced touch on different parts of the body, and also, of their reactions to passive movements of fingers, toes, legs, arms and head. This way, he identified somatic responses linked to homeostatic regulation mechanisms and adjustments in the autonomic nervous system (ANS), such as changes in respiratory rate, changes in body temperature, muscle relaxation, and so on (Cannon, 1929, 1932; Sterling & Laughlin, 2017). Sándor also realised that after such somatic reorganisation, his patients spontaneously shared their stories, memories, feelings, thoughts, and felt more emotionally regulated and better cognitively adapted to their life circumstances. He noted that body, emotions and mind harmonised as a coherent whole, after the activation of self-regulating and homeostatic mechanisms that acted at the levels of both soma and psyche. He also realised that the regular application of gentle touches, fostering as it did global homeostatic adjustments, promoted greater resilience, even in the chaotic, post-war environment.

Sándor grounded his method in Jung's psychology to give meaning to the spontaneous psychological contents that arose after a Calatonia session, the central technique of his method. In Jungian terms, these self-regulating mechanisms governing both soma and psyche work toward optimum physical states (soma) and the self-realisation (psyche) of the individual. In other words, for Jung, not only does the body obey the laws of homeostatic health-regulating mechanisms in order to keep itself functioning at optimum levels, but the psyche is also linked to mechanisms that promote optimum function. This maintains the psychological orientation of human beings bound to the fulfilment of their unique destiny: in the same way that the seed fulfils its destiny of becoming not just any tree, but an oak tree.

While many psychology professionals are certainly familiar with Jungian psychology, Jung's concept of the 'psyche as a self-regulating system' is not sufficiently valued in general psychology. Although not necessarily identified as such, this self-regulating aspect of the psyche can be observed in the EMDR (Eye Movement Desensitisation and Reprocessing) technique (Shapiro, 2014). EMDR releases or triggers the psyche's spontaneous ability to regulate the mind by guiding the patient to relive a traumatic incident, re-experiencing in measured doses the physical, emotional, and cognitive responses that occurred during the incident in question. When the patient is able to mobilise this memory in its three psychological dimensions (physical, emotional and mental), the therapist stimulates bilateral eye movement (Shapiro, 2014) to help release painful memories which the patient is then more able to process. The mental stabilisation achieved after EMDR is called the spontaneous flow of "adaptive thoughts" (and/or images, sensations), in which negative thought patterns diminish, and are replaced by a new adaptive narrative for the traumatic event. The innate dynamics of the psyche result in a similar self-regulating mental process on a daily basis, through dreams, fantasies, images, sensations, and other experiences, in a less intense manner, and without our being aware of them as such or even of having to understand them necessarily. Psychodynamic theories recognise this phenomenon, but unlike Jungian theory, do not see this process as guided by a higher principle that aims at psychic self-realisation.

Recent research appears to support the Jungian concept of autonomous self-regulation of the psyche, with a growing basis of scientific evidence which should encourage psychologists to consider this idea with interest. Since cognitive neuroscience identified the Default Mode Network (DMN), a set of interacting brain regions that facilitates spontaneous thoughts, daydreaming, and images, among other mental processes, scientists and clinicians have investigated the psychological function and importance of such neural connectivity (Andrews-Hanna, Smallwood, & Spreng, 2014). The DMN has been implicated in cognitive transitions, balancing internally focussed tasks and externally focussed tasks, keeping attention fluctuating between these two domains. Its function appears to be involved in both mind-wandering, imagination, and recollection as well as (external) contextual representations (Smith, Mitchell, & Duncan, 2018). The internally focussed mental process produced during DMN connectivity appears to revolve around self-reflective thoughts, reminiscence, the consideration of others' perspectives, and creativity. Such processes seem to occur as a 'needed' activity to keep the mind and emotions in more adaptive or regulated states, without the input of external stimuli, as if the mind were seeking an ideal psychological state through spontaneous meaning-making and self-narrative.

Thus, the concept of psychic self-regulation is highly pertinent to current developments in neuropsychology and cognitive neuroscience, even though this concept was defined by Jung nearly a century ago. Hence, the focus of this chapter is to elucidate the Jungian postulate of the psyche and its autonomous self-regulation capacity.

In this publication, the words "psychic", "psychical" and "psychological" meet the definition of "the totality of all psychic processes, conscious as well as unconscious" (Jung, 1971, p. 463). With that in mind, the psyche is here discussed as part of the ethos or philosophical foundations of Sándor's work, as well.

Psyche and Current Psychology

Simple as it may seem, to define the Jungian "psyche" is a daring endeavour. Even Jung himself elaborated on his understanding of the magnitude of this concept throughout his life and left the term broadly "open" as a comprehensive yet complex idea (Brooke, 2009; Jones, 2013; Yunt, 2001). He thought that trying to generate 'one' theory of the psyche would be an unsuccessful venture.

Many diagrams and maps of the human psyche (Jungian) are creatively portrayed on the Internet. However, these models represent only the finite model of the infinite psyche, whereas the psyche itself surpasses its human expression. According to Jung: "psyche is the greatest of all cosmic wonders and the *sine qua non* of the world as an object" (Jung, 1969, p. 225), as we can only relate to the world through our psyches. By psychic energy Jung means, "the total energy which pulses through all the forms and activities of the psychic system and establishes a communication between them" (Jacobi, 1968, p. 52). For Jung, "consciousness is a late-born descendant of the unconscious psyche" (1969, p. 453), and psyche is of a spiritual nature, an animating life-force that possibly expresses itself (without a self-reflective consciousness) throughout nature and certainly in animals:

> I do not wish to waste time in proving this point but will content myself with saying that never yet has any reasonable person doubted the existence of psychic processes in a dog, although no dog has, to our knowledge, ever expressed consciousness of its psychic contents. (Jung, 1969, p. 230)

This last sentence of Jung, that "no dog has, to our knowledge, ever expressed consciousness of its psychic contents", is an (anthropomorphically centred) expectation of reflective, human-like expression of consciousness. We do not know how our own consciousness is produced, much less that of animals, plants and planetary life, particularly in terms of what we call self-reflective consciousness (Fabbro, Aglioti, Bergamasco, Clarici, & Panksepp, 2015). Recent studies on ecology and biology on plant adaptation have shown that there is a plant-environment feedback cycle that modifies and adapts plant behaviours (Appel & Cocroft, 2014). Professor Chamovitz, at Tel Aviv University in Israel, says that "the rooting of plants – the fact that they are immovable – means they really need to be much more aware of their environment than you or me" (Gabbatiss, 2017). Therefore, the idea that the universe is interwoven into the psyche as Jung proposed, and that this same universe expresses some level of consciousness unknown to us, is plausible and charged with speculative-scientific value.

Thus, in a broader sense, the psyche is the "world", "woven into the fabric of the universe" (Hameroff, 2018), which could be interpreted in its human expression as an individual and unique experience of world development (objective and subjective) in each person, according to his or her ability to manifest it. Young-Eisendrath and Hall (1991) speak of a "constructivist" Jung, clearly visible in his definition below:

> Everyone makes for himself his own segment of the world and constructs his own private system . . . But the finite will never be able to grasp the infinite. . . . as a reflection of the world and man, (psyche) is a thing of such infinite complexity that it can be observed and studied from a great many sides. (Jung, 1969, p. 186)

Jung states that all we experience is psychic:

> . . . even physical pain is a psychic image that is experienced, and our sensory impressions – by all that they impose upon us, as a world of impenetrable objects occupying space – are psychic images, and only they are our immediate experience, for they alone are the immediate objects of our consciousness. (Jung, 1969, p. 456)

The origin of the word psyche supports the broader significance proposed by Jung: from the Greek verb ψυχω, Psyche means "to breathe, to cool, to blow" (Bailly, 1963, p. 2178), as the Spirit breathes life into human beings. In formal Greek, psyche is the word for butterfly, and the metamorphosis of the butterfly symbolises the spirit withdrawing from the body after death (Antonakou & Triarhou, 2017); therefore, the corollary must also be true, namely, that prior to the spirit withdrawing from the body it resides there throughout one's life. The word psyche is the root of the words psychology, psychiatry and psychopathology, words which long ago strayed from the above meanings (Askitopoulou, 2015; Bertolote, 2008; Browning, 2008; Crivellato & Ribatti, 2007).

In Jung's time, psychiatry did not have the compromised relationship with the pharmaceutical industry it does today. However, as a psychiatrist himself, Jung exposed in a lecture that:

> Psychiatry has been charged with gross materialism. And quite rightly, for it is on the road to putting the organ, the instrument, above the function.... Function has become the appendage of its organ, the psyche an appendage of the brain. In modern psychiatry the psyche has come off very badly. While immense progress has been made in cerebral anatomy, we know practically nothing about the psyche, or even less than we did before. (Jung, 1960, p. 160)

Jung notes that "the connection with the brain does not in itself prove that the psyche is an epiphenomenon, a secondary function causally dependent on biochemical processes" (Jung, 1969, p. 26). He continues, "the psyche deserves to be taken as a phenomenon in its own right; there are no grounds at all for regarding it as a mere epiphenomenon, dependent though it may be on the functioning of the brain" (Jung, 1969, pp. 21-22). As an example, in 2018, a 26-year-old graduate from an Ivy League university came to psychotherapy with depression. During the initial session, she told me that her psychiatrist had prescribed an antidepressant, which she had been taking for over a year. The patient added that she would have to keep taking the drug for five years because her psychiatrist reported that "scientific research has proven that patients who have taken antidepressant medication for less than five years from the initial diagnosis of depression have relapsed". I asked what had happened around the beginning of her depression, and she reported that she had got married, despite still being in love with an earlier boyfriend whom she had dated for four years.

No amount of medication will mend a broken heart, much less unravel the reasons and purpose that led this patient to make such a painful decision. James Hillman (1926-2011), a Jungian analyst who envisioned Archetypal psychology, proposes the idea that psychopathology (psyche-pathos-logos) refers to the "speech of the suffering soul" or the soul's suffering of meaning. The current medicalisation of the suffering soul might as well be labelled 'cosmetic psychiatry', in which Prozac takes on a role similar to that of Botox, in this case, to paralyse the 'expression' of the soul (Brandeis University, 2010; Conrad, 2007; Goldhill, 2017; Poitras, 2009; William, Martin, & Gabe, 2011; Yan, 2017).

Although Jung's definition of psyche is not synonymous with 'subjective experience of reality', "on the contrary, it is something objective, self-subsistent, and living its own life" (Jung, 1969, p. 448), in this patient's case, she was robbed of her subjective experience of the psyche, of the chance to make sense of her experiences, to understand her love and pain, and to expand her awareness of who she was in that situation and who she could become. In this kind of subjective experience lies the "plasticity" and "diversity" of the psyche, its "world" of possibilities for each of us.

Luhrmann (2000, p. 6) states that psychiatrists currently oscillate between two perspectives. Sometimes they discuss "mental anguish as if it were a heart disease: you treat it with medication, rest and advice about the right way to eat and live". On other occasions, they talk about this same anguish as being a result of "the kind of person you are: your intentions, your loves and hates, your confused and complicated past". Yet for many organisations, institutions, universities, and medical insurers, conventional psychiatry is a higher-order source of mind-brain knowledge with which clinical psychology must align, at the cost of losing the deeper meaning of life and of psychical reality. The psychologists who align with this "biological-pharmaceutical" view of psychological disorders become limited to using techniques of cognitive restructuring, emotional regulation, or other mechanistic approaches to the treatment of symptoms, without investigating the nature of the psyche (Jones, 2013) and its innate self-regulating mechanisms.

Expressing his frustration with this position of psychological science, Jung stated that "all modern 'psychologies without the psyche' are psychologies of consciousness, for which an unconscious psychic life simply does not exist" (Jung, 1969, p. 443). To Jones (2013), psychology with psyche, "in all its versions, concerns the holistic inner experience. [Psychology with psyche] provides a way of thinking about and working with inner experiences".

An anecdote illustrating this conventional view: in mid-1990s academia, one of my graduate professors in Florida gave a solemn definition of psychology as "the study of behaviour". I asked him, expecting a long answer about the history of psychology, "What happened to the old definition of psychology as the study of the soul?" To which, to my disappointment, he replied, "I have never heard of it".

Jung pointed out this split more than a century ago:

> It is really high time academic psychologists came down to earth and wanted to hear about the human psyche as it really is and not merely about laboratory experiments. It is insufferable that professors should forbid their students to have anything to do with analytical psychology, that they should prohibit the use of analytical concepts and accuse our psychology of taking account, in an unscientific manner, of "everyday experiences". I know that psychology in general could derive the greatest benefit from a serious study of the dream problem once it could rid itself of the unjustified lay prejudice that dreams are

caused solely by somatic stimuli. (Jung, 1969, p. 362)

It took about a century, after Jung made this statement, for the study of dreams to become a topic for scientific inquiry. But to this day, laboratory experiments take priority in the science of psychology. Psychology professor Richard Bentall, at Liverpool University (Knapton, 2016), points out that most research funding for psychological disorders in the UK is spent on brain scanners or gene sequencing machines, with almost nothing going toward the study of the psychological mechanisms or the social circumstances by which these problems develop.

Fortunately, there are many psychiatrists with integrity and "with psyche" (Ahn, Proctor, & Flanagan, 2009; Davies, 2013; Des, 2012; Gornall, 2013; Moore & Cross, 2014), who are embracing integrative perspectives to approach psychological disorders, and putting psychotropic drugs to their best and most necessary use. There is also an academic world "with psyche", which is challenging popular belief and the biological-pharmaceutical approach to psychiatry (Shorter, 1997), seeking to restore the integrity of psyche-soma, and working toward an understanding of the meaning of human experience.

Psyche and Unconscious

From its laboratories, academic cognitive-social psychology has contributed research evidence over the past twenty years about how "decision-making" and other higher order mental processes are carried out in the brain. They find that higher order mental processes are performed and resolved by what they term the "adaptive unconscious", not just as a subliminal influence for consciousness, but as a predominant or prevalent force (Bargh & Morsella, 2008, 2010; Damasio, 2010; Damian & Sherman, 2013; Masicampo & Baumeister, 2013; Nordgren, Bos, & Dijksterhuis, 2011; Wilson, 2002).

There are currently at least two emerging models based on these studies exploring how conscious and unconscious processes shape behaviours, feelings, and emotions, thoughts, and experiences (Baumeister & Bargh, 2014; Masicampo & Baumeister, 2013; Williams, Bargh, Nocera, & Gray, 2009; Winkielman & Schooler, 2011; Yuan, Ding, Liu, & Yang, 2015). One of these models for understanding the "adaptive unconscious" sees conscious and unconscious processes as complementary systems, not as competitors or opposites. In this view, unconscious and automatic processes are highly influential in the formation of the content of consciousness, although conscious thoughts are ultimately responsible for actions and decisions. Another model, however, suggests that "behaviour is usually determined by unconscious and automatic processes, while consciousness may occasionally intervene to override, regulate, redirect, and otherwise alter the stream of behaviour – often 'at a distance' - with unconscious processes filling in" (Baumeister & Bargh, 2014); in this view, it is understood that the "conscious mind is for talking".

The view that the unconscious predominates in human decisions requires a reassessment of how our "conscious rational self" fits within the larger picture (Sloman & Fernbach, 2017), challenging our "conscious-centric bias", as Bargh and Morsella (2008, 2010) call this self-referential idea that the conscious mind is "in command". Although this research is recent, Freud had already referred to our "naive narcissism", when he (1922) stated that:

> Man's desire for greatness is now suffering the third and bitterest blow coming this time from the current psychology [circa 1900], which is proving to the 'ego' of each of us that he is not the master of his own home, and who must be content with the leftover information coming from the unconscious about what happens in his own mind. (Freud, 1922, p. 246).

These two previous "bitter blows" refer to the theories of Nicolaus Copernicus (1473 – 1543) and Charles Darwin (1809 – 1882), which ended anthropomorphic worldviews: respectively, that the Earth was the centre of the universe, and that man was a being separate from the hierarchy of evolution. Now, social-cognitive psychology has dismantled the prerogative that our conscious mind represents our internal "legislative, judicial, and executive" powers operating within free will, to state that in fact all that control belongs to the unconscious (or non-conscious). This re-evaluation of our self-centred bias is based on research into the "autonomous systems of non-conscious (or unconscious) orientation", operating at the perceptual, evaluative, motivational, and emotional levels, all of them in non-conscious mutual cooperation (Bargh & Morsella, 2010; Smith & Lane, 2015). This new knowledge emphasises that deliberations of the "unconscious mind" precede the arrival of conscious reflection (Bargh & Morsella, 2008; Baumeister & Bargh, 2014; Bechara, Damasio, Tranel, & Damasio, 1997; Damasio, 2010; Dijksterhuis & Nordgren, 2006; Wilson, 2002).

This current view recognises that judgements, feelings, motivations, decisions, and other important higher mental processes occur outside the field of consciousness as a result of "evolutionary efficiency", that is, as a result of an evolutionary adaptation process (Wilson, 2002, p. 8). Evolutionary efficiency has shaped an "adaptive unconscious", a sort of "autopilot", operating under the radar of our consciousness to manage information, because consciousness has a small work-station incapable of handling the amount of sensory information that floods the organism at any given time (Wilson, 2002).

Jung (and Freud, too) described this influence of the unconscious at the beginning of the last century and called it the "personal unconscious":

> Everything of which I know, but of which I am not at the moment thinking; everything of which I was once conscious but have now forgotten; everything perceived by my senses, but not noted by my conscious mind; everything which, involuntarily and without paying attention to it, I feel, think, remember, want, and do; all the future

things which are taking shape in me and will sometime come to consciousness; all this is the content of the unconscious" (Jung, 1969, p. 245).

... besides these we must include all more or less intentional repressions of painful thoughts and feelings. I call the sum of these contents the 'personal unconscious'. (Jung, 1969, p. 179).

However, the definition of psyche for Jung extends far beyond the current definition of unconscious by scientists of social-cognitive psychology as it includes the collective unconscious. For Jung, the concept of a collective unconscious means a repertoire of genetically inherited patterns of behaviour, images and ideas, an inheritance from the total experiences of humankind over time:

> The collective unconscious comprises in itself the psychic life of our ancestors right back to the earliest beginnings. It is the matrix of all conscious psychic occurrences, and hence it exerts an influence that compromises the freedom of consciousness in the highest degree. (Jung, 1969, p. 155)

Both Jungian notions, of personal and collective unconscious, are validated by Damasio's statement below, almost word for word, establishing a dialogue between these two minds which extends over more than a hundred years:

> Our memories of things, of properties of things, of people and places, of events and relationships, of skills, of life-management processes - in short all of our memories, inherited from evolution and available at birth or acquired through learning thereafter - exist in our brains in dispositional form, waiting to become explicit images or actions. *Our knowledge base is implicit, encrypted, and unconscious.* (Damasio's emphasis; Damasio, 2010, p. 144)

And Jung validates Damasio's idea of a "dispositional form" with the idea of archetypes:

> The archetype is a possibility of representation that is given a priori. They are inherited with the brain structure – indeed they are [the brain's] psychic aspect . . . systems of readiness for action, and at the same time images and emotions. (Jung, 1970, p. 31)

Contemporary social-cognitive scientists exploring the influence of the unconscious on our conscious life have questioned our ability to access any self-knowledge, and also to have genuine free will, since most of the information necessary for having this free will and self-knowledge is under the control of the unconscious (Bargh & Morsella, 2008; Wilson & Dunn, 2004).

Opposing this view, Jung (1969) imagined the possibility of expanding consciousness through analytical psychotherapy, through the search for meaning and purpose, and through the pursuit of self-realisation (individuation) (Cambray, 2013). In the same way, Sándor felt that the combination of his somatic method with Jung's analytical psychology could increase self-knowledge, expansion of conscious awareness (as meta-awareness), self-regulation, social regulation and spiritual growth, furthering individual development and also social harmony (Armando, 2006; Farah, 2017; Lemos & Henry, 2005; Rios et al., 2010; Seixas, Rios, & Blanchard, 2009).

The Psyche-Butterfly

In his method, Sándor adopted Jung's (1969) understanding of the psyche and soma as a unit that expresses itself in a continuum of energy frequency. These frequencies have different manifestations, from a more ethereal (psychic) frequency to a denser (somatic) frequency, and these two manifestations, although distinct, are of the same essential origin and are therefore subordinated to only *one* "higher principle" that regulates both (Blanchard, 2012; Seixas et al., 2009). This higher, regulating or harmonising principle of this energy continuum at the physical (somatic) level acts through the homeostatic and self-regulating biological mechanism of the body; and psychologically the higher regulating principle acts through symbols generated in dreams, daydreams, fantasies, spontaneous thoughts, visual arts, music and other expressive activities and artistic languages (Arcuri, 2005; Arcuri & Catta-Preta, 2012; Armando, 2006). In short, at the psychological level, regulation manifests itself as the "flow of images and symbols" generated by psychic activity, not as biochemical measures.

This reality of the "psyche-soma continuum", with its single higher principle that governs the self-regulation of both aspects of this continuum, is illustrated in the case treated by the British National Health Service (NHS). The patient, a six-year-old boy, was brought for brief therapy with a complaint of aggressive and defiant behaviours at home and at school (Blanchard, 2010, 2011). The mother and the boy both attended the first session and I addressed the boy after his mother explained the reasons for bringing him to therapy. He was quiet, vigilant and guarded, and refused to engage in play therapy or talk to me. Using a doll, I showed him a sequence of touches and movements that I could teach his mother to do on him at home. To my surprise, he said he would like to receive the techniques.

After the somatic work, I offered him paper and pencil with which to draw. He seemed relaxed and at ease and drew (Fig. 1) a road with a rainbow to the right and a snail to the left, a tree in the centre and in the foreground a butterfly with its right wing shaded. He explained that the shaded wing of the butterfly was broken.

An initial psychological evaluation at the hospital revealed that his family had undergone drastic changes the previous year - first his parents had divorced, and then, six months later, his mother had moved in with her new boyfriend and his four daughters, all older than my patient, who until then had been an only child.

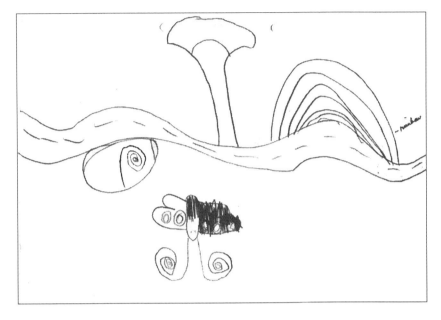

Figure 1

The pleasant bodily sensations evoked by subtle touch allowed this patient to "feel" his body again. Previously, his body had been a "place" of negative emotions and he could not relate to it - he could only act out without having any idea of why or for what reason he was behaving in this way. The sequence of gentle touches and playful movements mediated the soma-psyche flow, which in turn helped him express his inner emotional discomfort through a symbol that made sense to himself and to others.

From his experience emerged a psychical symbol that represented his difficult situation and its associated suffering. On the left side the snail, the physical-material aspect, symbolised the need to slow down the pace of the changes; on the right-hand side, the rainbow, the immaterial/celestial aspect, represented his need for protection and psychological care; and in the middle, the tree, a symbol of vitality, suggested the fulfilling of the potential implicit in the seed, the rooting of his life project. The butterfly's broken wing revealed his helplessness.

Such principles of self-regulation and self-organisation of soma and psyche encourage a less "directive" attitude on the part of the Jungian psychotherapist. The function of the therapist in this case is to tune in to the directions of the psyche as expressed in the patient's dreams, in his or her images, in fantasies, in artistic expressions, and also in somatic manifestations. The value of these psychical expressions is as important as the patient's narrative, since the contents of the narrative and those of the unconscious form a whole which only in this way gives us an integrated view not only of the situation but also of how the patient inserts himself into it with his strengths and vulnerabilities (Rios, Armando, & Regina, 2012).

Often the conscious narrative of patients is in direct conflict with what is expressed in the language of the unconscious. A classic example of this conflict is the unbalanced life of the businessman who neglects his feelings and his emotional needs in favour of his career, only to lose his meaningful relationships and develop symptoms that represent the neglected life of the psyche, e.g., vertigo, panic attacks, in more extreme cases, cardiac infarct or alcoholism, among other symptoms.

As a clinical example of this conflict between conscious and unconscious mind, a 40-year-old patient who was undergoing very invasive fertility treatments, reported, after a Calatonia session, that she felt "calm and peace" in her body, during its application. However, she added that she struggled with those feelings because she thought her body needed to focus on actively producing a baby and "not on being so lazy". There was certainly a huge discrepancy between the patient's expectations about her body and the experience her body provided, and the gap between her ego's desires and her somatic regulation provided scope for much analytical work.

By including Calatonia to facilitate restorative (homeostatic) adjustments, the therapist can help the patient to integrate these conflicts at various levels - somatic, sensory, emotional, cognitive, and spiritual. And so, psychotherapy follows a dynamic development informed by the homeostatic regulation of the psyche and soma that occurs during Calatonia, in somatic attunement (dyadic regulation) with the therapist (Armando, 2006; Delmanto, 2008; Farah, 2017; Gaeta, 2010; Horta et al., 2012; Penna, 2007; Rios et al., 2010; Seixas et al., 2009).

A Spiritual System with a Purpose

To paraphrase the intention expressed in Aristotle's quotation at the beginning of this chapter, the psyche contains the seed of a person's psychological development, the matrix of all potentialities for each individual. It is in this sense that Jung (1969) understood the psyche as a purposeful system in which psychological growth, expansion of consciousness, and self--realisation of the individual are the purpose that the psyche serves. Jung asserted that this idea of purpose or finality changes the perspective of how we look at the manifest contents of the psyche.

Jung's idea of psyche as an "intentional system" is similar to the current concept of "self-organisation", defined as a process whereby a system generates an observable ordering without the assistance of an outside agent. Self-organisation is present in molecular, biological, computational, psychological, and social systems, and even in planetary physics and cosmology (Aschwanden et al., 2018; Heylighen, 2001). It refers to a spontaneous order orchestrated by a systemic "driving force" (similar to Jung's definition of psychic energy) and a positive feedback mechanism (similar to Jung's idea of self-regulating mechanisms of the psyche). Interactions between the elements of the system evolve to a self-organised pattern, such as the planetary system itself, the spontaneous geometry of snow crystals, the murmuration of birds and all swarm behaviours of fish, bees, herds and other groups (Aschwanden et al., 2018).

This pattern of cohesiveness of a system is often triggered by random fluctuations within the system, with a resulting reorganisation that is sustained by all its components, creating "order out of randomness" (Aschwanden et al., 2018; Barton,

1994; Camazine et al., 2001; Heylighen, 2001; Kahn, 2013; Moussaid, Garnier, Theraulaz, & Helbing, 2009; Witzany, 2014). Anyone who has ever observed a flock of birds at dusk knows what a self-organised system is. It forms spontaneously from random fluctuations, with all members of the flock actively participating in the maintenance of this natural systemic organisation, shown as a marvellous synchronised dance in the air.

The intentionality of the psyche, sustained by its feedback and feedforward regulation (i.e., dreams, images, sensations, fantasies), is an example of the 'mechanisms' that maintain such self-organisation within an individual's lifespan. The psychical intentionality and its regulatory mechanisms are constantly seeking cohesion and sustaining the design of one's self-realisation, or "individuation" (Jung, 1969). This confirms what was said earlier - that a psychic system can never be considered as a "result" of brain function alone, as traditional psychiatry would have it.

To reason the psyche-brain controversy, there are many theoretical models and propositions that run parallel to the debate on brain-consciousness studies (Blackmore, 2006; Blanchard, 2012). A prevalent view in these debates, the quantum paradigm, proposes that the basis of the material world is non-material, "the visible order of the world is based on phenomena that transcend the materialism of classical physics" (Valadas Ponte & Schäfer, 2013); thus, supporting the Jungian idea of the immaterial psyche.

Going beyond quantum theory, Hameroff and Penrose (2014), the maverick scientists of consciousness and quantum biology, argue that the science of quantum mechanics is not complete without the theory of "orchestrated objective reduction" (OrchOR). They tell how consciousness appears in human experience without being an epiphenomenon of brain activity. Opposing the standard model that consciousness emerges from complex computation among brain neurons, Hameroff explains that in an OrchOR theory, consciousness happens before neuronal firing occurs, so the activation of neurons would be a consequence of consciousness and not its activating process. OrchOR theory is based on quantum vibrations of the protein chains (polymers) found in microtubules within the neurons:

> . . . vibrations which interfere, "collapse" and resonate across scale, control neuronal firings, generate consciousness, and connect ultimately to "deeper order" ripples in space-time geometry. Consciousness is more like music than [brain] computation. (Hameroff, 2018)

Similarly, Jung stated that "*our psyche is set up in accord with the structure of the universe, and what happens in the macrocosm likewise happens in the infinitesimal and most subjective reaches of the psyche* (Jung, 1963, p. 335)". Hameroff (2018) concludes that, "the nature of consciousness remains deeply mysterious and profoundly important, with existential, medical and spiritual implications".

To date, the psyche-soul-brain issue is far from settled, and it remains to be seen whether the Quantum or OrchOR theories can explain the brain-consciousness enigma (Bunge, 2012; Ishikawa, 2017). However, the present value of these ideas is to expand our views beyond the confines of materialistic science, which, in reducing psyche to brain, discards or denies meaning to human experience.

In the words of Dolan (2007), "ideas about the body, mind, self, consciousness, and soul will no doubt continue to be a matter of lively discussion as they have been for centuries", with "soul" and/or "psyche" possibly becoming topics of academic research in the near future (Pransky & Kelley, 2017; Preston, Ritter, & Hepler, 2013).

To conclude, Sándor's ethos aligns deeply with Jung's views on the nature and origin of psychic processes:

> . . . we can perhaps summon up courage to consider the possibility of a 'psychology with the psyche'—that is, a theory of the psyche ultimately based on the postulate

of an autonomous, spiritual principle. We need not be alarmed at the unpopularity of such an undertaking, for to postulate 'spirit' is no more fantastic than to postulate 'matter.' Since we have literally no idea how the psychic can arise out of the physical, and yet cannot deny the reality of psychic events, we are free to frame our assumptions the other way about for once, and to suppose that the psyche arises from a spiritual principle which is as inaccessible to our understanding as matter. It will certainly not be a modern psychology, for to be modern is to deny such a possibility. (Jung, 1969, p. 445)

Postmodernism has swallowed the modernity to which Jung refers above and more recently, postmodernism has been superseded by a new era of electronic media, biotechnology, climate change and ethos revolution. There is hope that some meta-postmodern wisdom may increasingly encourage the adoption of practices with the psyche, which will bring understanding to the soul of patients, and help them to find the meaning and destination of their lives. Communities, as 'larger self-organising systems', may also engage in this quest for the living psyche, by inspiring the imagination about our collective purpose and embracing the diverse significance of each individual within this purpose.

References

Ahn, W. K., Proctor, C. C., & Flanagan, E. H. (2009). Mental health clinicians's beliefs about the biological, psychological, and environmental bases of mental disorders. *Cognitive science, 33*(2), 147-182.

Andrews-Hanna, J. R., Smallwood, J., & Spreng, R. N. (2014). The default network and self-generated thought: Component processes, dynamic control, and clinical relevance. *Annals of the New York Academy of Sciences, 1316*(1), 29–52. https://doi.org/10.1111/nyas.12360

Antonakou, E. I., & Triarhou, L. C. (2017). Soul, butterfly, mythological nymph: psyche in philosophy and neuroscience. *Arq. Neuro-Psiquiatr., 75*(3). http://dx.doi.org/10.1590/0004-282x20170012

Appel, H. M., & Cocroft, R. B. (2014). Plants respond to leaf vibrations caused by insect herbivore chewing. *Oecologia 175,* 1257. https://doi.org/10.1007/s00442-014-2995-6

Arcuri, I. G. (2005). Psicologia Transpessoal, Arteterapia e Calatonia. *Hermes, 10,* 100-111.

Arcuri, I. G., & Catta-Preta, M. (2012). *Sonhos e Arte: Diário de Imagens.* São Paulo, SP: Primavera Editorial.

Armando, M. D. (2006). *Calatonia e Religiosidade – Uma Abordagem Junguiana* (Master's thesis). Pontifical Catholic University, São Paulo, BR.

Aschwanden, M. J., Scholkmann, F., Béthune, W., Schmutz, W., Abramenko, V., Cheung, M. C. M., ... Green, W. H. (2018). Order out of randomness: Self-Organization processes in astrophysics. *Space Science Reviews, 214*(2), 55-75.

Askitopoulou, H. (2015). Sleep and dreams: From myth to medicine in ancient Greece. *Journal of Anaesthesia History, 1*(3), 70-75. https://doi.org/10.1016/j.janh.2015.03.001

Bailly, A. (1963). *Dictionnaire Grec-Français.* 26e éd. Paris, FR: Séchan L. et Chantraine P.

Bargh, J. A., & Morsella, E. (2008). The unconscious mind. *Perspectives on Psychological Science: A Journal of the Association for*

Psychological Science, 3(1), 73–79.
Bargh, J. A., & Morsella, E. (2010). Unconscious Behavioral Guidance Systems. In C. R. Agnew, D. E. Carlston, W. G. Graziano, & J. R. Kelly (Eds.), *Then A Miracle Occurs: Focusing on Behavior in Social Psychological Theory and Research* (pp. 89-118). Oxford, UK: Oxford University Press.
Barton, S. (1994). Chaos, self-organization, and psychology. *Am Psychol., 49*(1), 5-14.
Baumeister, R. F., & Bargh, J. A. (2014). Conscious and unconscious: Toward an integrative understanding of human mental life and action. In J. W. Sherman, B. Gawronski, & Y. Trope (Eds.), *Dual-process theories of the social mind* (pp. 35-49). New York, NY: Guilford Press.
Bechara, A., Damasio, H., Tranel, D., & Damasio, A. R. (1997). Deciding advantageously before knowing the advantageous strategy. *Science, 275*(5304), 1293–1295. https://doi.org/10.1126/science.275.5304.1293
Bertolote, J. (2008). The roots of the concept of mental health. *World Psychiatry, 7*(2), 113–116.
Blackmore, S. (2006). *Conversations on Consciousness*. Oxford, UK: Oxford University Press.
Blanchard, A. R. (2010). Somatic integration to systemic therapy. *The Psychotherapist, 47*, 5-7.
Blanchard, A. R. (2012). A Consciência e sua Base no Corpo. In M. E. Spaccaquerche (Ed.), *O Corpo em Jung: Estudos em Calatonia e Outras Práticas Integrativas* (pp. 39-60). Sao Paulo, SP: Editora Vetor.
Blanchard, A. R. (2011). O corpo da família. *Hermes, 15*, 60-71.
Brandeis University. (2010, May 19). Medicalizing human conditions: A growth industry -- but what does it cost? *ScienceDaily*. Retrieved from www.sciencedaily.com/releases/2010/05/100517152536.htm
Brooke, R. (2009). The self, the psyche and the world: A phenomenological interpretation. *Journal of Analytical Psychology, 54*(5), 601-618. https://doi.org/10.1111/j.1468-5922.2009.01809.x

Browning, D. (2008). Internists of the mind or physicians of the soul: Does psychiatry need a public philosophy? *Zygon*, 43(2), 371–383. https://doi.org/10.1111/j.1467-9744.2008.00922.x

Bunge, M. (2012). Does Quantum physics refute realism, materialism and determinism? *Science and Education*, 21(10), 1601–1610. https://doi.org/10.1007/s11191-011-9410-z

Camazine, S., Deneubourg, J.-L., Franks, N. R., Sneyd, J., Theraulaz, G., & Bonabeau, E. (2001). *Self-organisation in biological systems. Princetown Studies in Complexity*. Princeton, NJ: Princeton University Press.

Cambray, J. (2013). *Synchronicity: Nature and psyche in an interconnected universe*. Mendocino, CA: University Press Audiobooks.

Cannon, W. B. (1929). Organization for physiological homeostasis. *Physiol. Rev., 9*, 399–431.

Cannon, W. B. (1932). *The Wisdom of the Body*. New York, NY: W. W. Norton & Company.

Conrad, P. (2007). *The Medicalization of Society: On the Transformation of Human Conditions into Treatable Disorders*. Baltimore, MD: Johns Hopkins University Press.

Crivellato, E., & Ribatti, D. (2007). Soul, mind, brain: Greek philosophy and the birth of neuroscience. *Brain Research Bulletin*, 71(4), 327–336. https://doi.org/10.1016/j.brainresbull.2006.09.020

Damasio, A. (2010). *Self Comes to Mind: Constructing the Conscious Brain*. London, UK: William Heinemann.

Damian, R. I., & Sherman, J. W. (2013). A process-dissociation examination of the cognitive processes underlying unconscious thought. *Journal of Experimental Social Psychology*, 49(2), 228-237.

Davies, J. (2013). *Cracked: Why Psychiatry is Doing More Harm Than Good*. London, UK: Icon Books.

Delmanto, S. (2008). *Subtle Touches: Calatonia*. São Paulo, SP: Summus Editorial.

Des, S. (2012). The psychiatric oligarchs who medicalise normality. *BMJ, 344,* e3135.

Dijksterhuis, A., & Nordgren, L. F. (2006). A theory of unconscious thought. *Perspect. Psychol. Sci., 1,* 95-109.

Dolan, B. (2007). Soul searching: a brief history of the mind/body debate in the neurosciences. *Neurosurgical Focus, 23*(1), E2. doi: 10.3171/foc.2007.23.1.2.

Fabbro, F., Aglioti, S. M., Bergamasco, M., Clarici, A., & Panksepp, J. (2015). Evolutionary aspects of self- and world consciousness in vertebrates. *Frontiers in human neuroscience, 9,* 157. doi: 10.3389/fnhum.2015.00157

Farah, R. M. (2017). *Calatonia – Subtle Touch in Psychotherapy.* São Paulo, SP: Editora Companhia Ilimitada.

Freud, S. (1922). *A general introduction to psychoanalysis.* New York, NY: Boni and Liveright.

Gabbatiss, J. (2017, January 27). "Plants can see, hear, smell – and respond". *BBC Earth.* Retrieved from http://www.bbc.com/earth/story/20170109-plants-can-see-hear-and-smell-and-respond

Gaeta, I. (2010). *Psicoterapia Junguiana – Novos caminhos na clínica – O uso de mandalas e Calatonia.* São Paulo, SP: Editora Vetor.

Goldhill, O. (2017, December 29). In the Dark: 30 years after Prozac arrived, we still buy the lie that chemical imbalances cause depression. *Quartz.* Retrieved from: https://qz.com/1162154/30-years-after-prozac-arrived-we-still-buy-the-lie-that-chemical-imbalances-cause-depression/

Gornall, J. (2013). DSM-5: a fatal diagnosis? *BMJ, 346,* f3256.

Hameroff, S. (2018, November 26). *Quantum Consciousness.* Retrieved from http://www.quantumconsciousness.org/content/overview-sh

Hameroff, S., & Penrose, R. (2014). Consciousness in the universe: a review of the "OrchOR" theory. *Phys. Life Rev., 11*(1), 39-78 https://doi.org/10.1016/j.plrev.2013.08.002

Heylighen, F. (2001). The science of self-organization and adaptativity. *The Encyclopaedia of Life Support Systems,* 1–26. https://doi.org/10.1.1.38.7158

Hillman, J. (1996). *The Soul's Code: In Search of Character and Calling.*

New York, NY: Random House.

Horta, E. V. P., Minicuci, M. C., Fontana, O. M., & Paschoa, V. L. F. (2012). *Jung & Sándor: Trabalho Corporal na Psicoterapia Analítica*. São Paulo, SP: Editora Vetor.

Ishikawa, S. (2017). A final solution to the mind-body Problem by Quantum language. *Journal of Quantum Information Science, 7*, 48-56. doi: 10.4236/jqis.2017.72005.

Jacobi, J. (1968). *The Psychology of C.G. Jung*. London, UK: Routledge and Kegan Paul.

Jones, R. (2013). Jung's "Psychology with the Psyche" and the behavioral sciences. *Behavioral Sciences, 3*(3), 408–417. https://doi.org/10.3390/bs3030408

Jung, C. G. (1960). The content of the psychoses (R. F. C. Hull, Trans.) (H. Read et al., Eds.), *The collected works of C. G. Jung* (Vol. 3, pp. 153-178). Princeton, NJ: Princeton University Press. (Original work published 1914).

Jung, C. G. (1963). Memories, dreams, reflections. New York, NY, US: Crown Publishing Group/Random House.

Jung, C. G. (1969). The structure of the psyche (R. F. C. Hull, Trans.) (H. Read et al., Eds.), *The collected works of C. G. Jung* (Vol. 8, 2nd ed.). Retrieved from http://www.proquest.com (Original work published 1931)

Jung, C. G. (1970). Mind and earth (R. F. C. Hull, Trans.) (H. Read et al., Eds.), *The collected works of C. G. Jung* (Vol. 10, 2nd ed.). Retrieved from http://www.proquest.com (Original work published 1931)

Jung, C. G. (1971). Psychological Types. (R. F. C. Hull, Trans.) (H. Read et al., Eds.), The *collected works of C. G. Jung* (Vol. 6, 2nd ed.). Retrieved from http://www.proquest.com (Original work published 1921)

Kahn, D. (2013). Brain basis of self: self-organization and lessons from dreaming. *Front. Psychol. 4*, 408.

Knapton, S. (2016, March 28). Mental illness mostly caused by life events not genetics, argue psychologists. *The Telegraph*. Retrieved from: https://www.telegraph.co.uk/news/2016/03/28/mental-illness-mostly-caused-by-life-events-not-genetics-argue-p/

Lavine, T. Z. (2011). *From Socrates to Sartre: The Philosophic Quest* (Kindle Edition). New York, NY: Bantam.

Lemos, L. H. C., & Henry, B. (2005). Psicoterapia e Toques Sutis. *Hermes, 10*, 18-25.

Luhrmann, T. M. (2000). *Of two minds: The growing disorder in American psychiatry*. New York, NY: Alfred A. Knopf.

Masicampo, E. J., & Baumeister, R. F. (2013). Conscious thought does not guide moment-to-moment actions — it serves social and cultural functions. *Frontiers in Psychology, 4,* 478.

Moore, A., & Cross, W. (2014). Understanding the unconscious mind: Jungian psychology and mental health nursing. *Issues in Mental Health Nursing, 35*(4), 306-313, DOI: 10.3109/01612840.2014.886753

Moussaid, M., Garnier, S., Theraulaz, G., & Helbing, D. (2009). Collective information processing and pattern formation in swarms, flocks, and crowds. *Topics in Cognitive Science, 1*(3), 469–497.

Nordgren, L. F., Bos, M. W., & Dijksterhuis, A. (2011). The best of both worlds: Integrating conscious and unconscious thought best solves complex decisions. *Journal of Experimental Social Psychology, 47*(2), 509-511. doi: 10.1016/j.jesp.2010.12.007

Penna, L. (2007). A calatonia e os níveis de consciência. *Hermes, 12,* 82-95.

Poitras, G. (2009). Business ethics, medical ethics, and economic medicalization. *Int J Business Governance Ethics, 4,* 372-389.

Pransky, J., & Kelley, T. M. (2017). How the formless comes into form: A process by which Universal Mind powers consciousness and thought to create people's psychological lives. *Cogent Psychology, 4*(1), 1307633. https://doi.org/10.10 80/23311908.2017.1307633

Preston, J. L., Ritter, S. R., & Hepler, J. (2013). Neuroscience and the soul: competing explanations for the human experience. *Cognition, 127,* 31-37.

Rios, A. M. G., Seixas, L. P., & Blanchard, A. R. (2010). The Body in

Psychotherapy: Calatonia and Subtle Touch Techniques. In Raya Jones (Ed.), *Body, Mind, and Healing After Jung: A Space of Questions* (pp. 228-250). London, UK: Routledge.

Rios, A. M. G., Armando, M. D., & Regina, A. C. B. (2012). Bases Neuropsicológicas do Trabalho Corporal na Psicoterapia. In M. E. Spaccaquerche (Ed.), *Corpo em Jung* (pp. 19-38). São Paulo, SP: Editora Vetor.

Sándor, P. (1974). *Técnicas de relaxamento*. São Paulo, SP: Editora Vetor.

Seixas, L. M. P., Rios, A. M. G., & Blanchard, A. R. (2009). "O Corpo para Jung". In P. Albertini, & L. V. Freitas (Eds.). *Jung e Reich – Articulando conceitos e práticas* (Chap 5). Rio de Janeiro, RJ: Guanabara Koogan.

Shapiro, F. (2014). The role of Eye Movement Desensitization and Reprocessing (EMDR) therapy in medicine: Addressing the psychological and physical symptoms stemming from adverse life experiences. *The Permanente Journal*, 18(1), 71–77. http://doi.org/10.7812/TPP/13-098

Smith, R., & Lane, R. D. (2015). The neural basis of one's own conscious and unconscious emotional states. *Neuroscience and Biobehavioral Reviews, 57*(10), 1-29. https://doi.org/10.1016/j.neubiorev.2015.08.003

Smith, V., Mitchell, D. J., & Duncan, J. (2018). Role of the Default Mode Network in Cognitive Transitions, *Cerebral Cortex*, 28(10), 3685–3696.

Sloman, S., & Fernbach, P. (2017). *The Knowledge Illusion: Why We Never Think Alone*. New York, NY: Riverhead Books.

Shorter, E. (1997). *A History of Psychiatry: From the Era of the Asylum to the Age of Prozac*. Hoboken, NJ: Wiley.

Sterling, P., & Laughlin, S. (2017). *Principles of Neural Design*. Cambridge, MA: The MIT Press.

Valadas Ponte, D., & Schäfer, L. (2013). Carl Gustav Jung, Quantum physics and the spiritual mind: A mystical vision of the twenty-first century. *Behavioral Sciences*, 3(4), 601–618.

Williams, L. E., Bargh, J. A., Nocera, C. C., & Gray, J. R. (2009). The unconscious regulation of emotion: Nonconscious reappraisal goals modulate emotional reactivity. *Emotion*, 9(6), 847–854.

William, S. J., Martin, P., & Gabe, J. (2011). The pharmaceuticalization of society: A framework for analysis. *Sociology of Health & Illness*, 33(5), 710-725.

Wilson, T. D. (2002). *Strangers to ourselves: Discovering the adaptive unconscious*. Cambridge, MA: Belknap Press of Harvard University Press.

Wilson, T. D., & Dunn, E. W. (2004). Self-Knowledge: Its limits, value, and potential for improvement. *Annual Review of Psychology*, 55(1), 493–518. https://doi.org/10.1146/annurev.psych.55.090902.141954

Winkielman, P., & Schooler, J. W. (2011). Splitting consciousness: Unconscious, conscious, and metaconscious processes in social cognition. *European Review of Social Psychology*, 22(1), 1–35. https://doi.org/10.1080/10463283.2011.576580

Witzany, G. (2014). Biological self-organization. *Intern. Journal of Signs and Semiotic Systems*. 3, 1-11.

Yan, J. (2017). Percentage of Americans Taking Antidepressants Climbs. *Psychiatric News*, 52(20), 1–1. https://doi.org/10.1176/appi.pn.2017.pp9b2

Yuan, J., Ding, N., Liu, Y., & Yang, Y. (2015). Unconscious emotion regulation: Nonconscious reappraisal decreases emotion-related physiological reactivity during frustration. *Cognition and Emotion*, 29(6), 1042-1053. doi: 10.1080/02699931.2014.965663

Young-Eisendrath, P., & Hall, J. (1991). *Jung's Self Psychology: A Constructivist Perspective*. New York, NY: Guilford Press.

Yunt, J. D. (2001). Jung's contribution to an ecological psychology. *Journal of Humanistic Psychology*, 41(2), 96–121. https://doi.org/10.1177/0022167801412007

11

The Calatonia of Sight: Learning to See the World with Relaxed Eyes and Greater Awareness

Vivian Farah Nassif
Maria Georgina Ribeiro Gonçalves

> *"The eye is the lamp of the body. If your vision is clear, your whole body will be full of light. But if your vision is poor, your whole body will be full of darkness. If then the light within you is darkness, how great is that darkness!"*
>
> Matthew, 6:22-23
>
> *"True vision requires much more than the eye, it takes the whole man, for what we see is no more and no less than what we are."*
>
> Richard Guggenheimer

Calatonia of Sight is a new field of therapeutic application of the classic technique of Calatonia pioneered by Pethö Sándor (1982).

Calatonia of Sight is a sequence of touches made to the face and head, analogous to a reproduction of the sequence of touches made to the feet (Delmanto, 1997; Farah, 2008; Sándor, 1982). The touches are performed at strategic points in the orbicularis, occipital and cervical regions, in which there is an enormous stimulation of the parasympathetic branch of cranial and vagus nerves (Hammer et al., 2015; O'Rahilly & Muller, 1982).

This application of Calatonia of Sight was created by Nassif (Gonçalves & Nassif, 2008), a former student of Pethö Sándor, through her work conducting therapy with individuals suffering from visual impairments. She formulated this method for use with the eye region, adapted from the Self-Healing method by Meir Schneider (1998) combined with Sándor's method. Schneider's method primarily works to integrate the body with visual perception, enhancing the individual's awareness of the body's ability to self-regenerate (Schneider, 2005).

The postmodern, technological world has made us more oriented towards the mental and cognitive, in detriment of our biological and psychological systems. The need for balance between the soma and the psyche has not gone away, but has merely been relegated to the background. The stress affecting our body and mind, so prevalent in modern life, frequently targets the performance of our eyes. As with any physical organ, the eyes can suffer from over use and stress (Kozeis, 2009), whether from many hours spent in front of the computer or from watching TV, reading, playing video games, for example.

In physiological terms, clinical observations (Gorodscy & Tosi, 1987; Lemos & Henry, 2005; Conte & Gabriel, 2009) reveal that Calatonia acts to regulate the autonomic nervous system and recondition both physical and psychological aspects of the individual. These experiences, using Calatonia, result in a greater harmonisation of muscle tone and lead to improvement in blood circulation (Cortese, 1998). Calatonia also contributes significantly to the reduction of anxiety and helps in recovery from depression (Benevides, 2006).

The Eyes

For decades now, there has been increased awareness of the need to care for the body in order to improve health. However, improved eye care and vision treatment have made progress only in the late 20th and early 21st centuries. Since then, vision has been the subject of numerous sophisticated studies, including advances in laser technology and other surgical techniques.

These technological advances have led to better understanding of the complexity of the visual system comprised of the eyes, optic nerves and cerebral cortex. The eyes receive light and transform photons into nerve impulses, which transmit them to the brain via the optic nerve. In the brain, this information is decoded into a visual image. The optic nerve is considered an extension of the brain into the eye, since the retina is composed of nervous tissue. We perceive/see mainly with our brains and only partially with our eyes (Schneider, 2005).

It is currently proposed that neocortical operations are essentially multisensory, and there is evidence that auditory and somatosensory processing occur in the visual cortex, and vice-versa. This pervasiveness of multisensory influences on all levels of cortical processing strongly suggests that the senses do not operate independently during real-world cognition (Ghazanfar & Schroeder, 2006). For instance, postural control is also associated with an integration of touch and vision (Jeka, Oie, & Kiemel, 2000). Because of this multisensory relationship, working with subtle touches in the visual area can potentially enhance the levels of sensorial integration, particularly in terms of body schema and body orientation.

The region surrounding the eyes holds psychosomatic relevance because muscle tension is affected by stress and emotions. Muscle tension in this region consists of the contraction and freezing of most of the muscles surrounding the eyes, eyelids, forehead and tear ducts, as well as of the deep muscles located at the occipital base of the cranium.

Vision and Conscious Vision

The balance between far-sightedness and near-sightedness as well as between central, detailed vision and peripheral vision, allows us to perceive our body in space, in relation to our surroundings and to other individuals.

Our urban landscape, dominated by high buildings, and our current lifestyle of staying indoors for long hours are aggravating factors that lead to limited use of farsightedness. This has resulted in overuse of our nearsighted vision.

As a consequence, we suffer from a lack of horizons both metaphorically and visually and this causes a unique form of stress which can also give rise to visual impairments and a diminution of our psychological universe. In fact, exacerbated eye use has become the rule for a population which today can no longer do without the constant use of computers and electronic devices in their daily lives.

Just as in music, where there are pauses between the notes, so, also, activity and rest should be part of the visual world for visual function to remain healthy and unimpaired.

The conscious gaze should be characterised by attention, focus and presence, in contrast to a vaguely automated look where the eye functions for basic but unregistered activities. This conscious vision is true vision, and it can expand continuously throughout life.

To understand the process of conscious vision we must consider the use of the eyes, brain and mind together (Kaplan, 2003). The mind and the emotions influence the selection of visual images so it becomes necessary to relax one's mind and stabilise one's emotions to see without "distortions". When we relax, some of the images, feelings and ideas that have been engraved in our memory but which, hitherto, have been inaccessible due to psychological blocks, can emerge, be analysed and understood. These psychological blocks can cause muscle strain that can make vision difficult.

The eyes, and consequently the capacity for visual perception, are intimately connected with the body, mind and emotions and are deeply affected by them. Symptoms of visual impairment appear in many mental health disorders, such as panic attacks, anxiety, stress, and post-traumatic stress disorder. For example, at the beginning of the 20th century and at the end of the 19th century, there were frequent cases of hysterical blindness, now known as conversion disorder (American Psychiatric Association, 2013) and dissociative disorder (Reed, 2010) – a form of blindness caused by the avoidance of all contact with inner and outer reality.

Anxiety also affects the visual field and may cause distorted, hazy or blurred vision. The eyes may become dry, red, watery or itchy, and oversensitive to light or spots on the visual field, and may even produce spontaneous visual effects when the eyes are closed. The depth of the visual field may oscillate with no apparent cause, and patients may see flashes or black objects in the corner of the eyes. During physiological or psychological stress, the sympathetic nervous system has a fight-or-flight response and the pupils become dilated, and visual attention is restricted to finding the best way to escape or to better visualise the threat.

Witnessing scenes and images impacts emotions and memories and vice-versa, and is the basis of visual flashbacks in post-traumatic disorders. When asleep and dreaming, during the phase of rapid eye movements (REM phase) the eyes also are working. They work by participating in the adjustment of memory, emotions, cognitive and physical processes, making vision an active part of unconscious life as well. The technique of Eye Movement Desensitization and Reprocessing (EMDR; Shapiro, 1995), used for the treatment of psychological trauma, incorporates rapid eye movements in psychotherapy sessions to facilitate the integration of traumatic experiences in an awakened state. The effectiveness of the EMDR technique evidences the close connection between the eyes and psychological life.

In therapy, eye contact between patient and therapist is "silent speech" and, combined with verbal communication, allows the nuances of the therapeutic relationship to be understood. Eye gaze informs the therapist of the fluctuating emotional states of the patient such as fear, suffering, sadness and more.

Eye Relaxation

Vision is processed through imperceptible and constant movements of the eyes. As we saw previously, even when we dream the eyes are moving and actively processing information. Considering the importance of vision for most of our day-to-day activities, relaxing the eyes is a key priority in taking greater care of oneself. A simple way to relax and lubricate your eyes is to gently blink.

As mentioned above Meir Schneider's Self-Healing method uses self-awareness exercises. Light is blocked from reaching the eyes by covering them with the palms of the hands. This position is maintained until you observe the blackness of your own eyelids. Stay in this position for a few moments. This exercise aims to interrupt optic nerve activity and to give the eyes time to rest.

Another exercise allows the eyes to adjust to different intensities of light by turning one's face towards the sun, keeping the eyes closed during the whole exercise and moving one's head slowly from side to side.

These eye-care techniques allow finely-detailed visual perceptions the time to recuperate so as to obtain an improvement in visual acuity. However, Ribeiro (2003) indicates in her lecture on balance and vision that the areas related to vision often carry so much latent tension that these exercises may not be sufficient to engender a state of relaxation:

> If we anxiously seek immediate results from eye improvement exercises, we fall into the trap of silent and harmful tension. The expectation of results provokes tension and this, in turn, makes any transformation difficult. (Ribeiro, 2003, p. 8).

Ribeiro (2003) further asserts that massage and relaxation techniques awaken somatosensory perception and prepare the visual system for greater readiness.

Subtle Touches (Sándor, 1974) to the skin in the eye region provide deep relaxation, which may engender a calming of the mind, relieving a state of vigilance or even hypervigilance, and allowing a state of quiet observation free from self-criticism.

In this state of consciousness, we are more likely to develop a much-needed sense of conscious vision, free from prejudgements and preconceptions.

Suzana Delmanto (1997), in her book Subtle Touches, notes that touches made to the eyes, head and neck, improve visual acuity and reduce stress. In cases of progressive visual impairment, this method aims to stimulate the regenerative capacities of the visual system, by lessening tensions that may be contributing to visual degeneration.

The process of acquiring conscious vision begins with the awareness of one's own body — of its limits and needs, as well as the interpretation of somatic images, thoughts and emotions, weaving an individual pattern of self-perception and worldview.

Calatonia of Sight seeks to relieve tension in the eyes and the mind through touch, to increase physical awareness of the body and to access somatic images associated with it, and thus improve visual readiness and well-being.

Calatonia of Sight

Calatonia of Sight has been used since 2007 in Brazil in the context of clinical psychotherapy and visual therapy. The effects of Calatonia of Sight have been observed and recorded for approximately ten years of clinical practice by Nassif (Gonçalves & Nassif, 2008), generating a body of consistent experiential knowledge. More scientific research is needed and will be developed for the further validation of the approach in the field of visual perception.

The sequence of touches used in Calatonia of Sight begins with the subtle touch stimulation of the areas around the eyes, forehead and temples.

The first four touches recreate a sequence analogous to the first four touches made to the toes in classic Calatonia, albeit in the region of the eyes where the orbicular, frontal and corrugator muscles are located. The thumbs are placed on the top of the forehead forming an arch (see number zero in Figure 1), and are kept there for the duration of the four initial touches.

The fifth touch, analogous to the touch made to the hallux (toe) in Calatonia, is made above and in the centre of the zygomatic bone (see number five in Figure 2).

The sixth touch is made in the region of the temples. The seventh touch is made just below the temporomandibular joint and both are analogous to the touches made to the soles of the feet in Calatonia (see number six in Figure 2).

The last two touches (in the occipital region and seven of the cervical vertebrae) are analogous to the touches made to the heel and calf in Calatonia.

The Calatonia of Sight may either be conducted on its own or immediately following the sequence of Calatonia made to the feet. The average duration is nine minutes, one minute for each touch, or 15 cycles of breathing at each point.

Clinical Observations

In clinical practice, it has often been noted that the onset of visual impairments is related to overstress, trauma or some unexpected event in one's life. It is usually something that the person could not see or did not want to see as it would result in breaking some established life pattern. Pathologies as a defence mechanism against a perceived vulnerability or threat; as a consequence, a psychological barrier (e.g., denial) may be created and may find a correspondence in the physical body.

In their anamnesis, when asked about possible connections between the visual impairment and stress, many patients report the presence of an intense stressor, such as a fight with family members, partners or an institution — some event that for that person was particularly difficult or even impossible to deal with satisfactorily. For example, a patient with vascular encephalopathy who was unable to see in a part of the visual field stated that when her husband left her with four small children, life had "faded" for her.

Calatonia of Sight is aligned with the principle taught by Sándor which is to accompany the patient's process without prior expectations and not to create expectations of spe-

The Calatonia of Sight: Learning to See the World with Relaxed Eyes and Greater Awareness

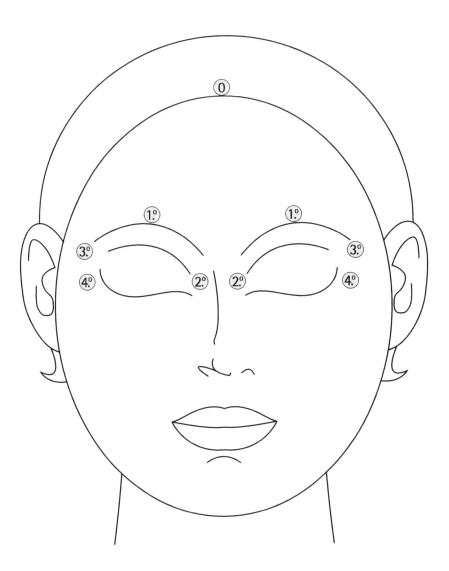

Figure 1

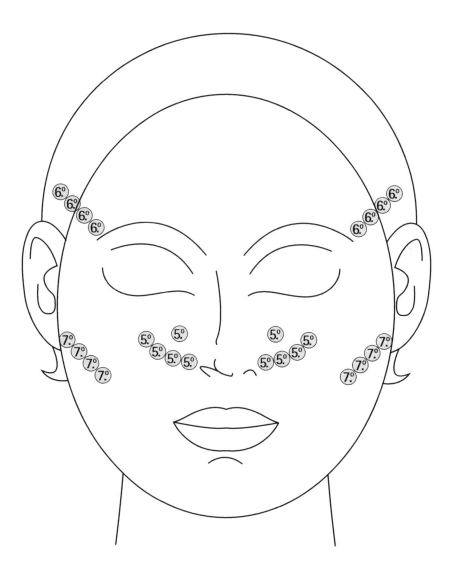

Figure 2

cific results in the patient. In the meeting between patient and therapist, a "field" is visualised as a "third point", in which the qualities of conscious, unhurried and careful observation of the patient can be held.

Clinical observations have shown that touches to the eye region promote deep relaxation, even in individuals who cannot normally rest their minds when they experience the classic Calatonia to the feet. Patients report that Calatonia of Sight induces a state of relaxation that starts from the face and spreads from the back to the feet in a segmental and profound way, as if perceiving this process from the axis of the body.

A few patients seen in private practice reported some discomfort during the first four touches of Calatonia of Sight, at the point where the thumbs join at the top of the head to form an arch (point zero in Figure 1). For others, when the same region was touched it promoted a feeling of great well-being described by one patient "as if the body came in from the outside through the top of the head" (sic). This difference may be a fruitful area for future observation and exploration of meanings.

In patients receiving regular Calatonia of Sight treatments, a layered loosening of the orbicularis and facial muscles was observed. Calatonia of Sight has also been shown to be effective in situations where there is an intense demand made of the individual's mental and visual skills. In the context of testing, evaluation and examination, these touches allow patients to gain enhanced calm and confidence. Some patients reported that when applied before bedtime these touches allowed them to fall asleep more quickly and be more well-rested afterwards.

Calatonia of Sight provides a space for the body, the eyes and the mind to unclench, and from that state we can perceive how our thoughts, emotions and tensions influence our vision of the exterior and the interior. "If we are to enter conscious vision, we need to become aware of how light affects us from within, as well as what it tells us about what goes on outside" (Kaplan, 2003, p. 16).

An older woman, who was brought to the first appointment by her daughter, did not wish to attend psychotherapy. She had already tried a modality of psychotherapy but had given up as she did not find the treatment to be effective. She showed obvious resistance to treatment. In the first interview, the therapist explained that the Calatonia method of therapy included a body-based approach and the patient accepted this option. After a sequence of tapping and massage with a foam ball on her back, she reported a sense of release and well-being. For this reason, she decided to continue treatment and became particularly responsive to Calatonia of Sight.

    She reported that the touches to her head made her feel "as if her thoughts were tidy and her head was light". Everything went surprisingly well until one of her daughters to whom she was most attached, said she was planning to move to another country. She started to show clear physical, emotional and mental changes. She did not sleep well, she felt sad, and negative thoughts took over her mind. She believed her daughter was doing something crazy, and was being irresponsible for leaving behind her career and an organised life. This continued until her daughter wrote her a letter so that she could read and re-read the real reasons and context behind her decision to move. Interestingly, reading the letter immediately calmed her down - her eyes were conveying the message to her brain and she could find peace.

    When she was distressed, rereading the letter gave her comfort, whereas verbal reassurances had no such effect as they formed only a temporary auditory register. Her daughter's move profoundly affected her balance and her therapy process, leading her to once again see herself as sick and insecure. She compared herself to the goddess Demeter who became increasingly desperate after her daughter Persephone's abduction. In her process of acquiring a more conscious mode of vision she knew that her daughter's choices challenged her, and that she had to learn to accept the decision that her daughter had made. Calatonia of Sight contributed by diluting her mental tensions and allowing her to re-evaluate ideas, feelings and emotions.

Another woman who was diagnosed with glaucoma and severe visual impairment in one eye, came to sessions after surgery to reduce the intraocular pressure which causes glaucoma. She had difficulty seeing and walking. She was leaning on her husband's arm as she was afraid of falling, even though she did not have any motor problems. She was depressed.

All her sessions were based upon exercises specifically formulated for vision, including the Meir Schneider Self-Healing method, massage and subtle touches. She received the classic Calatonia and Calatonia of Sight, and the latter was without a doubt her favourite point of therapy, where she was able to relax and feel good about herself.

After a few months, her improvement was obvious and she began to attend therapy unaccompanied. Her general outlook changed; she became cheerful, confident and smiling, and practised the exercises with dedication and ease when at first, she had felt incapable. Upon her return to the ophthalmologist, she showed a surprising overall improvement as well as an improvement in visual acuity.

Final Considerations

The technological revolution has created virtual possibilities that have changed how human beings relate to time, space, oneself and each other. These changes may suit the mind but not necessarily the body, which requires real-life interactions in real time-space boundary to achieve and maintain health and balance.

This new technology delivers information and mental stimulation that reach us mostly through our eyes, and deeply affects memory and our perception of the world: "the human being retains in memory about 11% of what he hears, three percent of what he smells, two percent of what he touches and 83% of what he sees" (Miranda, 2000, p. 255). If what we see makes up most of the content stored in our memory, are we aware of the images that formed and form us? When we are overstimulated by outside images that are wholly different from the images generated in moments of inner quietude, are we allowing ourselves to be alienated from our inner core?

Calatonia of Sight facilitates detachment from an excessive consumption of visual and mental information. It may help to break a stereotyped pattern of engagement with the external world. When this stereotyped pattern is broken, there is an opportunity for us to give our attention to inner images, thereby gaining greater "insight".

Most importantly, vision is associated with language, which names and attributes meaning to what we see. The language also creates a narrative which enables us to communicate what is seen. This narrative integrates visual process, perception, memory, discernment and meaning. For this reason, it becomes even more significant to include vision and the eyes as part of the therapy process. To improve one's psychological health means to 'see' oneself and others under a new light or from a different perspective; only then may a new narrative unfold.

Finally, Calatonia of Sight fosters an awareness of how we see the outside world and sensitises us to the images of our inner world, helping to integrate outer and inner vision. Such a process of integration paves the way for empathy and compassion for self and others (Arcuri, 2005; Armando, 2006; Penna, 2005).

References

American Psychiatric Association (2013). *Diagnostic and Statistical Manual of Mental Disorders (Fifth ed.)*. Arlington, VA: American Psychiatric Publishing.

Armando, M. D. (2006). A calatonia e o numinoso. *Hermes, 11*, 138-146.

Benevides, M. L. S. (2006). Calatonia: Um método de psicoterapia profunda em psicossomática. *Hermes, 11*, 7-19.

Conte, D. L., & Gabriel, M. S. (2009). Contribuição à Prática da Psico-oncologia "Toque-Sutil: Um método de trabalho corporal em Psico-oncologia". In Sociedade Brasileira de Psico-oncologia (SBPO). *Boletim Eletrônico, VI*(4).

Cortese, F. (1998). Cinesiologia Psicológica: Integração físio-psíquica. *Hermes, 3*, 32-37.

Delmanto, S. (1997). *Toques Sutis: Uma experiência de vida com o trabalho de Pethö Sándor*. São Paulo, SP: Summus Editorial.

Farah, R. M. (2008), *Integração psicofísica: o trabalho corporal e a psicologia de Carl Gustav Jung*. São Paulo, SP: Companhia Ilimitada.

Ghazanfar, A. A., & Schroeder, C. E. (2006). Is neocortex essentially multisensory? *Trends in Cognitive Sciences, 10*(6), 278 – 285.

Gonçalves, M. G. C. R., & Nassif, V. F. (2008). A Calatonia da Visao: Aprendendo a ver o mundo com olhos relaxados e mais conscientes. *Hermes, 13*, 22-31.

Gorodscy, R. C., & Tosi, S. M. V. D. (1987). *Calatonia: uma experiência clínica*. São Paulo, SP: Temas.

Guggenheimer, R. (1950). *Creative Vision in Artist and Audience*. New York, NY: Harper & Brothers.

Hammer, N., Glätzner, J., Feja, C., Kühne, C., Meixensberger, J., Planitzer, U., Schleifenbaum, S., Tillmann, B. N., ... Winkler, D. (2015). Human vagus nerve branching in the cervical region. PloS one, 10(2), e0118006. doi:10.1371/journal.pone.0118006

Jeka, J. J., Oie, K. S., & Kiemel, T. (2000). Multisensory information for human postural control: integrating touch and vision.

Experimental Brain Research, 134, 107-25.
Kaplan, R. (2003). Visão Consciente. São Paulo, SP: Mercuryo.
Kozeis N. (2009). Impact of computer use on children's vision. Hippokratia, 13(4), 230-231.
Lemos, L. H. C., & Henry, B. (2005). Psicoterapia e Toques Sutis. Hermes, 10, 18-25.
Miranda, E. E. (2000). Corpo: Território do Sagrado. São Paulo, SP: Edições Loyola.
O'Rahilly, R., & Muller, F. (1982). Basic Human Anatomy. Philadelphia, PA: W.B. Saunders.
Penna, L. (2005). O tempo e o espaço na calatonia. Hermes, 10, 92-100.
Reed, G. M. (2010). Toward ICD-11: Improving the clinical utility of WHO's International Classification of mental disorders. Professional Psychology: Research and Practice, 41(6): 457-464.
Ribeiro, M. F. L. (2003). Equilíbrio e Visão. São Paulo, SP. Unpublished manuscript, author hardcopy.
Sándor, P. (1982). Técnicas de Relaxamento. São Paulo, SP: Vetor.
Schneider, M. (1998). Manual de Autocura: Método Self-Healing. São Paulo, SP: Triom.
Schneider, M. (2005). Movimento para Autocura. Self Healing: um recurso essencial para a saúde. São Paulo, SP: Cultrix.
Shapiro, F. (1995). Eye Movement Desensitization and Reprocessing: Basic Principles, Protocols, and Procedures. New York, NY: Guilford Press.

12

Calatonia in Child Psychotherapy of Early Childhood Trauma

Ana Maria Galrão Rios

Our essentially social species depends on intersubjectivity for survival, which may explain why human beings are, for the most part, highly empathic. The mirror neuron system, described by Gallese (2008), provides us with the ability to automatically read the intention behind another's actions and forms one of the neurological bases for emotional resonance between all individuals; especially between a child and a mother. This chapter examines the use of somatic psychotherapy for the treatment of attachment issues.

For a healthy development, babies need a caretaker who is emotionally attuned. In addition to forming a bond, the adult caregiver needs to be able to respond to the child's demands efficiently in terms of physical and emotional needs (Araujo, 2011).

Although babies have an inborn ability to recognise the emotional states of other individuals (at their respective developmental level of resonance) and to communicate their own mental states, it is the adult's responsibility to attribute symbolic meaning to the child's expressions in the first place. An adult caretaker should mirror a baby's emotions to empathise with them, soothe them and provide a safe space for their expression. Communication between babies and caregivers is nonverbal, gestural and prosodic, and such communication is present throughout a child's life, built from the tonic dialogue between a child's body and the caregiver.

Siegel and Solomon (2003) state that integration of information, events and circumstances into a coherent and functional whole defines adequate development - a development in which anxiety does not become paralysing for the child. The quality of the early relationships that a baby establishes with caregivers will facilitate or hinder the on-going process of coherent integration of information, since psychological development takes place via intersubjectivity.

Children are exposed to high levels of anxiety, even chronic trauma, when there is a lack of access to sensitive caregivers capable of assigning proper meanings to the baby's expressions and of meeting their physiological and emotional needs in a timely manner. Overwhelming anxiety can be experienced, for example, when children are unable to understand or assign meaning to what is happening; thus, they feel unsafe. Outbreaks of anxiety may often occur before a functional ego has established itself. Trauma is defined here as an experience that cannot be integrated or understood within a coherent life narrative.

Relaxation techniques facilitate a patient's ability to re-experience traumatic elements in the therapeutic process (Siegel & Solomon, 2003). This is accomplished through a context of affective modulation, as the trauma is softened or lessened by being evoked in a welcoming environment. Verbal therapy has its limits and verbal interpretation loses its effectiveness when a traumatic episode was caused by inappropriate somatic dialogue between a child and her/his parents. That which occurred prior to the spoken word is best engaged outside a linguistic and rationalised approach. Siegel and Solomon (2003) state that the process of focussing on multiple levels also changes the subjective experience of mental states, which increases acceptance of intense and dysregulated emotional states.

The re-creation of memories triggered within an affectively regulated relationship with the therapist can lead to a new configuration of more integrated self-representations. This can occur through processes of codification, reorganisation and recoding. In this context, the adverse effects of traumatic re-experiencing gradually seem less devastating depending on the flexibility of the individual's psyche.

Therapy could then promote not only resilience in the face of adversities, but provide healthy development after the experience of trauma, helping in its elaboration within a more fluent and integrated narrative of life.

Psyches that Communicate: The Psyche and its Transformation in Somatic Psychotherapy

In child psychotherapy, we count on the possibility of a child being able to transform their behaviours and attitudes in the face of the difficulties they encounter in their development.

To achieve this transformation, child therapy offers playing, practising, creating and re-creating the world within the boundaries of the therapist's office, and the sense of pleasure that comes with it. Fantasy and role-play allow for the anticipation of future possibilities, experimenting with new resources, developing empathy through role exchange, and broadening one's understanding of reality. When they play, both therapist and patient drift together in a world full of symbols.

The way the patient relates to the therapist at the beginning of therapy is likely to reproduce the emotional tone found in previous relationships. When the therapist is able to observe the patterns of transference established through therapy, they are better equipped to understand the nature of the attachments that the patient tends to form. The engramic elements from previous relationships can remain operative throughout an individual's life.

Relaxation and body awareness techniques introduced in

child psychotherapy can facilitate diagnosis of the quality of the child's primary relationship with the mother. This work can promote the establishment of trust between the child and the therapist through this form of creative regression. It provides an opportunity for a transferential relationship to be established, with the conscious and unconscious dynamics that this entails.

Using the hypothesis of neuronal plasticity (Cozolino, 2010), we can see that the brain, in an attempt to adapt the individual to their circumstances, reinforces some neural networks as selected responses to the demands of life. But the brain is a social organ which is liable and open to influences and it can reconfigure itself and offer new adaptations when the social environment changes, bringing new challenges and new possibilities.

The patient's modes of perception, understanding, affect and action are organised according to his or her implicit memories (Siegel, 1999). These modes can be transformed at all stages of life when different meanings are attributed to psychological content and to verbal or non-verbal communication. They can also be transformed in therapy when the individual is unable to do so unassisted. A different self-perception in the individual's relationship with others can configure new neural networks or reconfigure previous ones.

Experiencing the self in therapy allows a re-creation of states experienced by the individual at the beginning Therapeutic environments offer holding, containing, setting boundaries, and attentiveness to the meaning of the child's behaviours, which may often be disorganised because they are new. From the outset, the therapist is expected to show syntony with the development of the child and this attunement often requires affective contact. Child psychotherapy is effective insofar as it is an experience-laden, embodied intersubjectivity (Johnson, 1987) that promotes the occurrence of new representations and integrations.

One of the factors that promote adequate psychological development is the ability to modulate affect, which is dependent upon communication between the right cerebral hemispheres of any two persons in reciprocal emotional resonance. Just as the brain matures and the psyche develops within meaningful interpersonal relationships early in life (Stern, 1997), so does progress in therapy depend on these same conditions. Therapists can use emotional attunement, attachment, tactile stimulation, containing and holding, and the capacity for symbolic understanding of the patient's symptomatology as transferential tools.

Non-verbal, tactile techniques, such as Calatonia and Subtle Touch, offer the experience of being together with another person in a way that can be both new and surprising, in contrast to previously established implicit patterns. This is possible because these techniques rely on a conditioning induced by regular, consistent, predictable and repetitive (although novel initially, and always unusual out of the therapy context) stimuli.

An emotionally engaged therapist can function as a kind of autobiographical assistant, allowing the patient to change their life narrative. In other words, the therapist must help the patient to construct their inner world, which both therapist and patient are capable of recognising through verbal and non-verbal communication. This inner world is distinct from the external world yet is related to it, thus, the patient can re-signify his or her experiences.

Interpretation of the content produced by the patient is useful for gaining a greater awareness of the patient's internal states. The accuracy of these interpretations improves when there is an empathic relationship between therapist and patient, and often allows for margins of error on the part of the therapist. The desynchronisations that eventually occur in these interpretations help the patient to discriminate between himself/herself and the meaning of the other, a differentiation that is a necessary part of the construction of their identity.

A person who has a good relationship with another allows that person to be different. In such a relationship mistakes are made and amended, and intrapsychic and interpersonal dimensions are discriminated. In the dance between approach and avoidance responses, a secure bond is established that gives rise to mistakes and apologies.

Syntony is a primarily unconscious process even though it is used consciously as a tool by the therapist, and it cannot be feigned. True emotional involvement with a child is required for their process to unfold. Thus, the patient-therapist relationship is strong enough to significantly change the child's expectations of the world and his/her ability to tolerate frustration and act creatively in the face of adversity. In a profound connection, both patient and therapist are transformed.

A Clinical Case Study

Bruna's grandmother sought therapy for her granddaughter who, at age seven, had paralysing anxiety attacks. She couldn't complete tests at school even when she studied hard for the subject, and suffered from insomnia, moodiness and irritability the week before the test. She was unwilling to accept help and wanted to do everything herself even when she had difficulty, often giving up before she had completed the exercises.

Bruna is an adopted child. At the age of two she was taken into foster care by the police after reports of maltreatment by her natural parents. She went to live with her four-year-old sister in an orphanage which she remembers as a nice place. They stayed there for two years. At the age of four they were adopted by a single woman, who had suffered from romantic disillusionment (she was abandoned by her fiancé shortly before their wedding), to enable her to find a fulfilling role in her life thereby avoiding depression.

At that time, Bruna only remembered that she thought it very strange to have to change her name. Their adoptive mother became increasingly depressed and was very impatient and angry with the children at first, and was then confined to bed, dying a year later. Bruna commented that although she was told that her mother had died from a heart attack, she thought that her mother actually died *"from her feelings"*. Their adoptive maternal grandmother took care of the girls. This grandmother, who had separated from her husband shortly before her daughter's death, raised the two children with the help of a nanny. In her will, their adoptive mother had left a trust fund for the two girls, which allowed the family to live in comfort and security.

Following her evaluation, Bruna showed signs of a resilient attitude: in a house-tree-person test, she drew a tree that burgeoned with fruit, and "everything that people need to live". She displayed an insecure connection to the therapist, expressed her annoyance at having to leave at the end of each session and became anxious during the holidays, when away from therapy. During periods of separation, she frequently wanted to take something from the therapist's office as a symbolic object. This was an attempt to ensure that she had something to remind her of the therapist's presence and to maintain her connection to the therapist.

From the beginning of therapy, she responded very well to body-based approaches. She often requested massages and subtle touch sequences and, even when joking or telling a story, she placed her foot in the therapist's lap for a massage. She often requested massages with creams, oils and alcohol gels to experiment with different textures and sensations. She greatly benefitted from therapy, even in sessions in which she became irritated and refused to say anything, sitting with her back turned to the therapist.

She showed an interest in gardening but often pulled the seedlings out from the soil as soon as they sprouted, not giving the carrots enough time to grow so they could be eaten. Radishes, beans and flowers met the same fate. While gardening, she began to play with mud and became interested in moulding the clay. However, showing the same anxious attitude she displayed at school, she couldn't model anything. She invariably became dissatisfied and destroyed her final work, and turned everything into a shapeless mess or, at most, a pizza.

The therapist understood that Bruna did not have a fixed

maternal figure and suffered many setbacks that prevented her from attributing a form to an undifferentiated mass. The therapist encouraged Bruna to work with plaster. Plaster powder mixed with water consists of a soft mass, which hardens while drying into a form. Bruna was supplied with a plaster mould which she could use to model and paint, and she was very happy with the initial result. After extensive exploration Bruna switched to different materials, using the same process but with chocolate, soap, and finally wax, to make candles.

Bruna went back to using clay after much experimentation with the different materials that therapy offered her. She was now able to manifest her inner content in a satisfactory way and began to mould snakes: "*they bite us and make us bleed; we defend ourselves by swallowing snakes but then snakes can bite us from the inside*". In one of the sessions during this period, she took the notebook that the therapist used to make notes at the end of each session and tried to maintain a sense of continuity by writing: "*Today was a very nice day because we discussed swallowing snakes. We are learning to heal the wounds. It's really cool*".

The snakes continued to be ever-present but instead of being swallowed, they moved into a more symbolic field by retreating to a doll's house, launching attacks from within and causing great turmoil. Slowly, the all-female family of Barbie dolls who lived there learned to deal with the snakes. The dolls drove the snakes out and put up protective mechanisms so they couldn't get back in through the doors and windows that also protected against the storms, earthquakes and other disasters that assaulted them. Usually, Bruna left all the parts of the house dismantled when she left at the end of each session, showing some anxiety but also laughing at herself and challenging herself: "*You want to see how I'll get on?*" In the next session, she built the house again and continued the game.

Shortly afterwards there was a play at her school to which Bruna invited the therapist, insisting strongly that she come. When the therapist set a boundary at this point, Bruna became very quiet for a few sessions until the day of the play, hoping that the therapist would attend. She then sent the following letter by post:

> São Paulo, November 18, 2005
> *I was sad because you didn't go to my play, but I imagined you watching me. You know, that's why I didn't say much in your office. But I really like you and sometimes we have to deal with this stuff.*
> *A big big kiss from Bruna.*

Bruna clearly had developed a permanent representation of the object of her desire, a guarantee of the continuity of attachment, the ability to build and repair, and a resistance to frustration without her anxiety giving way to disorganised behaviour.

Soon after she began to learn the (Catholic) catechism and to prepare for her first communion. She had to choose a godmother and thought about this very solemnly, because she understood that they would be her mother's substitute. Bruna described the following dream in therapy: "The city of São Paulo turned into a nightmare and we were walking down the street to buy bread. There were men who would go around beating people and beat them so hard until they were red and even the adults would cry. So, then Z. (her nanny) was walking with me and my sister to buy bread. My sister and I were small and so Z. took the beatings for me and my sister. And they hit her very hard. She was beaten instead of me. And then we managed to sneak away and get home". During the session in which Bruna recounted this dream, she later bathed and took care of a doll that represented her nanny and asked me to administer a relaxation technique on the doll. As I applied the relaxation technique on the doll, she told me that she had chosen her nanny to be her godmother. From that moment on, she started to refer to her nanny solely as "Dindinha" (auntie).

Bruna showed resilient behaviour right from the beginning of therapy. She was a good-natured survivor of severe trauma and saw it as funny having her name changed instead of doubting her own identity. She told her old name to friends in secret, saying that everyone had secret names. She said that if the therapist didn't have one, she could give her one. Bruna helped the therapist realise that her (Bruna's) life path held many secret names and that over time she could make greater sense of this contradiction.

Her resilience increased throughout the course of therapy, and the therapeutic relationship became ever stronger. She became more competent in school and in social relationships. She perceived and named her emotions more clearly and could express them properly. Gradually, she began resolving and balancing her internal and external demands. Her sister, however, who had much the same life story, had not yet managed to find a balance between competing demands, was unsuccessful at school and had serious difficulties in adjusting socially. Bruna was worried about her and asked me, "*Is she going to have a future or not?*", and asked herself: "*Am I going to have to take care of her?*". The significant differences in the levels of competence necessary to deal with adversity between the two sisters points to the multifactorial complexity in the development of resilience.

A few years after the end of therapy, Bruna, now a teenager, came back to the therapist. She was suffering from anxiety attacks again, triggered by her relationship with a boy she had fallen in love with at a holiday camp. Bruna said that she "*was using her exclusion glasses once again*".

This statement exemplifies the workings of implicit memory and its role in the dynamics of complexes (Cohen, 2013). When describing her feelings of anxiety, she could discriminate her dissociative mechanisms saying that "*I wanted to feel that when I was doing something, anything that I had chosen and wanted to do, I could feel it, concentrate on it. I feel like I'm outside of myself – I'm a dreamy and imaginative person, I just wanted to be there. I don't feel things*". She ended the session by saying, "*I came back to feel like myself again and to relax, talk and be massaged*".

Final Considerations

There are several body-based techniques suitable for use in child psychotherapy. The main technique used in Bruna's case was that of Calatonia (Sándor, 1974).

When physical contact is incorporated into child therapy in the form of a relaxation technique, it becomes an act of surrender: allowing one's body to be touched by another person trusting that they will not cause any harm; pledging to expand one's consciousness; and surrendering one's ego to the dynamics of the organising centre of one's personality, the Self (Jung, 1991).

Personality development runs along a path of organisation, disorganisation and reorganisation of patterns in a continuous flow of mental states, which presupposes occasional periods of imbalance leading to a trajectory of constant transformation. Supporting these phases of imbalance is necessary for the continuity of the patient's process. Often these periods are characterised by the emergence of new content from the unconscious, which does not have a structured form yet, hence it will not lend itself easily to communication. There are often no words to express this emergent experience.

So, even if there is an implicit knowledge of what is being lived, which forms the basis of understanding, we often need to be able to give this knowledge some conscious form of expression, "What can only be implicitly grasped at first must, at a later time, be recoded and described in language" (Knox, 2004, p. 10). This is true for all stages of life and is a fundamental aspect of analytical work.

The atmosphere of tranquillity provided by relaxation through Calatonia allows negative emotions to be re-experienced and freshly associated with more harmonious sensations. Hence, an individual's implicit memories may be anchored to more adaptive patterns in the future. Although not all the details of a patient's mental and emotional states can be translated into words, the sense of security afforded by being comfortably relaxed alongside another person facilitates this new reorganisation.

While explicitness or awareness of action planning and the patterns of how one perceives the world are key goals in child psychotherapy, often the transformation of unconscious patterns through tonic dialogue with the body is sufficient for enhancing well-being and resilience.

The images and expectations that children hold of their world and the internalisation of that world in terms of their subjective experience are shaped by several factors:

- shared experiences between the child and the primary caregivers;
- the child's ability to withstand temporary failures when emotionally attuning to the environment;
- the creation, withdrawal, resistance, construction and deconstruction of relationships;
- the oscillation between harmony and disharmony;
- the achievement of harmony by emotional modulation, a necessary step for psychological growth.

A healthy person is one who remains stable, flexible and positive when confronted with the mystery and insecurity that lie at the heart of existence. One must be creative in the face of challenges and able to find regulation and modulation in oneself, in one's body and in the unknown that lies within the body, in the hope of attaining the great experience of meaning which occurs in transpersonal containment (Jung, 1931).

References

Araujo, C. A. (2011). Psicologia Analítica. In F. B. Assumpção, & E. Kuczynski (Eds.), *Tratado de Psiquiatria da Infância e da Adolescência*. São Paulo, SP: Ed Atheneu.

Cohen, B. (2013). Tangled Up in Blue: A Reappraisal of Complex Theory. In J. Kirsch, & M. Stein (Eds.), *Why and How We Still Read Jung* (pp. 417-425). London, UK: Routledge.

Cozolino, L. (2010). *The Neuroscience of Psychotherapy: Healing the Social Brain*. New York, NY: Norton.

Gallese, V. (2008). Mirror neurons and the social nature of language: the neural exploitation hypothesis. *Social Neuroscience, 3*(3), 317-333.

Johnson, M. (1987). *The Body in the Mind: The Bodily Basis of Meaning, Imagination, and Reason*. Chicago, IL: University of Chicago Press.

Jung, C. G. (1968). Archetypes of the collective unconscious (R. F. C. Hull, Trans.). In H. Read et al. (Eds.), *The collected works of C. G. Jung* (Vol. 9/I, 2nd ed., pp. 3-41). Princeton, NJ: Princeton University Press. (Original work published 1954)

Jung, C. G. (1966). The aims of psychotherapy (R. F. C. Hull, Trans.). In H. Read et al. (Eds.), *The collected works of C. G. Jung* (Vol. 16, 2nd ed., pp. 36-52). Princeton, NJ: Princeton University Press. (Original work published 1931)

Knox, J. (2004). From archetypes to reflexive function. *Journal of Analytical Psychology, 49*, 1-19.

Sándor, P. (1974). *Técnicas de Relaxamento*. São Paulo, SP: Editora Vetor.

Siegel, D. & Solomon, M. F. (2003). *Healing Trauma: Attachment, mind, body and brain*. New York, NY: W. W. Norton.

Stern, D., (1997). *A constelação da maternidade*. Porto Alegre, RS: Artes Médicas.

13

Pethö Sándor's Method and Drawing: A Case Study

Lúcia Helena Hebling Almeida

This chapter describes a clinical case to demonstrate the value of integrating non-verbal expression (drawing) and somatic approach (Subtle Touch and Calatonia) coupled to Jungian psychotherapy, in the treatment of an adolescent with body image and self-esteem issues.

For Sándor, deep psychology is imbued with the idea of the opposite poles of tension and distension in constant action, and this rhythmic interchange produces homeostasis on a physiological level, while on the psychological level it appears as a drive for synthesis (Sándor, 1974, p. 10). This drive serves as an activating point for a new phase of integrative endeavour, in which consciousness is expanded following a period of crisis or conflict.

This integration can be observed both in terms of the body, which achieves a better posture, with less muscle tension and fewer physical symptoms, as well as in terms of improved psychological stability. A more (physically) relaxed and well-balanced individual carries this attitude over to their emotions, thoughts, relationships, and day-to-day life. Sándor's somatic techniques contribute to a process of muscle-tone regulation and to the spontaneous autonomic adjustment of the organism, allowing the patient to experience an exuberant outflow of unconscious content in safety, during a session.

Jungian psychotherapy (Jung, 1991) opts for a dialectic method based on genuine engagement and inquiry between therapist and patient, in which the therapist does not adopt a position of authority and superiority. This allows the individual to reveal himself as he is, wholly and without judgement.

Within this dialectic and integrative perspective, a patient led me to include drawing as a non-verbal therapeutic aid in her clinical treatment, to help this patient create symbols for her process and to anchor her progress in 'visible' indicators.

Drawing is a well-known and widely used instrument for psychological diagnosis as well as being a means of non-verbal communication in therapy. It allows freedom of expression in a way that bypasses the critical mind, whilst the somatic therapy gives the individual the strength to surrender to their inner processes. In this case, Jungian psychology provided a sound theory for understanding and integrating both, the symbolic (drawing) and bodily (somatic) processes that occurred in therapy.

The Body and the Formation of Identity: Implications for Somatic Psychology

Many writers have held forth on the body, body image and the formation of identity from a psychological perspective, noting that individuals build a sense of identity through their own experiences with the body within a social context (Dychtwald, 1984; Santin, 1992; Erikson, 1974; Schilder, 1981; Feldenkrais, 1979; Montagu, 1988).

Body image plays a role in identity development, being the created mental representation of one's physical self, and the thoughts and feelings that are associated with that perception. It is subject to distortions from internal elements such as emotions, moods, early experiences, and other idiosyncratic influences, as well as external elements, parental attitude, social media, and peer acceptance, for example.

It is therefore, a multidimensional construct that addresses the quality of one's experiences of one's body, particularly its appearance (Kamps & Berman, 2011). It encompasses dimensions such as self-perceptions, beliefs, attitudes, and cognitive, emotional and behavioural responses to one's appearance. It has two core facets: the degree of happiness with one's own body and the psychological value placed on appearance. The feelings resulting from the combination of all these elements can be positive, negative or both, linking body image to self-esteem (Kamps & Berman, 2011).

Erikson (1974) considers that the development of erogenous zones and muscle tone contributes to the development of a child's identity. This basic identity changes when adolescents start to explore various possibilities and begin to form their own identity based upon the outcome of their explorations. In this period, there may be great discomfort about their body and the changes they undergo, until they can adapt and accept bodily, emotional and cognitive changes, and as they grow, they reintegrate their sense of self.

Dychtwald (1984) highlights the concept that our "bodymind" is the result of emotional, psychological and psychosomatic experiences accumulated over the course of our life, as the ways we feel and act in the world affect, model and structure our body. Thus, a person who is rigid in terms of their patterns of thought and behaviour will also show this same rigidity in their body, such as muscular tension in their shoulders and neck, for example.

Schilder (1981) states that this postural model of the body is formed after a period of maturation and that this period is directly dependent on and connected to individual experiences, physical training and emotional attitudes generated by continuous contact with the outside world. He also highlights that an illness can modify this perception thereby impacting on one's body image, posture and libido of the body.

Individuals who dislike their own body usually have a corresponding negative self-image. This may impact their posture (kyphotic posture), or may make them to feel depressed, and often, may lead them to cut off contact with others. By contrast, if an individual begins to form a positive self-image, this may lead to their opening up in relationships, and to straightening or greatly attenuating their kyphotic posture (Almeida, 1999).

Montagu (1988) states that body awareness develops through the skin, stressing that tactile stimulation is of fundamental importance for a healthy development. He also observes that psychosomatic disturbances are associated with a lack of maternal care, and that these disturbances are more likely to occur in people with deprived early childhoods. Since the early studies of Montagu, research on the neuroscience of touch (Ravaja et al., 2017; von Mohr, Kirsch, & Fotopoulou, 2017), particularly research conducted in the past decade by McGlone and Olausson (McGlone, Wessberg, & Olausson, 2014), has emphasised the emotional and psychological significance of tactile history in human development (Feldman, 2004; Serino, & Haggard, 2010).

Currently, there are many different somatic approaches tailored according to each practitioner's views of the interface of body and psyche (Caldwell, 2018; Hartley, 2004; Heller, 2012; Kurtz, 2007; Marlock, Weiss, Young, & Soth, 2015; McNeely, 1989; Sandor, 1974), which provide extensive support and breadth for somatic psychology.

McNeely (1989) asserts that somatic therapy facilitates the identification of the content of a "complex" (Shultz & Shultz, 2009), as a core pattern of emotions, memories, perceptions, and wishes agglutinated around a theme or a universal pattern of experience, or archetype, such as motherhood or power. According to McNeely, somatic therapy helps in the resolution of a complex and fosters the development of one's potential held back because of the unconscious nature of a complex. The embodiment of a complex can be "seen" when a certain part of the patient's body is touched, thereby triggering the patient's awareness of memories, feelings, thoughts which had previously remained unconscious (Harris, 2000).

Feldenkrais (1979) reported using non-verbal directions and 'consciousness through movement' to improve a patient's range of motion, flexibility and coordination. As Feldenkrais explained, one moves according to one's perceived self-image, and reciprocally, by expanding perception and self-awareness, the self-image will change. As a consequence, new motivation and new behaviours will appear. The Feldenkrais's somatic re-education method has influenced many somatic psychotherapies, particularly the work of Levine (Payne, Levine, & Crane-Godreau, 2015) for the treatment of psychological trauma.

Guimarães (1990) also agrees with the importance of using somatic techniques and integrative methods in psychotherapeutic practice, as these methods allow for "a communication between intellectual and experiential learning in the patient's treatment" (Guimarães, 1990, p. 4). She asserts that a body-based approach provides a therapeutic bridge between physical symptoms and psychological symptoms.

The Use of Drawing in Jungian Psychology

Jung (1991) believed that artists projected part of their psyche onto matter or inanimate objects, as the alchemists did before them. Thus, the artist is not as free as he appears to be: his work will always be controlled by the rules of the unconscious psyche. According to Jung, the primary goal of modern artists is to express their inner vision of man and secondly to give vent to the spiritual and mundane aspects of the world (Jaffé, 1979). Similarly, individuals can express emotional disturbances not only verbally, but also by giving a visible form to their affects through images, such as by painting or drawing. Jung (Almeida, 1999) encouraged some of his patients to freely develop an image of a dream and to express it through dramatisation, writing, dancing, painting, drawing or modelling, because he realised that by combining the image with an action, the unfolding of unconscious processes could be observed.

Nise da Silveira (1981), a Brazilian pioneer in the field of psychiatry, based her work on Jung's psychology to treat hospitalised schizophrenic and psychotic patients. She understood, as Jung did, that artistic processes held elements that could offer therapeutic access to the subjectivity of the individual, mediating between the inner and outer world. Based on this principle, in the mid-1940s, she offered her psychiatric patients painting and art classes, a resource that is commonly used today in many mental health institutions. In addition, she saw drawing as a means of giving space and perspective to contain the invasive material streaming from the patients' unconscious. Therapeutic value can be found not in the work of art as a finished product, but in the process of creation that expresses one's subjectivity and allows for the elaboration of intra-psychic conflict (Giglio, 1994).

Furth (2004) took into account three important assumptions necessary for understanding the language of drawings, first that they originate in the same locus from which dreams emerge - the unconscious; second, drawings must be accepted as a valid and reliable method of communicating with the unconscious, and that they are equally reliable as analytical tools in psychotherapy; third, in the interpretation of drawings, it is assumed that mind and body are interconnected and that they communicate, so the body is also expressing itself in the drawing, not only the mind. For Furth, the cathartic effect of drawing allows the portrayed symbol to give new direction to the psychological energy, leading the person out of the conflict or paralysis, and thus assisting with the healing process.

Case Study

K was fifteen years of age and in the first year of secondary school; her parents took her to psychotherapy due to her aggressive behaviour and social withdrawal. She had almost no friends, barely got herself out of the house, and had low grades at school. K did not like her body because she was overweight, and wore only black clothes. In therapy, she presented symptoms of depression, spoke very little, and answered questions in monosyllables.

The images presented in this chapter were selected from the drawings made by K following the application of relaxation techniques, during our sessions of psychotherapy. The analysis of the drawings was paralleled with K's progress in therapy, and interpreted symbolically (Almeida, 1999; Chevalier & Gheerbrant, 1989; Machover, 1949; Moraes, 1979; Souzenelle, 1994).

K initially refused to do the Machover's Projective Drawings Test (Machover, 1949), which consisted of monochrome drawings of a house, a tree and a person, each one on an individual sheet of paper. However, she did agree to draw something of her own accord, and drew the following picture (Figure 1):

Figure 1

After her initial drawing, K's ability to express herself through drawings became clear, and I decided to use drawing as a therapeutic tool. I offered K relaxation techniques as part of her therapy, which she accepted. The sessions were divided into two parts: receiving somatic work first, followed by her drawing how she felt about her body afterwards. The somatic work started with a series of Subtle Touch techniques (Sándor, 1974).

I used the following passive relaxation techniques with this patient: a tennis-ball massage to the back and front of the body, a gentle face massage (Annex 1), the Michaux Relaxation Technique (Ferreira, 1974), spinal vibrations, and Calatonia (Sandor, 1974), which was made to the feet or hands in alternating sessions (Annex 2).

The type of relaxation technique used in each subsequent session was adjusted according to what K had drawn at the end of the previous session. For example, Calatonia could be applied in one session while the Michaux Relaxation Technique could be applied in another, and so on, depending on the area of the body that seemed to need more activation.

The first technique used was the tennis-ball massage (Annex 1) over the patient's whole body (back and front), followed by a gentle face massage. After that sequence, K drew the following picture (Figure 2).

Figure 2

The half-finished face indicates her difficulty communicating and interacting socially, as the face represents the individual's social front (Machover, 1949). This drawing confirms the basis for the concerns of K's parents, as it is indicative of someone who is very closed and insular.

In the following session the patient drew how she felt about her body (Figure 3), again following the tennis-ball massage and gentle face massage.

Figure 3

In Figure 3 we see the whole mouth. According to Chevalier and Gheerbrant (1989), the mouth is the opening through which air, words, and food pass – the opening to receiving nourishment and to voicing one's thoughts and feelings. The mouth is the first means by which we incorporate the world; the newborn child experiences the outside world at first-hand through their mouth.

This organ, which serves the breath (spirit) and enunciates words, logos, and singing, symbolises creative power and the insufflation of the soul. Thus, it represents the possibility of a higher state of consciousness, a power which creates order through reason.

All subsequent drawings were made after somatic work, in different sessions.

Figure 4

In Figure 4, the face appears, albeit covered by hair. The arms and legs are partially drawn, the neck is short and the shoulders align geometrically.

In Hebrew, the word corresponding to the neck is *tsavvar*, which contains the root word *tsadé* whose meaning is the divine hook which catches man to carry him up to the divine light. The 'stiff-necked' man is one who does not allow himself to be caught by the 'divine hook', who refuses, therefore, "to let himself spout forth at his source" (Souzenelle, 1994, p. 244).

The neck symbolises a bridge between the head (consciousness and thought processes) and the body which manifests unconscious physiological processes, instincts, the irrational world, and emotions (Almeida, 1999). The neck contains the throat, which reacts very rapidly and markedly to emotions and anxieties that may affect speech and communication.

The shoulders, here drawn in a geometric, squared and stylised way, are symbols of power and controlled force, according to Chevalier and Gheerbrant (1989). Shoulders represent the possibility of building, acting, completing a task, the power and capacity for protection, help, aid, responsibility and defence.

According to Souzenelle (1994), the Hebrew word for shoulder *(shekhem)* is used for the part of the body on which heavy loads are carried, and means 'term' or 'end'. The biblical meaning is 'to get up early', referring to the dealings with loads and work, and in this way, figuratively, the shoulders indicate a 'new dawn'.

The appearance of legs indicates the potential for interacting and closing distances in order to reach people or situations. In this sense, legs symbolise social commitments (Chevalier & Gheerbrant, 1989).

In Figure 5, the face has become softer and more cheerful and the body's contours have become more rounded, especially the shoulders, yet the body is still out of proportion. Only now the chest is represented.

Figure 5

Figure 6 represents a jump to a much broader expression. The hair is light and free-flowing and the face is graceful, the neck and shoulders are well-proportioned, the chest is sketched out and one can note the clavicle, the etymology of which is 'small keys'.

Figure 6

The chest is the region of the activated heart (Almeida, 1999), it evokes feelings, mood, affect, love, and some of its related physical manifestations, such as palpitations and tachycardia.

Chevalier and Gheerbrant (1989, p 260) noted that the Dogons of Mali, West Africa, view the clavicles as the seat of human nutrients. For this tribe each clavicle is a granary containing eight seeds that are associated with the four elements and the four cardinal points, among other things. They believe in the vitalising force of this bone, so much so that they crush animal clavicles to powder and mix it in with seeds to improve the yield of the harvest.

In Figure 7, the hair has been removed completely from the face, making it fully visible. According to Chevalier and Gheerbrant (1989), the face is the language of silence, because without saying anything, it shows our 'intimate self' to others, being more revealing than the rest of the body. When a face no longer expresses inner life, it becomes merely a mask:

> It is the seat of the sense organs and for this reason, it symbolises the evolution of the living being from darkness to light. It is the quality of its radiance that distinguishes the demonic face from the angelic. (Chevalier & Gheerbrant, 1989, p. 790)

Figure 7

The face, as the most expressive part of the body and most important communication centre, becomes the individual's social marker. It marks us out as an individual more than any other part of our body, and allows us to be identified as individuals.

The somatic techniques used in the 7th session were complemented by the Michaux relaxation technique (see Annex 2), as well as Calatonia performed on the feet.

Nine months after the start of therapy, the hands and feet were finally drawn in Figure 8. The number 'nine' (months) is charged with symbolism. According to Chevalier and Gheerbrant (1989), nine months appear to be a natural measure for the incubation of a creative process, which ends in fruitful culmination – such as pregnancy. The number nine represents the idea of a birth and new germination, beginnings and endings, the closing of a chapter.

Figure 8

Hands express the concept of activity, power and domination. In Far Eastern languages, the expressions 'to reach in' and to 'take one's hand' mean to start and finish a task (Chevalier & Gheerbrant, 1989). Feet represent a down-to-earth approach, but also power, decision, departure and arrival. Moraes (1979) conducted an extremely well-detailed review of feet and their symbolism in Calatonia, affirming the importance of feet for balance and movement as they provide support for the steadiness of the body and the personality, as well as for the flexibility 'to walk' in and out of the inner and outer world, figuratively.

Souzenelle (1994) reminds us that the feet increase the power of the body, hence the reason why practices such as acupuncture and reflexology focus so greatly on them. She also symbolically interprets the Christ washing the feet of his apostles as a gesture of blessing and healing. Christ says to Peter, "unless I wash you (your feet), you have no part with me" (John 13:8). Christ tells the apostle Peter that by having received the blessing, Peter can pass it on in the same way: "Now that I, your Lord and Teacher, have washed your feet, you also should wash another's feet" (John 13:14).

Figure 9

Figure 9 is more feminine and delicate, more well-proportioned and shows more sensibility. Its beauty speaks of a blossoming and healthy femininity. The female figure bears flowers that symbolise the product of an inner alchemy – a flowering, a return to one's centre, a unity, a resumption of the cycle of life. It is an archetypal image of K's soul and represents her spiritual centre, as well as "the attributes of spring, dawn, youth, rhetoric and virtue" (Chevalier & Gheerbrant, 1989, p. 437).

Conclusion

This chapter presents the idea described by Leloup (1996) that therapy involves taking care of one's body, and self, and the world, embracing the soul, its Peace, its Health and its everlasting Life. Through K's therapeutic process, a face is unveiled along with a renewed sense of identity. There is a clear depiction of how Subtle Touch techniques helped to restore a healthy development.

At the beginning of therapy, K showed a partial body image, because her emotional bluntness prevented her from closer contact with her body. One's body representation can be constantly modified by sensorimotor experiences – that is, the environment alters and refines body representation (Williams, 1983). In K's case, therapy provided the sensorimotor road on which to travel through what was symbolic, imaginary and real.

During her treatment, K did not take psychiatric medication - with the support of Sándor's techniques and psychotherapy, her depression subsided. As her body awareness improved, she lost weight, and her social avoidance ended. She became less aggressive with her parents and began to make friends. K's grades improved, and her beautiful drawings caught people's attention and revealed her artistic skills. At the end of the treatment, she was accepted by the university to study Style and Fashion.

Drawing is a useful technique for patients who have difficulty in abstracting and verbalising, it enables them to heal and reconstruct that which was considered inscrutable, incurable or lost (Alessandrini, 1996). The representation that K had of her body was disfigured, scattered, disproportionate and rootless, without depth. By giving form to her feelings and emotions in images, she was able to relate to them and assimilate them as a lived process (Almeida, 1999).

Awareness of one's body depends on body representations and involves both perceptual and motor elements as well as conceptual and cognitive ones.

The observation of K's progress through her drawings is a remarkable evidence of the mind-body processes that led to the treatment results. It is hoped that these results will inspire other psychotherapists to appreciate the usefulness of these techniques in clinical practice.

Annex 1 – Tennis-ball Massage

A gentle massage, using a tennis ball as an intermediary between the therapist's hand and the patient's body, made to the front of the body beginning on the foot which corresponds to the patient's dominant side of the body. The movements are then made travelling upwards towards the head, normally in a straight line except for the joints, where a circular motion is made. The same procedure is repeated on the patient's back.

Once completed, the patient turns back over to their front and soft strokes are made to the face, and the therapist ends by lightly rubbing the patient's scalp with their fingertips.

Annex 2 – Spinal Vibrations

The patient lies down on their stomach. The therapist brings their right index finger, middle finger and thumb together to vibrate each vertebra of the patient's spine, from the sacrum to the seventh cervical vertebra.

The therapist begins by gently placing their hand on the patient's sacrum and counting three respirations. On the fourth respiration, the therapist vibrates the vertebra by gently shaking it sideways. On every fourth respiration that the patient makes, the therapist moves the three right fingers (index, middle and ring finger) up the spine to the next vertebra, towards the cervical vertebrae.

If the patient breathes too quickly or too slowly, the therapist can follow their own calmer breathing rate. The most important thing is to follow a rhythm.

References

Almeida, L. H. H. (1999). *A psicologia organísmica, a psicologia junguiana e a utilização de desenhos: uma reflexão para a educação física* (Unpublished master's thesis). Paulista State University, Rio Claro, Brazil.

Caldwell, C. (2018). *Bodyfulness: Somatic Practices for Presence, Empowerment, and Waking Up in This Life*. Boulder, CO: Shambhala Publications.

Chevalier, J., & Gheerbrant, A. (1989). *Dicionário de símbolos*. Rio de Janeiro, RJ: José Olympio.

Dychtwald, K. (1984). *Corpomente*. São Paulo, SP: Summus.

Erikson, E. H. (1974). *Infancia y sociedad*. Buenos Aires: Horme S.A.E.

Feldenkrais, M. (1979). *Caso Nora*. São Paulo, SP: Summus.

Feldman, B. (2004). A skin for the imaginal. *Journal of Analytical Psychology*, 49: 285-311.

Ferreira, L. M. (1974). Relaxamento em Crianças com o método de Leon Michaux. In Petho Sandor (Ed.) *Técnicas de Relaxamento* (36-43). São Paulo, SP: Vetor.

Furth, G. M. (2004). *O mundo secreto dos desenhos: uma abordagem junguiana pela arte*. São Paulo, SP: Paulus.

Giglio, J. S. (1994). Técnicas Expressivas como Recurso Auxiliar na Psicoterapia: Perspectiva Junguiana. *Boletim de Psiquiatria, 27*(1), 21-25.

Guimarães, M. T. B. (1990). *Novos caminhos no processo educacional para alunos de graduação em psicologia: o método Feldenkrais* (Unpublished master's thesis). Pontifícia Universidade Católica de São Paulo, SP, Brazil.

Harris, J. (2000). *Jung and Yoga: The Psyche-Body Connection*. Toronto, ON: Inner City Books.

Hartley, L. (2004). *Somatic Psychology: Body, Mind and Meaning*. London, UK: Whurr Publishing.

Heller, M. C. (2012). *Body Psychotherapy: History, Concepts, and Methods*. New York, NY: W. W. Norton & Company, Inc.

Jung, C. G. (1991). *A dinâmica do inconsciente*. Petrópolis, RJ: Vozes.

Kamps, C. L., & Berman, S. L. (2011). Body image and identity formation: the role of identity distress. *Revista Latino Americana de Psicologia, 43*(2), 267–277.

Kurtz, R. (2007). *Body-Centered Psychotherapy*. Mendocino, CA: LifeRhythm.

Machover, K. (1949). *Proyeccion de la personalidad en el dibujo de la Figure humana*. Havana: Cultural S.A.

Marlock, G., Weiss, H., Young, C., & Soth, M. (2015). *The Handbook of Body Psychotherapy and Somatic Psychology*. Berkeley, CA: North Atlantic Books.

McGlone, F., Wessberg, J., & Olausson, H. (2014). Discriminative and Affective Touch: Sensing and Feeling. *Neuron. Cell Press. 82*(4), 737-755. doi: 10.1016/j.neuron.2014.05.001

McNeely, D. A. (1989). *Tocar: terapia do corpo e psicologia profunda*. São Paulo, SP: Cultrix.

Montagu, A. (1988). *Tocar: o significado humano da pele*. São Paulo, SP: Summus.

Moraes, L. P. (1979). *Calatonia: a sensibilidade, os pés, e a imagem do próprio corpo em psicoterapia* (Master's thesis, São Paulo University, SP, Brazil). Retrieved from http://bibliotecadigital.fgv.br/ojs/index.php/abp/article/view/18809.

Payne, P., Levine, P. A., & Crane-Godreau, M. A. (2015). Somatic experiencing: using interoception and proprioception as core elements of trauma therapy. *Frontiers in Psychology, 6*, 93. http://doi.org/10.3389/fpsyg.2015.00093

Ravaja, N., Harjunen, V., Ahmed, I., Jacucci, G., & Spapé, M. M. (2017). Feeling Touched: Emotional Modulation of Somatosensory Potentials to Interpersonal Touch. *Scientific Reports, 7*, 40504. http://doi.org/10.1038/srep40504

Sándor, P. (1974). *Técnicas de relaxamento*. São Paulo, SP: Vetor.

Santin, S. (1992). Perspectivas na visão da corporeidade. In A. Gebara, & W. W. Moreira (Eds.); *Educação física & esportes: perspectivas para o século XXI*. Campinas, SP: Papirus.

Schilder, P. (1981). *A imagem do corpo: as energias construtivas da psique*. São Paulo, SP: Martins Fontes.

Serino, A., & Haggard, P. (2010). Touch and the body. *Neuroscience* and Biobehavioral Reviews, 34(2), 224-236. doi: 10.1016/j.neubiorev.2009.04.004

Shultz, D., & Shultz, S. (2009). *Theories of Personality* (9th ed.). Belmont, CA: Wadsworth, Cengage Learning.

Souzenelle, A. (1994). *O simbolismo do corpo humano*. São Paulo, SP: Pensamento.

von Mohr, M., Kirsch, L. P., & Fotopoulou, A. (2017). The soothing function of touch: affective touch reduces feelings of social exclusion. *Scientific Reports*, 7, 13516. http://doi.org/10.1038/s41598-017-13355-7

14

Psychotherapy, Synchronicity and Subtle Touch

Beatriz Vianna Henry
Luiz Hildebrando Lemos

With regard to the use of subtle touch techniques in psychotherapy, the central issue is one of the relationship between the body and the psyche. As such, we will start from this point of duality and attempt to reconnect and bring together these opposing poles. Through this investigation we have formulated some additional questions and reflections that we would like to share with the reader.

Subtle Touch is a body-based technique which is applied methodically as an integral part of psychotherapy sessions. We have chosen to refer mainly to the basic sequence of Calatonia as described in the book *"Relaxation Techniques"* (Sándor, 1974), which is a unique form of touch and therefore the neural pathways generated by such contact with the skin are free of the conditioned responses associated with everyday forms of touch. The session, which is done in silence, begins when the instructions are given, followed by the sequence of touches, and ends when the therapist asks for the patient's observations. This state of silence allows both therapist and patient the opportunity for inner reflection.

The fact that the application of Calatonia is both all-encompassing and touches all levels of the individual – physical, emotional, mental, and spiritual (Armando, 2006; Farah, 2017; Sándor, 1974) – can be clearly seen from the patient's remarks at the end of the session when asked for her/his observations. Sensations, perceptual changes, emotional responses, visual images and passing thoughts are just some of the common outcomes from the experience. For example: "I felt I was sinking into my bed", "I felt as if I were floating in the air", "I felt something running through my body". An emotional response such as, "I suddenly felt a vague longing and I wanted to cry"; an image such as, "I saw myself floating in space and wires were coming out of my toes which were connected to your fingers and that was my connection to the Earth", or, "I had the feeling that my legs and arms were turned upwards, swaying, as if they were the tops of a tree in the wind and my belly were the roots".

Every therapist who uses this method has heard about and reported on patients making similar observations to the ones above. In order to be able to report on their observations the patient needs to pay attention to their organism as a whole and, more specifically, to the way unconscious content is made manifest. This once unconscious content appears as it is: distinct and detached from the ego, and as it takes shape, the patient is able to talk about it. The patient, encouraged to observe and record internal events, can develop an attitude towards them that takes into account the importance of unconscious elements for their own personal development. The patient develops the hard-won ability to be a non-interfering observer of background phenomena, which we define as part of the unconscious and in counterpart to consciousness. This active and careful attention to what occurs in the unconscious leads to a state of acceptance towards apparent inner chaos, allowing oneself a glimpse of the meaningful relationship between these two states of being.

Thus, the questions we ask at the end of a session of Calatonia are of fundamental importance as the technique will become part of a method of psychotherapy. It builds a bridge between the experiences elicited by the touches and their verbal expression: it defines the window through which we see, understand and act as psychotherapists.

There is a parallel between this form of body-based technique and the active imagination which Jung described as a way of experiencing and exploring the unconscious when we are awake. It consists in voluntarily lowering one's level of consciousness and waiting for the unconscious to freely produce an image, which we can then experience and eventually even "converse with". This "conversation with the personification of our complexes" (von Franz, 1979, p. 28) opens the way to what we call "unconscious content integration", which forms the goal common to all deep forms of psychotherapy: self-knowledge and psychological growth. The integration of unconscious elements requires us to transform our self-awareness, so that it is in harmony with our existing self-image. Usually, elements previously dormant within the energy field of a complex are projected onto the external world, because they are antagonistic to our self-image. We speak here of personal growth as all individuals function more effectively by knowing themselves better – by making their own choices rather than being impelled to act by reasons of which they are not aware – and consequently gaining a greater level of freedom.

We have to consider the fact that few people can claim that the elements of their unconscious mind are as real to them as the objects of the outside world, as Jung did in his memoirs (Jung, 1986). Most of us must walk a long road towards self-knowledge, on a path that has been trodden by those who came before us. Jung is one of these pioneers and has left us many indicators and signposts which enable us to face the journey with greater security. Thus, a first step on this journey is to experience at first hand a meaningful connection between the different levels of one's existence.

The training or conditioning which the patient undergoes

by the methodical application of Calatonia enables them to observe what happens in the background of the psyche without interfering with its flow. As therapists, by listening without judgement to the comments that patients make after a session of subtle-touch, we partake in the patient's search for meaning and connection, opening and maintaining a dialogue with the mobilised unconscious material, in the same way we do with dreams. Psychotherapy, as we understand it, does not have a definitive answer since it is a joint search, thus, a reductive interpretation is less desirable: "ah, that's because of such and such". We would be better able to participate in the patient's unique experience of their situation by being open to what they tell us. This is what Sándor did over the course of his life: he listened to his patients, and asked his students to record the experiences which resulted from their work experiences. This posture of openness is one of the key foundations of the method.

The silence and introspection that occur during the session of touches can lead to a regulation of muscle tone that most often produces a state of relaxation. In this state, a dialogue with the unconscious occurs and may result in psychophysiological reconditioning when it is experienced regularly, over time.

The connection between body and psyche is not merely one of cause and effect, as Jung discovered (1984b). A cause-effect relationship presupposes that the effector is distinct from that which is affected. When we consider the body and psyche as a duality with complex relationships that have not been fully unravelled, we are assuming that the boundaries between each pole of this duality are neither clear nor definite. This idea is analogous to one that appeared in the physics of the early twentieth century, in which the distinction between matter and energy became blurred when Einstein concluded that "a body's mass is a measure of its energy content" (Einstein, Lorentz, & Minkowsky, 1983), often simplified to "matter is energy". Heisenberg (1901-1976) formulated the 'uncertainty principle' in quantum mechanics in 1927, imposing constraints on the precision with which simultaneous measurements can be made on the location of an electron and its momentum (defined as the product of the mass and velocity of an object), the electron thereby lost its contour of matter. This phenomenon was also described when Louis de Broglie, in 1924, proposed the wave-particle duality, which states that electrons have both wave and corpuscular characteristics. Electrons behave in one way or another, depending on the specific experiment and the person conducting it. In this way, the observer's point of view is key to determining which aspect of reality will be highlighted. Thus, the duality of body and mind can also be considered in its complexity, subject to human experience and not as something definite and fixed.

Jung elaborated the concept of an *archetype*, defined as "an inherited and pre-existing disposition, a formative principle of instinctive power, which can be expressed through physical reactions or mental representations (images and ideas)" (Stein, 1978, p. 30). He suggested that "matter and spirit meet in the archetype" (Stein, 1978, p. 60). He used the term "Unus Mundus" to designate the unity of existence that forms the basis of the duality of psyche and matter, a transcendental whole that underlies the empirical world of appearances and which is not commensurate between the world of so-called matter and so-called psyche (Jung, 1984a; Jung, 1990; von Franz, 1974; Young & Dawson, 2002). Thus, two seemingly different things are interleaved in a way that we cannot easily access through our habitual state of awareness; they can only be seen through an expanded form of consciousness - that is, from another point of view.

Taking this view of reality, Jung formulated the concept of synchronicity which he used to express the inseparable link between psyche and matter, and the relation between internal and external events based on their analogy or meaning, leading to a causal ordination between events.

For Jung, causal methods alone are insufficient in accounting for psychosomatic issues: instead, there appears to be a relationship of synchronicity between the body and the psyche (Jung, 1984b). Just as one can causally link emotional states to physiological sequelae (e.g., fear to diarrhoea, stress to ulcer formation) there are psychosomatic phenomena for which it is impossible to seek a causal relationship, and a range of variations between one extreme and another.

Some observations made in the course of applying Calatonia exemplify the occurrence of this phenomenon of synchronicity: "It's hard to describe, but I swear the underside of my leg was fighting with my heel". This mental representation of physical tension or bodily representation of an emotional conflict can be read as a byproduct of synchronicity: two aspects, the corporeal and the mental, are linked through a synchronicity of meaning.

Another observation was made during a Calatonia session with a priest of a syncretic Afro-Brazilian religion, in whose rituals the priest often incorporates (channels) a spirit or entities. When the therapist conducted the sequence of Calatonia touches he (the therapist) had a creeping sense of fear. At the end of the sequence the patient reported that the entity he had manifested in his rituals had been present during the session.

We interpret this event as an example of synchronicity, whereby the therapist and the patient were interlinked: yet while the patient viewed this experience as an habitual event, the therapist felt it to be a uniquely frightening experience. Both patient and therapist had characteristics in common, such as empathy and a mutual connection, as well as a shared experience of the field of transference which forms the basis of the therapeutic setting. This observation corroborates Hans Dieckmann's research into transference and countertransference, in which he comes to the conclusion that "the Self constellates the synchronicity of fantasy in two individuals" (Young & Dawson, 2002, p. 160), and the observation of Schwartz-Salant that "therapy is a process in which two people mutually constellate the unconscious... the countertransference... is based on the development, both in the patient and the analyst, of the ability to experience and participate in a shared imaginary domain, which exists out of space, time and any notion of causality..."

(Young & Dawson, 2002, p. 161).

It's also common for anyone who works with subtle-touch techniques to hear, at the end of the sequence, something like this: "you seem to have guessed that it was my head" (or other part of the body) "that needed to be touched today". Something seems to be happening in the connection between the patient and the therapist during Calatonia, which somehow mobilises the therapist, even if they are not clearly aware of it, and spontaneously directs the therapist to touch certain areas of the patient's body. Sándor encouraged us to follow our intuition when applying Subtle Touch techniques. He also instructed us to imagine a point situated far above the Calatonia table, forming the point of a triangle between the therapist and the patient indicating a neutral, non-polarised point between the two, in order to avoid misunderstandings such as "passing energy to the other". This also provides the therapist with a means and motivation to become an instrument or vessel for something greater than their own desires and goals. This point, which Sándor called a "third point", is a mental representation of the archetypal world; its formation from three elements evokes the symbolism of the number three (Jung, 1984c; von Franz, 1974). "With the presence of the third term, tension is undone and the lost whole reappears" (Jung, 1979, p. 180) - by introspectively placing oneself in this archetypal field, the therapist re-conditions his attitude and point of view.

It is undoubtedly the first step on a path full of pitfalls to use subjective phenomena to guide one's actions, and it is therefore necessary to differentiate genuine intuition from one's desires and daydreams. This applies even more so to the training of therapists who seek to employ these methods of therapy in their own practice: they must necessarily go through a long phase of practical experience in applying and receiving the techniques. This ability can be developed through repeated sessions of Calatonia in the therapist's own process of analysis and supervision.

Thus, one can observe an additional effect of this way of

working - namely, an increase in the probability of synchronous phenomena. These events, in addition to creating a distinctive field of transference, are useful for guiding clinical action and frequently for understanding the time-course of analysis. Roderick Main (2007) surveyed how synchronicity phenomena are used in clinical practice, from Jung and his immediate disciples until 2007. Based on his survey, Main states that the frequency with which synchronicity occurs may depend on the therapist's focussed observation of synchronicity over the course of the therapy process.

Jung stated that synchronous phenomena most likely occur when there is an emotional intensity present which is brought about by the constellation of an archetype (Jung, 1984b). He states that this reaction is due to a corresponding decrease in the level of consciousness, and "Jung noted that there is a complementary relationship between the processes of consciousness and the phenomena of synchronicity. Thus, the phenomena of synchronicity always occur when a significant amount of psychic energy becomes submerged in the unconscious, i.e., becomes unconscious" (Frey-Rohn, 1971, p. 289).

However, these phenomena are also observed during Calatonia, in which an unconscious threshold is lowered through relaxation and the patient is led to adopt an attitude of observing without interfering with what is observed. Rather, this mental quieting allows for a change in one's mental disposition in such a way that the phenomena of synchronicity occur and can be perceived with greater clarity and equanimity, allowing for a greater integration of their underlying meaning.

It is interesting to find this insight in a book about ancient knowledge, with a different vocabulary and point of view:

> It is possible to read a closed book which one has not read before. It is possible, at will, to know the time by mentally evoking an image of a clock. Also, it is possible to remove all obstacles through the Fire of Space. People call this phenomenon clairvoyance, but it is better to call it

a burning vision. But one should note that this burning potential is not always the same. In addition, one should note that great shocks can improve this ability, just as total rest can. (Rörich, 1933, p. 148)

What this author calls burning vision, we can also call synchronicity.

Thus, in seeking to answer our initial question about the relationship between the body and the psyche, we comment on the place occupied by Subtle Touch techniques in psychotherapy. Summarising, these techniques: shift the levels of awareness and extend the inter- and intra-psychical exchange beyond the verbal; create a transferential field peculiar to this method; provide a regulation of physical, affective and mental tonus; and finally, attain a quietude that encourages the occurrence of phenomena of synchronicity, which may guide the therapeutic process towards the creation of meaning and transformation.

References

Armando, M. D. (2006). A Calatonia e o Numinoso. *Hermes*, 11, 138-146.

Farah, R. (2016). *Calatonia: Subtle Touch in Psychotherapy*. São Paulo, SP: Companhia Ilimitada.

Einstein, A., Lorentz, H. A., & Minkowski, H. (1983). *O Princípio da Relatividade*. Lisbon: Fundação Calouste Gulbenkian.

Frey-Rohm, L. (1971). *De Freud a Jung*. Mexico: Ed. Fondo de Cultura Econômica.

Jung, C. G. (1984a). *A Natureza da Psique*. Petrópolis, RJ: Ed. Vozes.

Jung, C. G. (1984b). *Sincronicidade*. Petrópolis, RJ: Ed. Vozes.

Jung, C. G. (1984c). *Psicologia e Religião*. Petrópolis, RJ: Ed. Vozes.

Jung, C. G. (1986). *Memórias, Sonhos e Reflexões*. Rio de Janeiro, RJ: Ed. Nova Fronteira.

Jung, C. G. (1979). *Interpretação Psicológica do Dogma da Trindade*. Petrópolis, RJ: Ed. Vozes.

Jung, C. G. (1990). *Mysterium Coniunctionis Vol 2*. Petrópolis, RJ: Ed. Vozes.

Main, R. (2007). Synchronicity and Analysis: Jung and After. European Journal of Psychotherapy and Counselling, 9(4), 359-371.

Roerich, H. (1933). *Mundo Ardente, vol 1 – Signos de Agni Yoga*. Rio de Janeiro, RJ: Fundação Cultural Avatar.

Sándor, P. (1974). *Técnicas de relaxamento*. São Paulo, SP: Ed. Vetor.

Stein, R. (1978). *Incesto e Amor Humano*. São Paulo, SP: Ed. Símbolo.

von Franz, M. L. (1974). *Number and Time*. London: Rider & Company.

von Franz, M. L. (1979). *A Alquimia e a Imaginação Ativa*. São Paulo, SP: Ed. Cultix.

Young-Eisendrath, P., & Dawson, T. (2002). *Manual de Cambridge para Estudos Junguianos*. Porto Alegre, RS: Artmed.

15

Calatonia and Resilience

Marilena Dreyfuss Armando

> *One of the simplest definitions of resilience is the resumption of new development after psychological trauma.*
> (Boris Cyrulnik, 2009)

Resilience is a fundamental aspect of psychological health and recovery from mental illness. For this reason, one of the goals in psychotherapy is to increase resilience to help patients manage anxiety, depression, trauma, among other issues, in a positive and adaptive manner. The use of somatic approaches such as Subtle Touch and Calatonia in clinical practice have demonstrated the potential of these techniques to increase resilience by strengthening the ego from its basis, the body. This chapter will examine some essential attributes of resilience, such as nourishing attachments and spiritual resources, understood here as an encompassing experience of an order higher than one's ego.

Pethö Sándor

To speak of Pethö Sándor is to speak of resilience. The life story of the founder of Calatonia is one of many examples of notable individuals who have been able to withstand vicissitudes, use them in their personal development and offer the results of this process to assist others.

Pethö Sándor graduated in medicine in 1943, specialising in gynaecology and obstetrics amid World War II. In 1945, at the end of the war, Hungary was invaded by Russia, a member of the allied coalition against Nazi Germany, because Hungary as well as neighbouring Bulgaria, Slovakia and Romania had been allied with the Axis powers (Germany, Italy and Japan). This led Sándor, along with his wife and two children aged two and three, to leave their home in Hungary in search of a country which could offer sanctuary. As they fled Hungary, Sándor worked continuously as a doctor in Red Cross hospitals in various refugee camps.

During this journey, there was one episode that clearly expressed both his humanitarian nature and his strength in the face of adversity. Whilst they were passing through Germany in May 1945, after the German surrender to the Soviet Union and the Allies, Sándor learned that his parents were in a nearby city held up on a train from Hungary, waiting for it to continue on its way. He was elated at the prospect of seeing them after such a long time. He met them in their carriage and, soon after being, his mother asked him for a glass of milk. After leaving the train to buy some milk at the station, he heard gunfire. He ran back and saw that the train had been strafed by American airplanes that had mistaken it for an enemy train - in it were only children and the elderly.

Sándor found his parents had been shot and killed. He did not hesitate to take care of the others who had been injured, as nothing more could be done for his parents. He worked tirelessly until the end of the day, when he walked to a nearby hill and only then allowed himself some moments of solitude to collect himself and express his grief. This attitude exemplified the way he lived his life: what came first was his work to help those who most needed it, a high form of altruism.

When he left Europe in 1949 he was a widower, his wife having died, at only 27 years of age, of pneumonia in a hospital which was not far from the refugee camps. He emigrated to Brazil with his two young sons, and there worked as a specialist in medicinal plants, as he had to wait a long time for his medical degree to be validated in Brazil. He later went to work in a chemical laboratory, which was one of the few options available to him until he mastered the Portuguese language.

By virtue of his open and multifaceted personality, he soon integrated himself within his local community, and as time went by, his neighbours frequently sought him out for medical advice. Little by little he began to offer psychotherapy to the local Hungarian community, as he was an avid reader and great admirer of Carl Gustav Jung's theoretical works. He set up his first psychotherapy practice in the mid-1950s and quickly became fully booked. He believed in charging his patients an affordable fee, and always accepted those who could only pay modestly.

Sándor was very sensitive towards his patients' needs and feelings and had a well-developed sense of intuition, as well as a remarkable erudition spanning several areas of human knowledge. In the 1960s, he spent most of his time teaching Jungian theory along with the somatic techniques he had created, and this specialisation differentiated him from other Jungian psychotherapists.

He also formed various groups for the study of Western esotericism (Hanegraaff, 2014). One phrase he liked to use, which aptly expressed his spiritual philosophy, was: "one should totally accept everything one experiences in life, even in the most arduous of situations, whilst remaining aware of the absolute uncertainty of living" (cited in classes).

Calatonia and Resilience

Constant changes in a complex and often threatening world, in which modernity, love, time, and life itself are excessively fluid, contribute to the construction of self-protective defences (Baumann, 2000, 2005, 2006). These defences prevent people from facing deeper and more complex inner issues which continuously accumulate throughout life, with the result that often they do not realise they are repeating the same defensive behavioural patterns. Consequently, many individuals do not develop an authentic resistance to adversity but rather a defensive structure based on fear and weakness, which often leads to depression, panic attacks, and so on.

According to Araujo (2006), stress is an inevitable aspect of the human condition, together with the other vicissitudes of modern life: unemployment, divorce, abuse and discrimination, drug addiction, chronic diseases, etc.

> Man, in the hypermodern age, is an individual who reveals different attitudes to his relations with himself, with others, with the world and with time. His existential anguish reveals itself in different ways: restlessness, voracity, dissatisfaction, stress and tension are just some of the mechanisms of psychosocial risk which affect his life (Araujo, 2006, p. 87).

The use of somatic techniques in psychotherapy, such as Calatonia and Subtle Touch, enhance one's ability to withstand stress, develop self-control and to perceive the body schema (Lemos & Henry, 2005). These are elements that contribute to the construction of identity and to building a new sense of self-confidence.

These techniques offer us the opportunity to establish a deeper therapeutic bond and trust through the reciprocity of touch. When the therapist touches the patient, he is also touched by the patient. As such:

The change which occurs with a touch also acts on the analyst. If the analyst is aware of the changes occurring in his own body, he can gain valuable information about himself and the patient, as a marker of transference and countertransference that would not otherwise be so clear. (Armando & Oliveira, 2002, p. 2)

The therapeutic bond that is then formed provides the patient with a secure and protected environment where he feels welcomed. In this context, the patient can unburden himself without fear of judgement, a factor that relieves his tension and facilitates the reduction and control of anxiety (Benevides, 2004), which contributes considerably to the development of resilience.

Another important element of touch is its integration with implicit memory (Siegel, 1999), which develops during the pre-verbal phase of infant development and is not directly accessible to consciousness. A therapist-patient interaction, mediated by touch, allows for the possibility of repatterning the implicit memories formed through the primordial relationship between mother and baby. By experiencing a new form of contact-touch at weekly intervals new neural circuitry is established, resulting not only in an expansion of synaptic plasticity but also in the relations with oneself and with others.

When Bowlby (1969) proposed that the mother-child relationship is founded on a set of innate signals from the baby, which requires closeness, he also established that this pattern is perpetuated throughout one's life as an adult. In the context of therapy, the therapeutic bond is also forged through the cognitive and emotional abilities of the patient, whether an adult or a child, through consistent application of care, and through the sensitivity and responsiveness of the therapist.

This theory is, in essence, a theory of regulation, and in this way Calatonia acts as a method for the facilitation of self-regulation and regulation of affective patterns. It also contributes to the modulation of the right cerebral hemisphere, through many afferent connections in the skin which regulate internal states and external relations with the environment.

Those individuals who do not receive a secure form of attachment may develop an aversive pattern of behaviour to novel situations, entering a state of anxiety because of their history of lack of response to their needs. In adults, as much as in babies, this anxiety can be located in the body. Thus, we can draw a parallel between the therapist and the individual's original caregiver (Rios, 2011).

Based on these views, the use of the Subtle Touch method as a non-verbal psychotherapeutic tool, aims to reach the layer of the unconscious where anxiety-inducing complexes are formed. Consequently, this process helps to rebuild early experiences in a trusting and safe environment. Trust and safety encourage a conscious surrender to the possibility of transforming one's fears and anxieties into resilient forms of behaviour.

This safe form of touch leads to a state of relaxation and to a decrease in vigilance levels in which a tonic dialogue with oneself (perceiving one's postural tension, physical pain, etc.) may occur. We refer here to tonic states as the basis of bodily states (Laranjeira, 2015). Implicit lifelong maladaptive patterns can be reorganised in this process in which psyche and body are treated and integrated, and meaning is ascribed to the patient's experience with the method. This opens up enormous possibilities for the reorganisation of the patient's affective life (Rios, Armando, & Regina, 2012).

The re-organisation of our affective life refers to the emergence of implicit patterns, images and sensations, which can be carefully nurtured and, if appropriate, interpreted within the patient's dynamics. However, when these emergent phenomena are more numinous or transcendent in quality, they may be simply accepted and validated to allow these phenomena to operate on implicit patterns without critical scrutiny or interpretation. The Subtle Touch techniques used by the trained psychotherapist follow a protocol that does not propose a religious or non-religious direction, leaving it totally up to the patient to attribute meaning to the numinous experience during their process.

Resilience and Spirituality

Today, spirituality is recognised for its role in the development and protection of the ego, and as a key agent of resilience. Spirituality can be understood as a deep feeling of transcendence, of belonging to something greater which unites us all and gives meaning to one's life, which may or may not include religion.

Tavares (2002) refers to spirituality as one of the deepest roots of human aspiration, stating that many studies directly link resilience to spirituality:

> One of the empirical studies which merits attention is that of Peres et al. (2007), showing that religious practices can have an important influence over how people interpret and deal with traumatic events – promoting resilient perception, positive learning experiences and self-confidence when dealing with adversity. (Tavares, 2002, p. 45)

Newberg, D'Aquili and Rause (2002) state that the highest level functions of the human mind developed from very simple neurological circuits linked to basic survival functions, such as those responsible for procreation, and that these circuits later became responsible for spiritual experiences. They reached these conclusions through an experiment monitoring brain activity in two groups: one group composed of Tibetan Buddhist monks in a state of meditation and the other composed of Franciscan nuns in a state of concentrated prayer. They identified a "religious brain" in human beings, and the structures which form part of this network developed from much simpler and more basic circuits. By using special technology, researchers identified the parietal lobes as playing a key role during this transcendental state. Both the left and right parietal lobes play a determining role in self-transcendence, the personality trait measuring predisposition to spirituality (Urgesi, Aglioti, Skrap, & Fabbro, 2010). Concerning the experience of the numinous in Calatonia, the parietal lobe integrates sensory information, including proprioception, the main sensory receptive area for the sense of touch as well as the major sensory inputs from the skin (touch, temperature, and pain receptors), relayed through the thalamus to the parietal lobe (Penfield & Rasmussen, 1950), which may substantiate some of the findings in clinical practice.

Newberg, D'Aquili and Rause (2002) state that there seems to be evidence of neurological processes which evolved to allow human beings to transcend material existence and to connect to the deepest and most spiritual part of themselves, which is perceived as "an absolute and universal reality" (Newberg et al., 2002, p. 9).

During an electroencephalographic examination which was carried out to monitor the effects of transcendental meditation on one patient, Persinger (1987) noted that this patient had an electrographic "abnormality" in the right temporal lobe. The patient reported that at the moment in which that "abnormality" was registered, she had felt 'the presence of God'.

Motivated by this and other findings, Persinger developed a method whereby patients were first blindfolded and then led into a soundproof chamber before donning a special helmet. Through this helmet, weak and complex magnetic fields generated by a computer were directed to particular areas of their brains. Many of the patients reported having felt the presence of a 'sentient being', and that this sense of presence corresponded to the prototype of the divine.

Marino (2005) explained that, since ancient times, experiences and beliefs about the existence of gods are normal properties of the human brain, having developed in our species as cognitive functions to facilitate our adaptability. Marino (2005) reasons that its primary function must have been to reduce anxiety about self-preservation and self-dissolution, which, had it not been controlled, would have interfered with our mechanisms of adaptation. Marino concludes that the experience of a subtle presence is an intrinsic property of the human brain, which leads us to think that spirituality is at the service of human resilience against perceived vulnerability.

Menegatti-Chequini (2011) refers to spirituality as the understanding of our sense of connection to a supreme and collective purpose, and for this reason, is a factor of resilience. For her, this connection transcends religious belief or practice and creates a state of communion with the universe. As such, spirituality is a factor capable of promoting and mediating resilience by transcending the sense of individual weakness and vulnerability.

In one study on the interrelationship between resilience and spirituality in cancer patients undergoing Jungian psychotherapy, Menegatti-Chequini (2011) found that the term resilience may define a process through which situations of adversity can be surpassed by transforming them into aspects of spiritual development. Jung (1978) defined religiosity, the term he used then to refer to what we now call spirituality, as directly linked to the relationship of the ego with the archetype of the Self.

Resilience and Contact with the Self

The Jungian concept of Self, as a unifying principle within the human psyche and as the origin and goal of psychic life, gives meaning and purpose to our actions, integrating them into a coherent whole. Rios (2008) states that the Self is experienced in the psyche as an instance of organisation and integration, greater than habitual consciousness, associated with totality and wholeness. In each individual there is an essential aspect of psychological development that leads to perceiving oneself as being connected to a higher plane (Rios, 2008).

Rios says that "from the standpoint of this higher plane, the struggles of daily life take on a new and expanded meaning because fantasies, dreams, infirmity, the accidental and the coincidental become potential messages from the invisible Partner (Self, in Jungian terms) with whom we share our life" (Rios,

2008, p. 10). Because of these encompassing and all-knowing attributes, the Self is equated to this higher plane, and thus with the experience of the numinous.

Jung (1978) used numinous to designate that which is sacred and deprived of rational characteristics, an intense psychic force. Jung took the term 'numinous' from Rudolf Otto (1992), who explained that the term "described the sacred, abstracted from its moral element and, even further, from the rational element" (p. 14). In Armando (2006), the numinous presents itself as a confrontation (of the ego) with a psychic force that holds a yet unrevealed meaning – such as one's true calling. It comes as a passion, or an ideal, an out-of-ordinary experience, a calling, a potent image or intuition which generates an emotional charge of such intensity as to transform one's routine, life and ultimately the whole individual.

The numinous experience is striking for marking one's relationship with transcendence, with soul connection, with that which lies beyond earthly realms, and for this reason, the experience of contact with the numinous is always transformative and moving.

The research conducted by Armando (2006) with students on the course in Body-Based Techniques at the Sedes Sapientiae Institute in Sao Paulo intended to describe their experience of the numinous. These students were instructed to take part in three sessions of Calatonia and to report their observations, first verbally and then as a written account. They were unaware of the research objectives; in the experiment briefing they were only informed that the study was being conducted as part of the researcher's Master's investigation. The following accounts detail the demographic characteristics and reports from two of the participants:

Participant A

The first participant was Carmen (alias), aged 28, single, a professional psychologist, a Kardecist (spiritism religion), with no previous experience of Calatonia.

When applying for a place on the course, Carmen said she was interested in studying Analytical Psychology and Body-Based Techniques because she was fond of Jungian psychology and had several problems with her body (she was obese). She did not like physical contact and the idea of being touched during Calatonia was unpleasant to her. She hoped to be able to resolve this issue during the course.

At first, she did not participate in practical exercises with Calatonia in class. The students are not obliged to participate in practical classes, since one of the underlying principles of the programme is that: if the body is touched before it is ready ,its psychological defence mechanisms are exacerbated. Gradually, she engaged with some somatic exercises and when subjects were being selected for this study, she was one of the first participants to volunteer. At that time Carmen had already undergone bariatric surgery and was no longer obese - with a healthy body mass index (BMI) she appeared to be feeling much better about her body and physical contact.

First session:

Carmen came to the initial session feeling a little anxious, saying it was the first time she was going to receive Calatonia. We had good rapport, as was already made clear during the course. After explaining all the details, I proceeded to apply the sequence of touches and Carmen described her experience as follows:

> It was the first time I had received Calatonia – it was also the first time that images came to me during body-based therapy.
> Initially, as always, I tried to slow my breathing but trying to do so only made me more anxious and my breathing became quicker and shorter. Then I began to concentrate on my legs and they felt lighter and seemed to tingle at the same time. It reminded me of PMS, and I even wondered if I was menstruating or not as it was the clos-

est sensation which came to mind. The feeling of lightness and presence then extended to my whole body and sometimes I felt my body weighted down ... I saw an image. This image, which came after a few hours of the sequence, made me think of the people who say that they died for a few moments and that they saw a tunnel. I saw someone coming towards me – as there was a lot of light behind them, all I could see was a dark "shadow" with light all around its outline, and dots of lights all around it. I also saw an elephant above me, on my right side; it was a drawing. I think it was pink, and it even had a skirt on, it was sitting down. When I tried to look, it disappeared.

When you touched me on the heel, I remembered a game from my childhood and the children's song "It rocks the coffin, it rocks you too, it taps you on the bum and hides away", but the word 'coffin' scared me when I thought of it and another children's song came to mind: "the agouti runs, in Auntie's house, vines run through, in Grannie's house, the handkerchief in my hand, fell to the floor, beautiful girl of my heart".

There was a moment when I thought I had fallen asleep. But no, I had just been very relaxed, I had given myself over completely. That was when I noticed that my breathing was excessively calm, evenly spaced and longer than at the beginning of Calatonia.

I felt I needed a touch on my head, which was when you stopped touching the lower part of my body and gave me a touch on the head. At the same time, I saw two elephants – strong and masculine – sitting back to back (leaning against each other), with their feet on the ground and their "knees" up by their chest, their upper legs were supported on the "knees". These two elephants became four very quickly - all on their backs and leaning against each other! It was great ... that's all I have to say!

Second session:

Carmen was less anxious when she arrived for the second session but was still not completely at ease which was due, by her own account, to the novelty of the experience. We continued to enjoy good rapport. The following is a report of the session:

> As far as I knew, I did not need to expect anything from the sequence, I cannot deny I had some expectations, and perhaps for that reason I had fewer physical sensations than the first time, and this time I had images right at the beginning, in the middle and at the end of the sequence; they seemed to be divided into parts this time. As for the images: at the beginning of the sequence I saw a butterfly – I felt as if I were the butterfly and was flying over a lake, then I was the one looking at that butterfly, it flew over the lake and left "marks", "waves" in the water, it even looked like it had a bit of a tail!
> It was a beautiful butterfly with blue and pink colours, I saw it from the side and its wings were pointed (they weren't rounded). Then I saw a butterfly flying upwards in a spiral, and right then I was reminded of the development process – which occurs in a spiral. This butterfly also had a bit of a tail – I thought that was very interesting! In the middle of the sequence I saw a triangle – I thought it was a pyramid but it wasn't, it was a triangle, and a strong yellow light was shining from its peak. I thought it was the sun but the image came closer and closer and when it was very close I saw an eye at the point of the triangle with light shining all around it.
> When I felt the touch to my head I saw a lake and drops of water began to fall on the surface, making those rings on the lake, and suddenly it began to rain and I thought my eyes were the lake, and I felt my eyes blink frenetically. It began to rain harder and gradually began to stop, lessening until I began to see a few rings forming on the lake,

with fewer and fewer rings until it stopped raining completely. The rain stopped together with the final touch to the head. For me, the most <u>wonderful</u> bodily sensation is the breathing, which becomes calmer, and almost stops.

Third session:
This time Carmen was calmer when she arrived, as she had already adapted to the experience. The report she handed in a week later was as follows:

> I started to see a river, I saw a girl playing on the banks of this river with another girl – it reminded me of the film Nell and the scenes from the film started to play out. What really stood out for me was the image of one hand touching another, the moment in which the girl's hands took the woman's hand and the man's hand and brought them up to each other's faces. I thought that was so beautiful! I remember seeing animals, I saw an owl, an elephant and a rat.
> When I felt the touch to my head, I saw the Earth as a globe and then a hand was placed on it and more hands came out, until the globe was completely covered by hands (of all sizes and races – white, black, indigenous, Asian, etc.). When the hands were taken off I saw that the globe wasn't there anymore, instead there was the head of a figure, I think it was Indian – I don't really understand these Indian images that I've had as I've never had much contact with Indian culture, I started to research them a bit more because of Calatonia.

After thirty days:
I loved the Calatonia sessions! I felt more relaxed and moved … I never thought it would move me so much … I thought nothing would happen, much less thought I would experience images, and I had so many! And they were amazing! The figure of the elephant was incredible,

they were Indian images which I'd never encountered before – it must be the collective unconscious ... I really don't know! I looked it up on the internet, that image of an elephant, and I was surprised to find the very same one ... coloured pink... sitting down with its legs crossed... later, when I wasn't even having sessions of Calatonia, I heard that it opens paths ... and it's true. How life changes, I must have changed eighty percent of the person I was before, to be the person I am today!

I came out of the sessions in a really thoughtful mood, I even had the urge to do therapy but it wasn't possible yet, but I think that things are going very well and I'm managing to deal with my feelings ... and situations positively, and without forgetting to take everything in, or almost everything!

There was a session in which I felt as if I were untethered to my body, as if my spirit had really let go of my body! It was a wonderful sensation! The session in which I saw the rain was also great ... I felt closer to God!

Personal concept of numinous:
What is numinous to me? I think it is something higher, superior, divine even!

Participant B

The second participant was Dalva (alias), aged 54, divorced, two children, a professional psychologist, Catholic, with previous experience of Calatonia (during the course).

Dalva has been a therapist for thirty years and has managed to attain great professional success. She treats many patients in her practice, gives lectures and even has time to work as a volunteer in a *favela (slum)*. She was smiling when she arrived for the session and was visibly prepared to go through the experience she had volunteered for. She said that it had been a long time since she had last received Calatonia, which was a shame because she liked it so much. The "ambience" created was one of lightness and mutual empathy. We talked about her current emotional state, so we could investigate any potential impediments to the application of Calatonia. As there were none, we agreed to proceed to the application of the sequence (of touches). She was asked about her current emotional state before the start of each of the sessions. Here are the transcripts of the accounts:

First session:
I had an image of a thread, as if my index finger was connected to a long line that went along my finger and outwards. It was shining and white. It reminded me of the painting of 'The Creation of Adam', in the Sistine Chapel. I feel the same way as I had felt when I was there (she said this while crying). That painting is a representation of not being alone. It is the union of God with man. I think I've lost that connection with God; my finger isn't there because the other finger isn't there either. That bond was lost when my father died and it's only now that I'm realising it. I still do not know what I'm going to do with all this.

Second session:
I saw a lot of connecting strands, as if it were a collage, a connecting thing. A long, long strand of female hair, a large strand of hair that turned into two strands that grew and became one. I felt a 'field of energy' and a vibration in the 'field' and very subtle movements in my feet, which were connected with my spine. It was as if my body formed a rectangle which divided and made very subtle movements between the parts, it felt like a flower opening. It was an inner dance. The feeling was very pleasant. The movement became smoother and suddenly stopped. It felt like a rose bud. I felt thin and long. The touches made me feel unaffected by everyday life.

Third session:
There were a lot of disjointed images which rapidly dispersed. There were some absurd things: Shrek and the desire to have my own swamp. One image that stood out was that of going through a dark tunnel and suddenly having the image of the cathedral in Brasilia. It was as if everything had gone dark and suddenly there was a very intense light above me that reminded me of the cathedral. A feeling of great relaxation. I felt your hands on my legs when in fact they were already on my head. There was a very strong force between my legs which kept them apart. Very strong. Then it went away. I lost all sense of time. When you went to touch my head, it seemed to last for a long time, and the sensation on my head was very pleasant; one of safety and support.

After thirty days:
The experience of the fingers was very strong. It lasts to this day. Something opened which has still not closed. It has to do with God directly, whatever that means. I still don't know what it means. I had a Catholic education, I studied in a college run by nuns for 12 years. Even though I haven't formally followed my religion it left a mark on me, it made me a religious person – it gave me my own internal religiosity. That began to break down when I went to university. I started to question everything, to be very rational. Afterwards I gradually took it up again, until the death of my father when it was broken all at once, this connection between the ego and something greater, without my being able to see it. Things became shallow. With the image which came to me in Calatonia, the situation became much clearer. It caught me by surprise, I was not expecting it. While when I saw it in the Sistine Chapel it was very intense – I got neck pain from so much looking up. But it didn't have the effect of the image during Calatonia. It is still inside me, every time I remember it

I cry. It reconnected me to this inner religiosity, which is very strong, which is mine alone. And that changes a lot because it reestablishes a series of internal connections, between the ego and the unconscious.

Personal concept of numinous:
Something greater than the Ego, something which the Ego does not have the resources to access, so it takes on an attitude of admiration. It encompasses the Ego but not in the sense of being swallowed, in the sense of being encompassed.

Final Thoughts

The experiences reported by Dalva and Carmen reveal their awareness of a profusion of symbolic images, saturated with meaning. These images are not interpreted in this chapter because the intention is not to delve into their personal meaning but to illustrate that images, such as those experienced by the participants, are archetypal in nature.

Images can be considered numinous because of their strong emotional impact on the individual - the symbols they express capture the person - they cause such an impression that they can engage, motivate, and transform. By emerging, they direct psychical energy where it needs to go to move the individual to a more balanced life and towards an expanded consciousness. Aspects of one's life that were previously neglected, abused, unknown or misused may be reorganised by the appearance of archetypal images, which intend to foster integration of those aspects and personal growth. The contact with the numinous nature of archetypes can be transformative: the images that emerged during the process of Calatonia of Carmen and Dalva gave back to them a spirituality which had lain dormant.

The development of spirituality has a great influence in increasing the resilience factor. Menegatti-Chequini (2011, p. 154) understands "spirituality as a state of reverence towards life, characterised by acceptance and love for oneself, for others and for life", in such a way to promote re-signification of situations of adversity and resilience in the real-world. For her, this process also fosters a society that is ethical, cooperative, and compassionate, thus, more resilient as well.

This chapter also highlights the importance of including some form of somatic approach to psychotherapy in order to be able to work psycho-somatically on pre-verbal experiences, which are not consciously accessible. This will enhance the potential for developing new neural pathways, making a positive contribution to the transformation of early patterns determined by mother-child attachment – patterns that have an impact on the development of resilience.

By lessening egoic activity, Calatonia enhances contact with the unconscious. Thus, it enables the emergence of a symbolic cascade that may lead to what Jung called individuation, understood here as the alignment of psychical energy under the guidance of the Self, directing the person beyond the collective consciousness to become one's genuine self. According to Bezinelli (2005), it:

> ... reveals an important point: the sense of predestination that accompanies this process, the feeling that there is a line, a guiding thread, a *spiritus rector*, an "intelligence" that stitches together the events of life and that makes us recognise that this is our life – no one else's. That things are what they must be, for good or ill, if they were not, it would not be our life. That everything is in place (Bezinelli, 2005, p. 91).

This process may be seen, on the one hand, as the relative capitulation of the ego, its longings and goals in the first half of life, giving way to the novel directives of the higher Self, usually in midlife. On the other hand, it may be seen as the development of a resilient being in the face of this new configuration.

The goal of analytical psychology has always been to help

people find meaning in their lives by analysing their conscious and unconscious mind. By seeking to engage deeper layers of being through touch – the first and closest form of communication between people – Calatonia can become an important means to facilitate the analytical process.

Hoeller speaks about the need for an experiential spirituality:

> Jung has shown that the greatest help for humanity in its state of spiritual distress, its condition of forlornness, is to be found in inner spiritual experience. By way of this kind of experience, the individual not only acquires various grades of *gnosis* – insight, consciousness, awareness of the true realities of being – but also receives *pistis*[1], trust, experiential faith, which alone ensures the survival and continuity of the effort of individuation. (Hoeller, 1982, p. 156)

In Jung's words:

> No matter what the world thinks about religious experience, the one who has it possesses a great treasure, a thing that has become for him a source of life meaning, and beauty, and that has given a new splendour to the world and to mankind. He has *pistis* and peace. (Jung, 1969a, p. 105)

In conclusion, if the psyche has a religious function (Jung, 1969b), this function is then reliant on development, and consequently will seek newer and evolving forms of expression. Calatonia has been, over sixty years, an excellent path towards opening a channel for the religious function to express itself, and for this reason, one can think of Calatonia as the beginning of a resilience-building process, born of Sándor's creative ability to resist and foster resistance.

---

1. Pistis, Greek for trust, faith, believe. (Bailly, 1963)

References

Araujo, C. A. (2006). Novas Idéias em Resiliência. *Hermes*, 11, 85-95.
Armando, M. D. (2006). A Calatonia e o Numinoso. *Hermes*, 11, 138-146.
Armando, M. D. (2006). *Calatonia e Religiosidade – uma abordagem junguiana* (Unpublished master's thesis). Pontificial Catholic University, São Paulo, Brazil.
Armando, M. D., & Oliveira, L. (2002). Tocar e Ser Tocado. *Jung e Corpo: revista do curso Jung e Corpo do Instituto Sedes Sapientiae*, 2, 19-24.
Bailly, A. (1963). *Dictionnaire Grec-Français*. Paris: Hachette.
Bauman, Z. (2000). *Modernidade Líquida*. Rio de Janeiro, RJ: Zahar.
Bauman, Z. (2005). *Amor Líquido*. Rio de Janeiro, RJ: Zahar.
Bauman, Z. (2006). *Medo Líquido*. Rio de Janeiro, RJ: Zahar.
Benevides, M. L. S. (2006). Um método de psicoterapia profunda em psicossomática. *Hermes*, 11, 6-19.
Bezinelli, J. (2005). O Mal. *Hermes*, 10, 80-91.
Bowlby, J. (2002). *Apego e perda: a natureza do vínculo*. São Paulo, SP: Martins Fontes.
Cirulnik, B. (2009). *De Corpo e Alma*. São Paulo, SP: Martins Fontes.
Hanegraaff, W. J. (2014). *Esotericism and the Academy: Rejected Knowledge in Western Culture*. Cambridge, UK: Cambridge University Press.
Hoeller, S. A. (1982). *The Gnostic Jung and the Seven Sermons to the Dead*. Wheaton, IL: Quest Books.
Jung, C. G. (1969). Psychology and religion. In H. Read et al. (Eds.), *The collected works of C. G. Jung* (Vol. 11, 2nd ed., pp. 3-107). Princeton, NJ: Princeton University Press. (Original work published 1940)
Jung, C. G. (1969). On the nature of the psyche (R. F. C. Hull, Trans.). In H. Read et al. (Eds.), *The collected works of C. G. Jung* (Vol. 8, 2nd ed., pp. 159-234). Princeton, NJ: Princeton University Press. (Original work published 1954)
Jung, C. G. (1978). *Psicologia e Religião* (Complete Works Vol. XI/1). Petrópolis, RJ: Vozes.

Laranjeira, C. D. (2015). Os Estados Tônicos como Fundamento dos Estados Corporais em Diálogo com um Processo Criativo em Dança. *Rev. Bras. Estud. Presença,* 5(3), 596-621. http://www.seer.ufrgs.br/presenca

Lemos, L. H. C., & Henry, B. (2005). Psicoterapia e Toques Sutis. *Hermes, 10,* 18-25.

Marino, R. (2005). *A Religião do Cérebro.* Rio de Janeiro, RJ: Gente.

Menegatti-Chequini, C. (2011). Resiliência e Espiritualidade. In C. A. Araujo, M. A. Mello, & A. M. G. Rios (Eds.), *Resiliência – teoria e práticas de pesquisa em psicologia.* São Paulo, SP: Ithaka.

Newberg, A., D'Aquilli, E., & Rause, V. (2002). *Why God won't go away.* Toronto, ON: Ballantine.

Otto, R. (1992). *O Sagrado.* Rio de Janeiro, RJ: Edições 70.

Persinger, M. A. (1987). *Neurological bases of God beliefs.* New York, NY: Praeger.

Rios, A. M. G. (2011). A Resiliência na Infância. In C. A. Araujo, M. A. Mello, & A. M. G. Rios (Eds.), *Resiliência– teoria e práticas de pesquisa em psicologia.* São Paulo, SP: Ithaka.

Rios, A. M. G. (2008). *Um estudo junguiano sobre a imagem de Deus na infância dentro da tradição cristã* (Unpublished master's thesis). Pontifícia Universidade Católica, São Paulo, Brazil.

Rios, A. M. G., Armando, M. D., & Regina, A. C. B. (2012). Bases neuropsicológicas do trabalho corporal na psicoterapia. In M. E. Spaccaquerche (Ed.), *Corpo em Jung.* São Paulo, SP: Vetor.

Siegel, D. (1999). *The develop mind.* New York, NY: The Guilford Press.

Tavares, J. (2002). A resiliência na sociedade emergente. In J. Tavares (Ed.), *Resiliência e educação.* São Paulo, SP: Cortez.

Urgesi, C., Aglioti, S. M., Skrap, M., & Fabbro, F. (2010). The Spiritual Brain: Selective Cortical Lesions Modulate Human Self-Transcendence. *Neuron, 65*(3), 309–319.

16

Calatonia: Novel Insights from Neuroscience

Anita Ribeiro Blanchard

This last chapter introduces the reader to several groundbreaking results from neuroscience underlying the use of Calatonia and to the integration of dreams in Sándor's method. These topics are presented in greater depth in a separate publication, called "Integrating Calatonia in Psychotherapy and Trauma Therapy: Novel Insights from Neuroscience" (Blanchard, 2020). This soon-to-be-published book is designed for clinical psychotherapists seeking a firm grasp on the latest results from neuroscience, and how they might explain the efficacy of Calatonia and Subtle Touch (ST) approach. This essay briefly highlights some of these developments to, hopefully, attract the reader's interest for more in-depth information.

An Approach to Psychophysical Self-Regulation

First of all, it is important to situate the Calatonia method within the context of other somatic and body-based techniques. Calatonia is not directed towards the cure of a specific symptom, such as the treatment of somatic or psychological weaknesses, character armour, knots of tension, and/or trauma held in the body; nor is it intended for the attainment of precise results, such as posture correction, soothing anxiety, or the activation or release of emotions. Although somatic techniques that do focus on specific results are valuable for addressing significant aspects of the soma-psyche relationship, Calatonia is not an interventionist approach; rather, it can be considered a technique that mediates overall well-being and self-regulated states.

Pethö Sándor (Kirsch, 2000) welcomed many of the alternative somatic approaches known in the 1960s and included several of them on his beginner course in somatic psychotherapy. In "*Técnicas de Relaxamento*" (Sándor, 1974), he described Faust's (1966) techniques for active relaxation and breathing in the treatment of neurasthenia (a previously devised classification for symptoms of fibromyalgia), and of neurosis and vegetative dystonia (now known as ANS dysregulation). Sándor also highlighted the work of Stokvis and Wiesenhütter (1963) and their relaxation and auto-suggestion methods, similar to autogenic training, for treating shifts in somatic tension caused by stress and negative thinking; Reich's body armouring (1961), which described exercises for releasing tension in body regions undergoing chronic muscular contraction; Schultz's autogenic training (1967) technique; and Jacobson's progressive relaxation (1938). Sándor placed great value on methods to heighten one's self-awareness, particularly for training psychotherapists in the use of body-based techniques. Consequently, he included a practical module on his advanced theoretical courses that covered not only the somatic techniques he had developed, but also weekly training sessions in the Feldenkrais (1979) and Eutony (Alexander, 1981; Bal, 2014) methods.

However, within the context of the numerous somatic methods available today (Barratt, 2010; Herbert, 2017; Heller, 2012; Knaster, 1996; van der Kolk, 2015), Sándor's Calatonia stands out as one that promotes global psycho-physiological readjustments that lead to optimal homeostatic values and stability of the internal milieu, instead of focussing on treating specific symptoms and disorders (Farah, 2008; Gorodscy & Tosi, 1987; Sándor, 1974). Calatonia promotes the reorganisation and strengthening of one's self-regulatory mechanisms extending towards brain regulation (large-scale brain synchronisation and metastability) in dyadic regulation with the therapist. Interpersonal synchronisation occurs spontaneously among individuals and groups (Cacioppo et al., 2014; Gipson, Gorman, & Hessler, 2016; Hove & Risen, 2009; Koole & Tschacher, 2016; Orsucci et al., 2016), however, it can be orchestrated to create a fine-tuned dyadic regulation for therapeutic purposes.

Allostatic and homeostatic self-regulation (Damasio & Damasio, 2016; Pezzulo, Rigoli, & Friston, 2015) in Sándor's view refers to the continuous re-organisation of the psyche-soma relationship around inner and outer changes and events. This interweaving of allostatic and homeostatic forms of regulation is maintained through a flexible combination of bottom-up homeostatic reflexes and top-down allostatic behaviours, the latter encouraged by a deepening self-awareness about one's needs and well-being. An example of such a combination of allostatic and homeostatic regulation is an individual's proactiveness (allostatic regulation) to avoid stress by getting enough rest and sleep - before that need becomes critical and triggers regulation by negative feedback, such as falling asleep at an inappropriate place and time (Clark, Watson, & Friston, 2018; Modell et al., 2015).

In today's world, homeostasis and self-regulated states have become fragile. Untold numbers of people live in chronic physical and psychological dysregulation, with no awareness of their own needs as they push their organism to the limit. They tolerate high levels of stress and physical and emotional pain, all of which is exacerbated by the inequality, frustration, racism, social exclusion and inherent uncertainty experienced in many aspects of life. These circumstances are extremely damaging to the organism and may lead to symptoms that call for improved adaptation to the individual's environment and a greater balance between needs and demands. When a traumatic event is added to this volatile mix, the individual may be left utterly "shattered".

Once unstable or dysregulated states become chronic patterns, restoring one's optimal homeostatic values and self-regulatory potency usually requires disrupting a pre-existing somatic and/or psychological pattern of dysregulation, which may have been involuntarily caused by maladaptive responses to the stressful situations that led to their formation (Damasio & Damasio, 2016). Under these circumstances, Sándor's technique of Calatonia is an effective treatment for steadily and cumulatively "dissolving" the pervasiveness of maladaptive patterns, by targeting global homeostatic balance.

These optimal homeostatic values vary from individual to individual, because they refer to both the regulation and stability of "regulated variables", such as blood pressure and temperature (for which the body has control sensors to warn of errors), and "nonregulated variables" such as heartbeats that can be altered by the autonomic nervous system (ANS) or modified by lifestyle, e.g., athletes have different values for heartbeat than sedentary people (Cooper, 2008; Gordon, 2003; Kringelbach & Berridge, 2017; Modell et al., 2015; Leventhal, Brissette, & Leventhal, 2003; Zajicek, 1999). Thus, Calatonia is open-ended in its results because each person has a unique optimal 'homeostat setting'.

This "unique homeostat setting" is influenced not only by one's developmental phase and life circumstances at the time of treatment, but also by one's biogenetic predispositions, epigenetics, personality and temperament, attachment and family history, and relational patterns, among other elements (Beaty et al., 2016; Gratton et al., 2018; Jung, 1959; Nostro et al., 2018).

Neuroscience and Brain Networks in Calatonia

There are several key findings from neuroscience about the neural substrates through which Calatonia operates to foster self-regulatory mechanisms of the psyche and soma and improve well-being. The best way to approach these findings is

by breaking them down into aspects that can be investigated in isolation (Blanchard, 2020), bearing in mind that these aspects work in synergy during a session of Calatonia:
- Dyadic regulation in resting-state neural connectivity (Deco, Kringelbach, Jirsa, & Ritter, 2017), which leads to increases in the synchronisation and metastability of large-scale networks, such as the Default Mode Network (DMN; Smallwood & Schooler, 2015), and the subsequent generation of cognitive processes such as mind wandering (Blanchard, 2020).
- The orienting reflex, affecting mostly bottom-up attentional and motivational patterns. In clinical psychology, motivation should be viewed as a concept of equal importance to resilience; however, very few treatment approaches take into consideration the fact that "motivation", at its base, is of an autonomic, instinctual nature (DeGangi, 2012, 2017). During Calatonia, the engagement of the orienting reflex helps to reorganise the individual's motivational and appetitive systems, reinstating a healthy drive to live (Blanchard, 2020). This drive cannot be defined in terms of any specific "quality of drive", such as sexual libido, as it was conceived by Freud (Baker, 1982) – again, here the quality of this reinstated motivation will match the individual's peculiar make up;
- Cortical-subcortical large-scale networks, which act to modulate global brain connectivity and synchronisation patterns through the rhythmic segregation and integration of neural populations acting in concert to code for complex stimuli and concepts (Goldberg, Harel, & Malach, 2006; Gollo, Zalesky, Matthew Hutchison, Van Den Heuvel, & Breakspear, 2015; Hari & Parkkonen, 2015; Santangelo, 2018). By proposing a quiet, non-task-oriented approach in resting-state functional connectivity, coupled with a steady, slow-paced influx of unusual passive stimuli, Calatonia provides the appropriate environment in which brain regulation may occur;

- The "grooming" system in the mammalian nervous system, primarily composed of C-tactile mechanoreceptors (CT receptors; Brauer, Xiao, Poulain, Friederici, & Schirmer, 2016; Iggo, 1960; Iggo & Muir, 1969; Olausson et al., 2002), and recently identified as part of the human social-affective system. The stimuli in Calatonia activate polymodal C-receptors (low-threshold unmyelinated free nerve endings and nociceptors) as well. These receptors are implicated in the modulation of pain (Monroe, 2009); they are sensitive to subtle touch and are slow to conduct their information to the brain, carrying sensory information of an affective-emotional quality;
- The discriminative-spatial system, associated with Merkel's cell-neurite complex receptors and the Ruffini corpuscle, a type of skin proprioceptor (Blanchard, 2020). Both are low-threshold (sensitive to light touch) and slow-adapting (keep responding to the stimulus), lightly myelinated nerve endings (Birznieks, Macefield, Westling, & Johansson, 2009; Ciaunica & Fotopoulou, 2017; Ebisch et al., 2016; Grion, Akrami, Zuo, Stella, & Diamond, 2016; Macefield, 2005; McGlone, Wessberg, & Olausson, 2014; Mountcastle, 2005). These are the most sensitive fibres responsive to subtle touch, more so than the CT receptors, and conduct medium-speed impulse conduction to the brain while remaining slow to inhibit the activation of "noticing" stimuli, as they "stay focussed" on the stimulus to investigate its perceptual features (e.g., location, direction, pressure);
- Interhemispheric cerebral connectivity via the corpus callosum, which mediates integrative higher-order cognitive functions (Compton et al., 2008; Compton, Feigenson, & Widick, 2005). By means of bi-lateral and simultaneous sustained touch, Calatonia activates connectivity through the corpus callosum (Blanchard, 2020);
- Engagement of cutaneous nerves, which are not sensory *per se*, but regulate the endocrine system both locally

(within the dermis) and globally (the whole organism via the Hypothalamus, Pituitary and Adrenals, HPA axis; Slominski et al., 2012). The engagement of cutaneous nerves during Calatonia may explain the frequently observed resetting of the endocrine system to healthier homeostatic values;

• The combination of attentional systems engaged in processing the location and quality of touch delivered in Calatonia. These systems are activated independently from the global networks, via connections with the thalamus, one of them being the parietal attentional system, known for its highly associative function with other areas of the brain (Daffner et al., 2003; Goldberg et al., 2006; Rushworth, Paus, & Sipila, 2001).

Just as with music, the "ensemble" of all the above elements performs within a "tempo", a rhythm based on sustaining each point of contact (touch points) for approximately three minutes. This 'tempo' creates compatibility between the patient's rhythm and the therapist's rhythm, a harmonisation that is conducive to dyadic regulation, and strengthens the naturally occurring interpersonal synchronisation on a therapeutic level (Cacioppo et al., 2014; Hove & Risen, 2009). The importance of establishing a conscious pace in therapeutic relationships cannot be emphasised enough (Fosha, 2001, 2009; Koole & Tschacher, 2016; Schore, 2009; Siegel, 2012), because our physiology follows rhythms (heartbeat, breathing cycles, brainwaves, pace of walking, and so on) and "rhythms are a prominent signature of brain activity" (Jones, 2016).

In Calatonia, the modulation of cortical oscillation via paced somatosensory stimuli also facilitates integration of the basic notion of selfhood. From early infancy to adulthood, selfhood is built through physical contact and proximal interaction with others via skin-to-skin interactions, before one develops the ability to share mental states in distal face-to-face interactions (Ciaunica & Fotopoulou, 2017; Hallam et al., 2014; Naruse & Hirai, 2000; Szirmai, 2010).

Below is a summary of the chapters (in Blanchard, 2020) that systematise these above elements into neuroscientific hypotheses:

Brain Connectivity and Brain Dynamics in Psychotherapy: The Occurrence of Mind Wandering and Apperceptive Processes in Calatonia

Ahead of his time, Sándor (1974) formed an all-encompassing conceptual paradigm of how individuals restore their self-regulatory mechanisms through therapy by including the "global regulation of brain states" in his analysis. The notion of brain "regulation" has only recently been characterised by cognitive neuroscience (Gollo et al., 2015; Hari & Parkkonen, 2015; Kelso & Tognoli, 2009; Tognoli & Kelso, 2014): there is now a consensus that the brain works through the communication, integration and synchronisation of distinct brain areas, considered as component parts within an information-processing paradigm of the brain, within a rhythmic time-scale that equates to a "novel chronoarchitecture" (Gollo et al., 2015).

By using passive, gentle stimulation, with the patient in a resting-state position similar to that employed in magnetic resonance imaging, Calatonia immediately engages the neuronal connectivity between key brain areas associated with a resting-state network (RSN). According to Lee and Frangou (2017), the spontaneous brain activity that occurs during this state is "organised into resting-state networks (RSNs) involved in internally-guided, higher-order mental functions (default mode, central executive and salience networks) and externally-driven, specialised sensory and motor processing (auditory, visual and sensorimotor networks)". RSNs are thought to reflect "a constant inner state of exploration, in which the brain at rest remains in a state of predictive readiness but does not commit to specific network configurations until required" (Lee, Moser, Ing, Doucet, & Frangou, 2018).

The high-amplitude, low-frequency EEG waves present in RSNs reflect the synchronous alternation between the firing and inactivity of a large population of neurons. This type of activity is associated with corresponding "synchronised states", as opposed to desynchronised states (with low-amplitude high-frequency spikes) that are related to behavioural activation. Synchronised brain states are believed to be functionally linked to the consolidation and processing of brain activity and connectivity, while desynchronised brain states occurring during periods of heightened activity may indicate increased variability and adaptability.

A healthy RSN functional architecture is defined by high within-network cohesion and between-network integration together with high dynamic metastability and synchrony strength; the opposite, (i.e. disrupted connectivity and lack of metastability) are features of many psychological disorders (Fox et al., 2005; Kelso & Tognoli, 2009; Lee, Doucet, Leibu, & Frangou, 2018).

Metastability refers to "a subtle blend of integration and segregation. Tendencies for brain regions to express their individual autonomy and specialised functions (segregation, modularity) coexist with tendencies to couple and coordinate globally for multiple functions (integration)" (Tognoli & Kelso, 2014), and is believed to be the key principle underlying neuro-cognitive organisation. In simpler words, the brain at rest oscillates between a state of pre-readiness for action in any necessary specific brain network configuration and a state of internally-orientated higher-order mental functions. This metastability (or a stable global rhythm), an oscillation between segregation into specific networks and synchrony within large-scale brain networks, equates to a healthy whole-brain organisation – and it may be through this principle that brain connectivity is regulated in response to internal and environmental factors.

A plausible hypothesis, presented in greater detail in Blanchard (2020), is that Calatonia may help to "reset" healthy levels of integration-segregation and metastability within the large-scale cortical-subcortical networks that form part of the RSNs. Whilst many somatic therapies rely on the behavioural engagement of patients in actively achieving self-regulated states, these heightened states of activity are not necessarily conducive of whole brain regulation, which Calatonia targets by engaging RSNs.

The psychological counterpart of the RSN connectivity mobilised during Calatonia is evident in the activation of one of the large-scale networks that emerge within the metastability process, the Default Mode Network (DMN; Wang, Verkes, Roozendaal, & Hermans, 2020), in which a variety of internally-guided higher-order cognition is processed.

DMN connectivity generates cognitive processes such as, emotional states attributed to oneself or others, autobiographical memory, self-reflective thought and insights, moral reasoning, imagining the future, mind wandering, and perspective-taking. These are fundamental psychological processes that regulate one's mind and emotions, and the functioning and development of the DMN can be disrupted by stress. Early life stress was found to disrupt the DMN and to compromise the natural occurrence of "internally directed cognition when not engaged in goal-directed tasks, episodic memory, and social or self-referential information processing" (Wang et al., 2019). Sándor's method works by facilitating the internal and external environment of the individual (through safe dyadic regulation, passive stimulation and a cognitive state unconstrained by task demands), which are necessary for the constellation of RSNs and consequently affect the connectivity and metastability of the large-scale DMN, and potentially the synaptic plasticity occurring through long-term potentiation (LTP; Bliss & Cooke, 2011) within this network.

Among the cognitive processes occurring within the DMN, an apperceptive process refers to a recursive state of awareness, whereby the mind engages in introspection or reflection of its own inner states, a meta-awareness about one's own situations. The probability of apperceptive processes occurring appears to increase in response to the subtle sensory stimuli present in Calatonia (Blanchard, 2020). In psychotherapy, the integration of the content of this apperception when they are reported by the patient after a session of Calatonia, as well as the integration of other content emerging from the unconscious (e.g., images and fantasies) is an intrinsic aspect of Sándor's method (Blanchard, 2020).

The Orienting Reflex and Stimulus Novelty in Somatic Psychotherapy

The "orienting response", also known as an "orienting reaction" or "orienting reflex" (OR; Nogueira, 2016), is when an organism has an automatic reaction to the perception of a novel stimulus in its environment. The OR is a set of bodily indicators that signal the biological relevance of an environmental stimulus.

A striking feature of the orientation response is that attention is directed to the novel event before it is even identified, with the purpose of appraising the value of the novel stimulus (Bernstein, 1979; Blackford, Buckholtz, Avery, & Zald, 2010; Block et al., 2017; Bradley, 2009; Bradley, Keil, & Lang, 2012). This spontaneous response is different from a response to potential threat or aversive stimulus: instead of eliciting an avoidant reaction, the orienting reflex encourages exploration, engagement and curiosity (Bradley, 2009).

Sándor purposefully thought of different ways of creating ORs by using inordinately light touch and other forms of stimulation, such as passive movements that cannot be voluntarily performed by the patient (e.g., rotating the patient's finger sideways), murmurs and other non-threatening sounds directed towards specific parts of the body, and small vibrations applied to bone projections and protuberances, such as the spinous process (Delmanto, 2008; Farah, 2017).

Calatonia triggers an OR due to its non-invasive nature (experienced as either of neutral or pleasant affect) and the novelty of its touch stimuli; each touch is static and sustained softly at each of the ten points of contact on the body. A light and stationary touch is often a strange sensory percept, particularly on the feet, as they are used to rough contact with stimuli on the ground and to carrying the heavy load of our body weight. The hands and feet are the body parts most involved in Calatonia, and form part of a body area (not including mucosa) covered by hairless (glabrous) skin. This feature sets the extremities of one's limbs apart from other body regions in terms of their importance and somatosensory coverage, as they are areas specialised towards very fine exploratory and adaptive functions. One's feet and hands are used actively and constantly, and as such, the experience of passive gentle touch on very precise points of these areas can easily throw the organism into a state of perceptual, emotional and cognitive surprise.

The positive implications of using the OR in psychotherapy are immense. For instance, clinical depression can be viewed as a "disorder of motivation" due to the loss of interest, curiosity and pleasure described in this illness, from the most basic physiological levels (sleep, appetite and sexual drive) to higher-order cognitive processes such as negative affective framing. As Pavlov (1927) posited, the OR forms the biological basis for the highest forms of curiosity, imagination, science, and knowledge of the world around us. The highest forms of the instinctive drive that we call motivation can be equated, on a cognitive level, to "experiencing enthusiasm" (from Ancient Greek, *enthous* 'possessed by a god, inspired'). Thus, by activating the organism with a spontaneous, instinctual, autonomic reflex such as an OR, one can engender the reorganisation of motivational states at not just physical but emotional (zest for life) and cognitive (curiosity and interest) levels as well (Blanchard, 2020; Vuilleumier, 2005).

Calatonia has been successfully employed to treat depression (Assaly, 1996; Benevides, 2006; Machado Filho, 2002; Rios, Seixas, & Blanchard, 2010) and even post-war depression (Sándor, 1974), by re-balancing the appetitive and reward systems of the brain. As an effective tool in psychotherapy, Calatonia is believed to recalibrate several key brain networks, leading to increased connectivity across segregated neural circuits whilst decreasing the connectivity of more circular feedback loops within core regions within brain networks associated with psychological symptomatology (Blanchard, 2020).

The Skin-Touch System in Calatonia

In Blanchard (2019), the skin-touch system is discussed from its evolutionary standing among other senses to the specific ways in which touch receptors and skin proprioceptors are exquisitely engaged in Subtle Touch and Calatonia method. Most clinicians are aware and mindful of the role of the skin-touch system in one's affective-emotional development, however, very little therapeutic use is made of the cognitive-discriminative and homeostatic factors that play out in the skin-touch system – the integration of emotional, cognitive and homeostatic factors is a central aspect explained in Blanchard (2019). It is in this connectivity that vigilance, fear, pain can be regulated to more adaptive levels in response to new non-threatening stimuli (Calatonia). These integrated events make Calatonia a highly valuable tool for establishing balanced communication between the affective and discriminative areas of the brain.

Another aspect of using the skin and touch as a therapeutic tool refers to the phenomenology implicated in the skin-touch system. Below are presented some elements of this phenomenology and how they play out in Calatonia. Touch is the 'first sense' (Fulkerson, 2014) and as such, the most intrinsically involved with mechanisms for safeguarding the survival and integrity of the organism, a primary cause for the evolution of the epidermis. As such, touch is the one sense that inevitably provides an immediate 'feeling' concerning which stimuli are present within and outside the confines of the body, a vital instinct for ensuring the organism's well-being (Damasio & Carvalho, 2013).

Touch differs from other senses such as vision, audition and olfaction, because tactile information arises, by definition, through tangible contact with the body, implying a more direct connection between the outside world and our mental representations. Tactile stimulation directly informs us of the characteristics of an object (or stimulus), or about the present state of one's body (Fulkerson, 2014). Attention directed towards touch is always a dual or divided form of attention from the perspective of cognitive neuroscience, while the attentional process itself may not even be acknowledged by the conscious mind, it oscillates between the stimulation itself (exteroceptive, exploratory) and one's responses to it (interoceptive, introspective).

Such impressions are common observations in Calatonia: patients may report feeling the quality of the touch, its pressure, temperature and duration; or may notice the street noises, the firmness of the bed, the softness of the blanket, with an emphasis on the perception of the outside world (exteroceptive attention). Alternatively, patients report having mental images of varying colours, hearing the noises of their abdomen, feeling an itch or "pins and needles", having sensations of "electric currents" coursing through their body, or experiencing contradictory feedback about their body's spatial position, its weight or lightness, etc., without reference to the stimulus itself, in which case their attention is clearly directed to the state of their organism (interoceptive and proprioceptive attention). Other reactions include a fluctuation of attention between these two states of awareness, or creating associations between the quality of the stimuli and an inner state: by remembering a fact, by labelling the touch as supportive, gentle or non-threatening, which may lead them to integrate multidimensional elements of the stimulus (Almeida, 1999; Armando, 2006; De Santis, 1976; Farah, 1996; Gabriel, 2001; Gonçalves, Pereira, Ribeiro, & Rios, 2007; Lorthiois, 2012; Rios, Armando, & Regina, 2012).

This seemingly casual process reveals perhaps the most important psychological aspect of the dual-integrative nature of touch. It allows individuals: to experience their physical boundaries and to perceive the quality of another's presence, to gain interoceptive self-awareness and awareness of the stimuli or environment. Several cognitive-affective associations may arise from the free flow of this dual attention, particularly in non-threatening and sustained touch, fuelled by one's life history, as well as a balance between interoceptive and exteroceptive attention.

This context is made more complex by the fact that touch conveys more prosocial emotions such as love, compassion, gratitude, and admiration than any other sensory modality (Hertenstein, Keltner, App, Bulleit, & Jaskolka, 2006; Sauter, 2017), which supports a notion of touch as the social-affective sense *par excellence*. At less explicit but equally important levels, touch allows the emergence of a visceral somatic resonance between interacting individuals, which is likely to form the basis for emotional contagion and empathy (Chatel-Goldman, Congedo, Jutten, & Schwartz, 2014).

Simply observing someone being touched activates in the observer's brain the same somatotopic area that corresponds to the part of the body where the other person is being touched. This forms a "vicarious touch" effect on the observer, and even more, it activates mirror-like responses in the insula, an important area for the processing of empathy (Banissy & Ward, 2013; Fitzgibbon, Ward, & Enticott, 2014; Keysers et al., 2004; Kuehn, Mueller, Turner, & Schütz-Bosbach, 2014; Schaefer, Heinze, & Rotte, 2012). This vicarious activation of the observer's brain also correlates to a specific personality trait, 'openness to experience': high scores in 'openness to experience' correlate to a magnification of brain responses to vicarious touch (Schaefer, Rotte, Heinze, & Denke, 2013). This points to the importance of skin-touch experience in formative aspects of the personality. "Vicarious touch" provides us with the subjective "capacity to understand the tactile experience of others, and by extension to understand others as experiencing selves" (Wood, Gallese, & Cattaneo, 2010). Whenever I applied Calatonia to children treated within the National Health Service (NHS, UK), I always encouraged the child's parents to stay in the room and simply be 'present' because I felt it would facilitate 'an understanding' of the child's process on some level.

In addition, signals and source strengths represented within the somatosensory cortex are about a fifth weaker to self-produced touch than external touch (touch delivered by someone else). In other words, being touched by another has a stronger impact than self-produced touch (Hesse, Nishitani, Fink, Jousmäki, & Hari, 2010).

Finally, alone among the health professions (medicine, nursing, physiotherapy, and occupational and speech therapy), psychotherapy is the only one that has not integrated touch as a mandatory part of its curriculum, to our profession's detriment. This lack of hands-on training in mainstream psychology leaves the clinician in a limbo of physical-somatic "detachment" and "disconnection" in the consulting room, and "out-of-touch" with the unavoidable reality of the physicality of the therapist-patient relationship. Body-based techniques that involve structured touch sequences and use a standardised application protocol, such as Subtle Touch and Calatonia, increase the therapists' confidence to employ them and bring depth and strength to the therapeutic alliance. In this sense, non-verbal synchrony between therapist and patient (Koole & Tschacher, 2016) can be safely enhanced with Sándor's method.

Working with Dreams in Calatonia and Subtle Touch

Jung (1969) regarded the psyche as a self-regulating system similar to the body and saw dreams as an aspect of the psyche's regulatory response. This has tremendous implications for the way we understand dreams, and specifically, nightmares.

If dreams are symptoms of an individual's psychological regulation, nightmares are not just the mind spinning out of control in response to trauma, nor are they a symptom of a "dysregulated brain". From the perspective of psychological balance, however painful and relentless nightmares may be, they remain a self-regulating response to trauma, i.e., an attempt to restore psychological balance. Nightmares manifest through the psychic effort to integrate material that has been rejected or which has been felt to be too intense, usually from a traumatic experience (Kalsched, 2004). As such, nightmares seek to maintain the individual's psychic integration while putting pressure on the consciousness of the dreamer to resolve situations of heightened vulnerability by assimilating traumatic experiences.

When I was working with severely abused and neglected children between the ages of 18 months and 17 years, for a nonprofit organisation in the USA, I found it was extremely important to keep in mind the "purpose" of their vivid and relentless nightmares. In addition to interpreting their dreams as expressions of the children's inner struggles with traumatic experiences (Kalsched, 2004), I understood that their nightmares were a "preparation for possible disasters in the future". At that time, a public defence lawyer told me that ninety percent of that particular population would end up being their clientele in the legal system when they became adults - if they survived to adulthood. Despite all the services available to those children via the social welfare system, their future was not guaranteed, and many would recreate the traumatic experiences of childhood as adults. Thus, the victimisation suffered by those children called for increased vigilance in order to reduce any future risks of re-traumatisation (Lipmann, 1988; Nielsen, 2010; Ofer, 2017; Revonsuo, 2000; Valli et al., 2005; Valli & Revonsuo, 2009). Revonsuo (2000) proposed that one of the functions of dreams is to simulate threats in preparation for waking life, which may have played an adaptive role in natural selection (Revonsuo, 2000; Revonsuo, Tuominen, & Valli, 2015; Zabriskie, 2004).

During that period, I found out that gentle somatic work could change these children's capacity to relate to their environment and could also help them to develop the discernment that had not been taught to them by their dysfunctional parental figures in the course of their development. This was facilitated through consistent experiences of well-being in dyadic regulation with the therapist, by feeling confident and relaxed in the presence of others, instead of experiencing constant hypervigilance and heightened stress levels. Thus, these children could achieve mastery of the environment through resilience and self-confidence, changing the pattern of responses they modelled from their original environment (Blanchard, 2011; Gonçalves, 2012; Gonçalves et al., 2007; Haase et al., 2016; Rios et al., 2012). These changes appear to decrease the frequency of impulsive reactions, increase ability to tolerate frustration, as well as reduce the chances of intergenerational propagation of the traumas they would otherwise experience, by replacing hypervigilance with resilience (Egeland & Susman-Stillman, 1996; Kundakovic & Champagne, 2015; Rios, 2011; Schechter et al., 2007).

Evolved adaptations often tend to benefit the species as a whole; similarly, dreaming may provide an adaptive benefit to our species not merely to each individual (Revonsuo, 2000). Thus, despite burdening traumatised children and adults, nightmares have the potential to foster integration and the resolution of high-priority issues, serving an adaptive role to the dreamer (even at the cost of psychological dissociation), as well as that of other individuals directly affected by the dreamer, in the present and in the future.

A vulnerable individual is compromised and compromises the whole group – or as the Basque proverb would have it, "a thread usually breaks at its thinnest point", that is, the fragility of the individual may threaten to interrupt the "lineage". Thus, a traumatic event provokes a strong reaction in the individual psyche, since it is just as important for the individual to recover from it, as it is for the safety of the species (Blanchard, 2020).

In Calatonia, dreams and nightmares are observed in tandem with the rhythmic self-regulation of the organism. Patients often report dreams after a session of Calatonia, or sometimes during the session, and the contents of the dreams can be perceived as the psychological counterpart of the global self-regulation of the organism. A simple example, a 10-year-old child, after a session of Calatonia asked me if I had noticed that his body jumped during the session, which I did not notice, but that was how he experienced it. He told me that his mind drifted into a "dream" during the session, and in this dream, he saw his dog with a damaged paw; he reached out to hold its damaged paw and, to his shock, the paw "fell off" the body of the dog into his hand. I asked him to draw that image, and to tell me more about his dog (standing for his emotional life). This process was the beginning of noticing (at his level of development) some aspectes of his sel-esteem, guilt, and his unattended emotional experiences within the family life, which he had never brought to therapy before as a (conscious) complaint.

Within the scope of this publication, the above summary is expected to contribute to the current discussion on the integration of neuroscientific knowledge and somatic psychotherapy. In a future publication, these neuroscientific topics in Pethö Sándor's method will be addressed in greater depth, emphasising aspects relevant not only to somatic therapies but also to psychotherapeutic practice in general.

References

Alexander, G. (1981). Eutony: The holistic discovery of the total person. New York, NY: Felix Morrow.

Almeida, L. H. H. (1999). A psicologia organísmica, a psicologia junguiana e a utilização de desenhos: uma reflexão para a educação física (Unpublished Master's thesis in Motricity Science). Universidade Estadual Paulista, Rio Claro, Brazil.

Armando, M. D. (2006). Calatonia e religiosidade – Uma abordagem junguiana (Unpublished Master's Thesis in Clinical Psychology). Pontifícia Universidade Católica de São Paulo, São Paulo, Brazil.

Assaly, R. C. H. (1996). Trabalho Corporal: Um Breve Relato de uma Experiência na Periferia de São Paulo. Hermes, 1, 116-122.

Baker, E. (1982). Sexual Theories of Wilhelm Reich. Journal of Orgonomy, 20(2).

Bal, G. (2014). Viver a Eutonia. Hermes, 19, 64-75.

Banissy, M. J., & Ward, J. (2013). Mechanisms of self-other representations and vicarious experiences of touch in mirror-touch synesthesia. Frontiers in Human Neuroscience, 7(112). http://doi:10.3389/fnhum.2013.00112

Barratt, B. B. (2010). Critical Theory and Practice in Psychology and the Human Sciences. Basingstoke, UK: Palgrave Macmillan.

Beaty, R. E., Kaufman, S. B., Benedek, M., Jung, R. E., Kenett, Y. N., Jauk, E., ... Silvia, P. J. (2016). Personality and complex brain networks: The role of openness to experience in default network efficiency. Human Brain Mapping, 37(2), 773–779. https://doi.org/10.1002/hbm.23

Benevides, M. L. S. (2006). Calatonia: um Método de Psicoterapia Profunda em Psicossomática. Hermes, 11, 6-19.

Bernstein, A. S. (1979). The Orienting Response as Novelty and Significance Detector: Reply to O'Gorman. Psychophysiol- ogy, 16, 263-273.

Birznieks, I., Macefield, V. G., Westling, G., & Johansson, R. S. (2009). Slowly Adapting Mechanoreceptors in the Borders of the Human Fingernail Encode Fingertip Forces. Journal of Neuroscience, 29(29), 9370–9379. https://doi.org/10.1523/JNEUROSCI.0143-09.2009

Blackford, J. U., Buckholtz, J. W., Avery, S. N., & Zald, D. H. (2010). A unique role for the human amygdala in novelty detection. NeuroImage, 50(3), 1188–1193. http://doi.org/10.1016/j.neuroimage.2009.12.083

Blanchard, A. R. (2011). O Corpo da Família. Hermes, 15, 60-71.

Blanchard, A. R. (2020). Integrating Calatonia in Psychotherapy and Trauma Therapy: Novel Insights from Neuroscience. (Manuscript in preparation)

Bliss, T. V., & Cooke, S. F. (2011). Long-term potentiation and long-term depression: a clinical perspective. Clinics (Sao Paulo, Brazil), 66 Suppl 1(Suppl 1), 3–17.

Block, S. R., King, A. P., Sripada, R. K., Weissman, D. H., Welsh, R., & Liberzon, I. (2017). Behavioral and neural correlates of disrupted orienting attention in posttraumatic stress disorder. Cognitive, Affective, & Behavioral Neuroscience, 17(2), 422–436. https://doi.org/10.3758/s13415-016-0488-2

Bradley, M. M. (2009). Natural selective attention: Orienting and emotion. Psychophysiology, 46(1), 1–11. http://doi.org/10.1111/j.1469-8986.2008.00702.x

Bradley, M. M., Keil, A., & Lang, P. J. (2012). Orienting and Emotional Perception: Facilitation, Attenuation, and Interference. Frontiers in Psychology, 3, 493. http://doi.org/10.3389/ fpsyg.2012.00493

Brauer, J., Xiao, Y., Poulain, T., Friederici, A. D., & Schirmer, A. (2016). Frequency of Maternal Touch Predicts Resting Activity and Connectivity of the Developing Social Brain. Cerebral Cortex, 26(8), 3544–3552.

Cacioppo, S., Zhou, H., Monteleone, G., Majka, E. A., Quinn, K. A., Ball, A. B., … Cacioppo, J. T. (2014). You are in sync with me: Neural correlates of interpersonal synchrony with a partner. Neuroscience, 277, 842–858. https://doi.org/10.1016/j.neuroscience.2014.07.051

Chatel-Goldman, J., Congedo, M., Jutten, C., & Schwartz, J.-L.

(2014). Touch increases autonomic coupling between romantic partners. *Frontiers in Behavioral Neuroscience, 8.* 343 https://doi.org/10.3389/fnbeh.2014.00095

Ciaunica, A., & Fotopoulou, A. (2017). The touched self: Psychological and philosophical perspectives on proximal intersubjectivity and the self. In C. Durt, T. Fuchs, & C. Tewes (Eds.), *Embodiment, enaction, and culture: Investigating the constitution of the shared world* (pp. 173-192). Cambridge, MA: MIT Press.

Clark, J. E., Watson, S., & Friston, K. J. (2018). What is mood? A computational perspective. *Psychological Medicine, 48,* 2277 – 2284. https://doi.org/10.1017/ S0033291718000430

Compton, R. J., Feigenson, K., & Widick, P. (2005). Take it to the bridge: An interhemispheric processing advantage for emotional faces. *Cognitive Brain Research, 24*(1), 66–72.

Compton, R. J., Carp, J., Chaddock, L., Fineman, S. L., Quandt, L. C., & Ratliff, J. B. (2008). Trouble Crossing the Bridge: Altered Interhemispheric Communication of Emotional Images in Anxiety. *Emotion, 8*(5), 684–692. http://doi.org/10.1037/a0012910

Cooper, S. J. (2008). From Claude Bernard to Walter Cannon. Emergence of the concept of homeostasis. *Appetite, 51*(3), 419-427 https://doi.org/10.1016/j.appet.2008.06.005

Daffner, K. R., Scinto, L. F., Weitzman, A. M., Faust, R., Rentz, D. M., Budson, A. E., & Holcomb, P. J. (2003). Frontal and parietal components of a cerebral network mediating voluntary attention to novel events. *Journal Cognitive Neurosci.* 15(2), 294-313.

Damasio, A., & Carvalho, G. B. (2013). The nature of feelings: Evolutionary and neurobiological origins. *Nature Reviews Neuroscience, 14,* 143-152. https://doi.org/10.1038/nrn3403

Damasio, A., & Damasio, H. (2016). Exploring the concept of homeostasis and considering its implications for economics. *Journal of Economic Behavior and Organization, 126,* 125–129

De Santis, M. I. (1976). *O discurso não-verbal do corpo no contexto psicoterápico* (Unpublished Master's thesis in Clinical Psychology). Pontifícia Universidade Católica do Rio de Janeiro, Rio de Janeiro, Brazil.

Deco, G., Kringelbach, M. L., Jirsa, V. K., & Ritter, P. (2017). The dynamics of resting fluctuations in the brain: Metastability and its dynamical cortical core. *Scientific Reports, 7*(1).

DeGangi, G. A. (2012). *The Dysregulated Adult: Integrated Treatment Approaches.* Cambridge, MA: Academic Press.

DeGangi, G. A. (2017). *Pediatric Disorders of Regulation in Affect and Behavior.* Cambridge, MA: Academic Press.

Delmanto, S. (2008). *Subtle Touches: Calatonia, A life experience with Pethö Sándor's work.* São Paulo, SP: Summus.

Ebisch, S. J. H., Salone, A., Martinotti, G., Carlucci, L., Mantini, D., Perrucci, M. G., ... Gallese, V. (2016). Integrative Processing of Touch and Affect in Social Perception: An fMRI Study. *Frontiers in Human Neuroscience, 10.* https://doi.org/10.3389/fnhum.2016.00209

Egeland, B., & Susman-Stillman, A. (1996). Dissociation as a mediator of child abuse across generations. *Child Abuse Negl., 20*(11), 1123-32.

Farah, R. M. (1996). O Trabalho Corporal com Idosos como Estímulo ao Processo de Individuação. *Psicologia Revista, 3,* 62-73.

Farah, R. M. (2008). *Integração Psicofísica – o trabalho corporal e a psicologia de C. G. Jung.* São Paulo, SP: Companhia Ilimitada.

Farah, R. (2017). *Calatonia: Subtle Touch in Psychotherapy.* São Paulo, SP: Companhia Ilimitada.

Faust, J. (1966). *Aktive Entspannungsbehandlung.* Stuttgart, DE: Hippokrates-Verlag.

Feldenkrais, M. (1979). *Caso Nora.* São Paulo, SP: Summus.

Fitzgibbon, B. M., Ward, J., & Enticott, P. G. (2014). The neural underpinnings of vicarious experience. *Frontiers in Human Neuroscience, 8,* Article ID 384.

Fosha, D. (2001). The dyadic regulation of affect. *J Clin Psychol.* 57(2), 227-242.

Fosha, D. (2009). Positive Affects and the Transformation of Suffering into Flourishing. *Annals of the New York Academy of*

Sciences, 1172, 252-262.

Fox, M. D., Snyder, A. Z., Vincent, J. L., Corbetta, M., Van Essen, D. C., & Raichle, M. E. (2005). From the Cover: The human brain is intrinsically organized into dynamic, anticorrelated functional networks. *Proceedings of the National Academy of Sciences*, 102(27), 9673–9678. https://doi.org/10.1073/pnas.0504136102

Fulkerson, M. (2014). *The First Sense: A Philosophical Study of Human Touch*. Cambridge, MA: MIT Press.

Gabriel, M. S. A. (2001). *Métodos do Trabalho Corporal: uma proposta sutil* (Unpublished Master's thesis). Universidade Estadual Paulista "Julio de Mesquita Filho", Assis, Brazil.

Gipson, C. L., Gorman, J. C., & Hessler, E. E. (2016). Top-down (prior knowledge) and bottom-up (perceptual modality) influences on spontaneous interpersonal synchronization. *Nonlinear Dynamics, Psychology, and Life Sciences*, 20(2), 193–222.

Goldberg, I. I., Harel, M., & Malach, R. (2006). When the Brain Loses Its Self: Prefrontal Inactivation during Sensorimotor Processing. *Neuron*, 50(2), 329–339.

Gollo, L. L., Zalesky, A., Matthew Hutchison, R., Van Den Heuvel, M., & Breakspear, M. (2015). Dwelling quietly in the rich club: Brain network determinants of slow cortical fluctuations. *Philosophical Transactions of the Royal Society B: Biological Sciences*, 370(1668). https://doi.org/10.1098/rstb.2014.0165

Gonçalves, M. I. C. (2012). O toque sutil em criança intitucionalizada. In M. E. Spaccaquerche (Ed.), *O Corpo em Jung: Estudos em Calatonia e Outras Praticas Integrativas* (pp. 215-230). Sao Paulo, SP: Editora Vetor.

Gonçalves, M. I. C., Pereira, A. P., Ribeiro, A., & Rios, A. M. G. (2007). Subtle Touch, Calatonia and other Somatic Interventions with Children and Adolescents. *USABP Journal*, 6(2), 33-47.

Gordon, E. (2003). Integrative neuroscience. *Neuropsychopharmacology*, 28, S2–S8. https://doi.org/10.1038/sj.npp.1300136

Gorodscy, R. C., & Tosi, S. M. V. D. (1987). *Calatonia: uma experiência* clínica. São Paulo, SP: Temas.

Gratton, C., Laumann, T. O., Nielsen, A. N., Greene, D. J., Gordon, E. M., Gilmore, A. W., ... Petersen, S. (2018). Functional brain networks are dominated by stable group and individual factors, not cognitive or daily variation. *Neuron, 98*(2), 439–452. https://doi.org/10.1016/j.neuron.2018.03.035

Grion, N., Akrami, A., Zuo, Y., Stella, F., & Diamond, M. E. (2016). Coherence between Rat sensorimotor system and hippocampus is enhanced during tactile discrimination. *PLoS Biol 14*(2), e1002384. https://doi.org/10.1371/journal.pbio.1002384

Haase, L., Stewart, J. L., Youssef, B., May, A. C., Isakovic, S., Simmons, A. N., ... Paulus, M. P. (2016). When the brain does not adequately feel the body: links between low resilience and interoception. *Biol. Psychol. 113*, 37–45. doi: 10.1016/j.biopsycho.2015.11.004

Hallam, G. P., Webb, T. L., Paschal, S., Miles, E., Niven, K., Wilkinson, I. D., ... Farrow, T. F. D. (2014). The neural correlates of regulating another person's emotions: an exploratory fMRI study. *Frontiers in Human Neuroscience, 8*, 1–12. https://doi.org/10.3389/fnhum.2014.00376

Hari, R., & Parkkonen, L. (2015). The brain timewise: how timing shapes and supports brain function. *Philosophical transactions of the Royal Society of London. Series B, Biological sciences, 370*(1668), 20140170. doi:10.1098/rstb.2014.0170

Heller, M. C. (2012). *Body Psychotherapy: History, Concepts, and Methods.* New York, NY: W. W. Norton & Company.

Herbert, C. (2017). *Overcoming Traumatic Stress – A self-help guide using cognitive behavioural techniques.* London, UK: Robinson, Little Brown Book Group.

Hertenstein, M. J., Keltner, D., App, B., Bulleit, B. A., & Jaskolka, A. R. (2006). Touch communicates distinct emotions. *Emotion, 6*(3), 528–533. https://doi.org/10.1037/1528-3542.6.3.528

Hesse, M. D., Nishitani, N., Fink, G. R., Jousmäki, V., & Hari, R. (2010). Attenuation of Somatosensory Responses to Self-Produced Tactile Stimulation, *Cerebral Cortex, 20*(2), 425–

432. https://doi.org/10.1093/cercor/bhp110

Hove, M. J., & Risen, J. L. (2009). It's All in the Timing: Interpersonal Synchrony Increases Affiliation. *Social Cognition, 27*(6), 949–960. https://doi.org/10.1521/soco.2009.27.6.949

Iggo, A. (1960). Cutaneous mechanoreceptors with afferent C fibres. *J Physiol, 152*, 337–353.

Iggo, A., & Muir, A. R. (1969). The structure and function of a slowly adapting touch corpuscle in hairy skin. *J Physiol. 200,* 763–796.

Jacobson, E. (1938). *Progressive Relaxation.* Chicago, MI: The University of Chicago Press.

Jones, S. R. (2016). When brain rhythms aren't 'rhythmic': implication for their mechanisms and meaning. *Current opinion in neurobiology, 40,* 72-80.

Jung, C. G. (1959). *Psychological types.* New York, NY: Pantheon.

Jung, C. G. (1969). On the nature of the psyche (R. F. C. Hull, Trans.). In H. Read et al. (Eds.), *The collected works of C. G. Jung* (Vol. 8, 2nd ed.). Retrieved from http://www.proquest.com (Original work published 1954)

Kalsched, D. (2004). *The Inner World of Trauma.* Hove, UK: Brunner-Routledge.

Kelso, J. A. S., & Tognoli, E. (2009). Toward a Complementary Neuroscience: Metastable Coordination Dynamics of the Brain. *Downward Causation and the Neurobiology of Free Will,* 103–124. https://doi.org/10.1007/978-3-642-03205-9_6

Keysers, C., Wicker, B., Gazzola, V., Anton, J. L., Fogassi, L., & Gallese, V. (2004). A Touching Sight: SII/PIV activation during the observation and experience of touch. *Neuron, 42*(2), 335–346.

Kirsch, T. B. (2000). *The Jungians (A Comparative and Historical Perspective).* London, UK: Routledge.

Knaster, M. (1996). *Discovering the Body's Wisdom: A Comprehensive Guide to More than Fifty Mind-Body Practices That Can Relieve Pain, Reduce Stress, and Foster Health, Spiritual Growth, and Inner Peace.* New York, NY: Bantam.

Koole, S. L., & Tschacher, W. (2016). Synchrony in Psychotherapy:

A Review and an Integrative Framework for the Therapeutic Alliance. *Frontiers in psychology, 7,* 862. doi:10.3389/fpsyg.2016.00862

Kringelbach, M. L., & Berridge, K. C. (2017). The affective core of emotion: Linking pleasure, subjective well-being, and optimal metastability in the brain. *Emotion review: Journal of the International Society for Research on Emotion, 9*(3), 191199.

Kuehn, E., Mueller, K., Turner, R., & Schütz-Bosbach, S. (2014). The functional architecture of S1 during touch observation described with 7T fMRI. *Brain Structure & Function, 219*(1), 119–140. http://doi.org/10.1007/s00429-012-0489-z

Kundakovic, M., & Champagne, F. A. (2015). Early-life experience, Epigenetics, and the developing brain. *Neuropsychopharmacology, 40*(1), 141-53.

Lee, W. H., Doucet, G. E., Leibu, E., & Frangou, S. (2018). Resting-state network connectivity and metastability predict clinical symptoms in schizophrenia. *Schizophrenia research, 201,* 208–216.

Lee, W. H., & Frangou, S. (2017). Linking functional connectivity and dynamic properties of resting-state networks. *Scientific reports, 7*(1), 16610.

Lee, W. H., Moser, D. A., Ing, A., Doucet, G. E., & Frangou, S. (2018). Behavioral and Health Correlates of Resting-State Metastability in the Human Connectome Project. *Brain topography, 32*(1), 80–86.

Leventhal, H., Brissette, I., & Leventhal, E. A. (2003). The common-sense model of self-regulation of health and illness. In L. Cameron, & H. Leventhal (Eds.), *The Self-Regulation of Health and Illness Behaviour* (pp. 42–65). Abingdon, UK: Routledge.

Lipmann, P. (1988). On the private and social nature of dreams. *Contemp. Psychoanalysis, 34,* 195-221.

Lorthiois, C. (2012). Os Toques Sutis na educação – Um re-ligar do corpo com a cabeça. In M. E. Spaccaquerche (Ed.), *O Corpo em Jung: Estudos em Calatonia e Outras Praticas Integrativas.* São Paulo, SP: Editora Vetor.

Macefield, V. G. (2005). Physiological characteristics of low threshold mechanoreceptors in joints, muscle and skin in human subjects. *Clinical and Experimental Pharmacology and Physiology, 32,* 135–144. https://doi. org/10.1111/j.1440-1681.2005.04143.x

Machado Filho, P. T. (2002). A Calatonia e a Depressão. *Hermes, 7,* 6-15.

McGlone, F., Wessberg, J., & Olausson, H. (2014). Discriminative and affective touch: Sensing and feeling. *Neuron, 32*(4), 737-755. https://doi.org/10.1016/j.neuron.2014.05.001

Modell, H., Cliff, W., Michael, J., McFarland, J., Wenderoth, M. P., & Wright, A. (2015). A physiologist's view of homeostasis. *Advances in Physiology Education, 39*(4), 259–266. https://doi.org/10.1152/advan.00107.2015

Monroe, C. M. (2009). The effects of therapeutic touch on pain. *Journal of Holistic Nursing: Official Journal of the American Holistic Nurses' Association.* https://doi.org/10.1177/0898010108327213

Mountcastle, V. C. (2005). *The Sensory Hand: Neural Mechanisms of Somatic Sensation.* Harvard, MA: Harvard University Press.

Naruse, K., & Hirai, T. (2000). Effects of slow tempo exercise on respiration, heart rate, and mood state. *Perceptual and Motor Skills, 91*(3 Pt 1), 729–740. https://doi.org/10.2466/pms.2000.91.3.729

Nielsen, T. A. (2010). Dream analysis and classification: The reality simulation perspective. In M. Kryger, T. Roth, & W. C. Dement (Eds.), *Principles and Practice of Sleep Medicine* (pp. 595-603). New York, NY: Elsevier.

Nogueira, M. (2016). Resposta de orientação musical: Uma hipótese para a origem do dispositivo de sentido. *Música Hodie, 16*(1), 54–70.

Nostro, A. D., Müller, V. I., Varikuti, D. P., Pläschke, R. N., staedter, F. H., Langner, R., & Eickho, S. B. (2018). Predicting personality from network-based resting-state functional connectivity. *Brain Structure & Function, 223*(6), 2699–2719. http://doi.org/10.1007/s00429-018-1651-z

Ofer, G. (2017). Personal, group and social dimensions of dreams. In R. Friedman, & Y. Doron (Eds.), *Group analysis in the land of milk and honey*. London, UK: Karnac.

Olausson, H., Lamarre, Y., Backlund, H., Morin, C., Wallin, B. G., Starck, G., ... Bushnell, M. C. (2002). Unmyelinated tactile afferents signal touch and project to insular cortex. *Nat Neurosci. 5*, 900–904.

Orsucci, F. F., Aas, B., Schiepek, G., Reda, M. A., Giuliani, A., Gipson, C. L., ... Hessler, E. E. (2016). Special Issue: Interpersonal Synchronization. *Nonlinear Dynamics, Psychology and Life Sciences, 20*(2), 1–3.

Pavlov, I. P. (1927). *Conditioned Reflexes*. Oxford: Oxford University Press.

Pezzulo, G., Rigoli, F., & Friston, K. (2015). Active inference, homeostatic regulation and adaptive behavioural control. *Progress in Neurobiology, 134,* 17 – 35.

Reich, W. (1961). *Selected Writings: An Introduction to Orgonomy*. New York, NY: The Noonday Press.

Revonsuo, A. (2000). The reinterpretation of dreams: An evolutionary hypothesis of the function of dreaming. *Behavioral and Brain Sciences, 23*(6), 877–901. https://doi.org/10.1017/S0140525X00004015

Revonsuo, A., Tuominen, J., & Valli, K. (2015). The Avatars in the Machine: Dreaming as a Simulation of Social Reality. *Open MIND, 32*(38). https://doi.org/10.15502/9783958570375

Rios, A. M. G. (2011). A Resiliência na Infância. In C. A. Araujo, M. A. Mello, & A. M. G. Rios (Eds.), *Resiliência – Teoria e práticas de pesquisa em psicologia*. São Paulo, SP: Ithaka.

Rios, A. M. G., Armando, M. D., & Regina, A. C. B. (2012). Bases neuropsicológicas do trabalho corporal na psicoterapia. In M. E. Spaccaquerche (Ed.), *O Corpo em Jung: Estudos em Calatonia e Outras Praticas Integrativas*. São Paulo, SP: Vetor.

Rios, A. M. G., Seixas, L. P., & Blanchard, A. R. (2010). The Body in Psychotherapy: Calatonia and Subtle Touch Techniques. In R. Jones (Ed.), *Body, Mind, and Healing After Jung: A Space of Questions* (pp. 228-250). London, UK: Routledge.

Rushworth, M. F. S., Paus, T., & Sipila, P. K. (2001). Attention systems and the organization of the human parietal cortex. *NeuroImage,* 13(6), 353. https://doi.org/10.5761/atcs.oa.13-00279

Sándor, P. (1974). *Técnicas de relaxamento.* São Paulo, SP: Editora Vetor.

Santangelo, V. (2018). Large-Scale brain networks supporting divided attention across spatial locations and sensory modalities. *Frontiers in Integrative Neuroscience, 12.* https://doi.org/10.3389/fnint.2018.00008

Sauter, D. A. (2017). The Nonverbal Communication of Positive Emotions: An Emotion Family Approach. *Emotion Review,* 9(3), 222–234. https://doi.org/10.1177/1754073916667236

Schaefer, M., Heinze, H. J., & Rotte, M. (2012). Embodied empathy for tactile events: Interindividual differences and vicarious somatosensory responses during touch observation. *NeuroImage,* 60(2), 952–957. https://doi.org/10.1016/j.neuroimage.2012.01.11

Schaefer, M., Rotte, M., Heinze, H.-J., & Denke, C. (2013). Mirror-like brain responses to observed touch and personality dimensions. *Frontiers in Human Neuroscience, 7,* 227. http://doi.org/10.3389/fnhum.2013.00227

Schechter, D. S., Zygmunt, A., Coates, S. W., Davies, M., Trabka, K. A., McCaw, J., ... Robinson, J. (2007). Caregiver traumatization adversely impacts young children's mental representations of self and others. *Attachment & Human Development, 9*(3), 187-205.

Schore, A. N. (2009). Relational trauma and the developing right brain: An interface of psychoanalytic self-psychology and neuroscience. *Annals of the New York Academy of Sciences,* 1159, 189–203. https://doi.org/10.1111/j.17496632.2009.04474.x

Schultz, J. H. (1967). *O treinamento autógeno.* São Paulo, SP: Mestre Jou.

Siegel, D. J. (2012). *The Developing Mind.* New York, NY: The Guilford Press.

Slominski, A. T., Zmijewski, M. A., Skobowiat, C., Zbytek, B., Slominski, R. M., & Steketee, J. D. (2012). Sensing the environment: regulation of local and global homeostasis by the skin's neuroendocrine system. *Advances in anatomy, embryology, and cell biology, 212*, v–115.

Smallwood, J., & Schooler, J. W. (2015). The Science of Mind Wandering: Empirically Navigating the Stream of Consciousness. *Annual Review of Psychology, 66*(1), 487-518.

Stokvis, B., & Wiesenhütter, E. (1963). *Der Mensch in der Entspannung*. Stuttgart, DE: Hippokrates-Verlag.

Szirmai, I. (2010). How does the brain create rhythms? *Ideggyógyászati Szemle, 63*(1–2), 13–23. https://doi.org/10.1080/136 03116.2012.693402

Tognoli, E., & Kelso, J. A. (2014). The metastable brain. *Neuron, 81*(1), 35–48.

Valli, K., & Revonsuo, A. (2009). The threat simulation theory in light of recent empirical evidence: A review. *American Journal of Psychology, 122*(1), 17–38. https://doi.org/10.1017/S0140525X00004015

Valli, K., Revonsuo, A., Pälkäs, O., Ismail, K. H., Ali, K. J., & Punamäki, R. L. (2005). The threat simulation theory of the evolutionary function of dreaming: Evidence from dreams of traumatized children. *Consciousness and Cognition, 14*(1), 188–218. https://doi.org/10.1016/S1053-8100(03)00019-9

van der Kolk, B. (2015). *The Body Keeps the Score: Brain, Mind, and Body in the Healing of Trauma*. New York, NY: Penguin Books.

Vuilleumier, P. (2005). How brains beware: Neural mechanisms of emotional attention. *Trends in Cognitive Sciences, 9*(12), 585-594. https://doi.org/10.1016/j.tics.2005.10.011

Wang, H., Verkes, R.-J., Roozendaal, B., & Hermans, E. J. (2019). Toward Understanding Developmental Disruption of Default Mode Network Connectivity Due to Early Life Stress. *Biological Psychiatry: Cognitive Neuroscience and Neuroimaging, 4*(1), 5–7.

Wood, R., Gallese, V., & Cattaneo, L. (2010). Visuotactile empathy within the primary somatosensory cortex revealed by short-latency afferent inhibition. *Neuroscience Letters*,

473(1), 28–31. https://doi.org/10.1016/j.neulet.2010.02.012

Zabriskie, B. (2004). Imagination as laboratory. *The Journal of analytical psychology, 49,* 235-242.

Zajicek, G. (1999). Wisdom of the body. *Medical Hypotheses, 52*(5), 447-449.

Authors

Lúcia Helena Hebling Almeida
Clinical Psychologist, Doctorate degree in Mental Health from the University of Campinas (UNICAMP), Master's degree in Psychomotricity from the State University of São Paulo (UNESP), specialist trained in the Subtle Touch psychophysical integration method, at the Sedes Sapientiae Institute. E-mail: dra.luciahelena@hotmail.com.br

Marilena Dreyfuss Armando
Clinical Psychologist, Master's in Jungian Psychology from the Pontifical Catholic University of Sao Paulo (PUC/SP), specialist trained in the Subtle Touch Psychophysical Integration method, at the Sedes Sapientiae Institute, adjunct professor of Body-based Techniques at the Sedes Sapientiae Institute and Paulista University (UNIP). E-mail: maridrey@terra.com.br

Anita Ribeiro Blanchard
Registered Psychologist (PUC/SP/Brazil), Licensed Mental Health Counsellor (USA), HCPC registered and British Psychological Society Chartered Counselling Psychologist (UK), PhD Candidate at the University of Barcelona, specialist trained in the Subtle Touch Psychophysical Integration method, at the Sedes Sapientiae Institute. E-mail: anitarblanchard@gmail.com

Rosa Maria Farah *(in memoriam)*
Clinical Psychologist, Master's in Jungian Psychology, specialist trained in the Subtle Touch Psychophysical Integration method, at the Sedes Sapientiae Institute, former professor and coordinator of the 'Body in Psychotherapy' programme of the professional psychologist course at PUC/SP.

Irene Gaeta (Arcuri)
　　Jungian Analyst (IAAP), Doctorate in Clinical Psychology (PUC/SP), Master's in Gerontology, certificate in Art Therapy and Health from the Medical School at the University of São Paulo (USP). Coordinator and adjunct professor of graduate studies in Jungian Psychotherapy at UNIP and adjunct professor of the 'Body in Psychotherapy' programme of the professional psychologist course at PUC/SP. E-mail: iarcuri@uol.com.br

Maria Irene Crespo Gonçalves
　　Clinical Psychologist (USP), specialist trained in Psychomotricity at the Sedes Sapientiae Institute, specialist trained in Couples Therapy at the J. L. Moreno Institute, and a member of the International Society for Sandplay Therapy ISST. E-mail: irenecrespo1@yahoo.com.br

Maria Georgina Ribeiro Gonçalves
　　Clinical Psychologist (retired), specialist trained in the Subtle Touch Psychophysical Integration method, at the Sedes Sapientiae Institute, former adjunct professor and internship supervisor at PUC/SP.

Claudia Herbert
　　HCPC registered and BPS Chartered Clinical Psychologist, Associate Fellow of the British Psychological Society (BPS), Applied Psychology Practice Supervisor (RAPPS), Cognitive Behavioural Psychotherapist (UKCP/BABCP), EMDR Consultant and EMDR Child & Adolescent Consultant (all EMDR Europe accredited), Schema Therapist (ISST), International Trauma Specialist. Trained in several body-oriented healing methods, including Calatonia and Subtle Touch. E-mail: claudia.private@oxdev.co.uk

Beatriz Vianna Henry
Clinical Psychologist (USP), BA in Mathematics (Presbiteriana Mackenzie University), specialist trained in the Subtle Touch Psychophysical Integration method, at the Sedes Sapientiae Institute, researcher at the 'Imaginal Laboratory' at the Institute of Psychology at USP.
E-mail: bianry@gmail.com

Luiz Hildebrando Campos Lemos
Clinical Psychologist (USP), specialist trained in the Subtle Touch psychophysical integration method, at the Sedes Sapientiae Institute, researcher at the 'Imaginal Laboratory' at the Institute of Psychology at USP.
E-mail: lhclemos@gmail.com

Marie-Céline Lorthiois
Pedagogue, Master's in Educational Psychology (PUC/SP), specialist trained in the Subtle Touch Psychophysical Integration method, at the Sedes Sapientiae Institute, and international Circle Dance facilitator.
E-mail: pedagogiaprofunda@gmail.com

Paulo Toledo Machado Filho
Psychiatrist, Jungian Psychotherapist specialising in body-based techniques, Sociologist, Master's in Social Anthropology (USP), specialist in Analytical Psychology and the body-based approach, adjunct professor and Coordinator of the 'Jung & the Body' programme at the Sedes Sapientiae Institute. E-mail: ptmachadof@uol.com.br

Vivian Farah Nassif
Occupational Therapist (USP), specialist trained in the Subtle Touch Psychophysical Integration method, at the Sedes Sapientiae Institute, certified therapist in the Meir Schneider's Self-Healing method by the San Francisco School for Self-Healing. E-mail: vivinassif@uol.com.br

Ana Maria Galrão Rios
> Clinical Psychologist, Master's and Doctorate in Jungian Studies (PUC/SP), specialist in the Subtle Touch Psychophysical Integration method, with a diploma from the 'Jung & the Body' programme granted by the Sedes Sapientiae Institute. Adjunct professor of the 'Jung & the Body' programme at the Sedes Sapientiae Institute, coordinator of the Personality Development course within the graduate programme for Jungian Psychotherapy at UNIP.
> E-mail: anamariagrios@uol.com.br

Leda Maria Perillo Seixas
> Clinical Psychologist, specialist trained in the Subtle Touch Psychophysical Integration method, at the Sedes Sapientiae Institute, Master's in Jungian psychology (PUC/SP), supervisor and adjunct professor of the 'Body in Psychotherapy' programme of the professional psychologist course at PUC/SP. PhD candidate (2020) in Religious Sciences. Founder and editor of *Hermes*, an online indexed journal for Jungian, somatic and integrative studies.
> E-mail: ledapseixas@uol.com.br

Sandra Maria Greger Tavares
> Psychologist, Master's in clinical psychology, PhD in Developmental Psychology and post-doctorate in Social Psychology from the Institute of Psychology at USP, scientific researcher at the Health Institute of the State Health Department of São Paulo, and specialist trained in the Subtle Touch Psychophysical Integration method, at the Sedes Sapientiae Institute. E-mail: gregerusp@gmail.com

Annex:
Brief Description of the Calatonia Technique

Calatonia consists of a sequence of nine delicate touches, applied bilaterally to the patient's toes, upper aspect of the soles, arches, heels, calves, and a tenth touch in which the patient's head is support by the therapist's hands; the touch is sustained for 1 to 3 minutes at each point. Patients do not have to undress, just remove their shoes, socks, jewelry, contact lenses and lie on a massage table.

Initial Supine Position

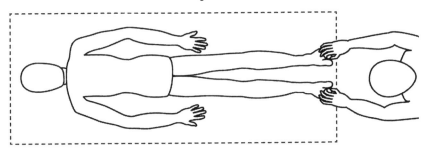

Order of the Sequence of Touches (1-7)

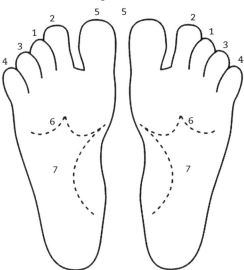

Calatonia: A Therapeutic Approach that Promotes Somatic and Psychological Regulation

Supporting the Heels (8)

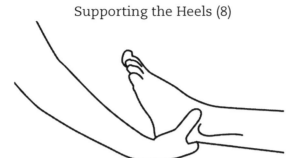

Supporting the Calves (9)

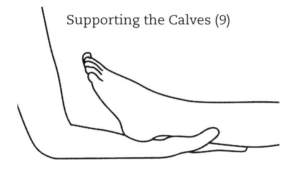

Supporting the Head (10)

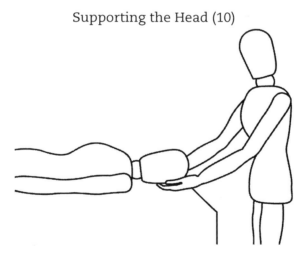

Made in the
USA
Middletown, DE